We Were Dancing on a Volcano

Bloodlines and Fault Lines of a Star-Crossed Atlanta Family
1849-1989

Joseph Gatins

The Glade Press
www.gladepress.blogspot.com

Permissions.
Joseph F. Gatins Jr.'s 1901 college-era photo, courtesy of Hargrett Rare Book and Manuscript
Library, University of Georgia Libraries. Rawa-Ruska prisoner of war punishment camp line
drawings and photo, courtesy of *Ceux de Rawa-Ruska*

FIRST EDITION

Printed on acid-free paper.

Interior design by J.L. Saloff, Saloff Enterprises, www.Saloff.com
Photo layout and cover design by Honor Woodard, http://silvermoonfrog.blogspot.com

Library of Congress Catalog Number: 2009908870

Cataloging-in-Publication
Gatins, Joseph.
    We were dancing on a volcano : bloodlines and fault lines of a star-
    crossed Atlanta family : 1849-1989 /
    Joseph Gatins. -- 1st ed.
        p. cm.
        Includes bibliographical references and index.
        ISBN-13: 978-0-578-02779-1
        ISBN-10: 0-578-02779-8

    1. Gatins, Joseph--Family. 2. Atlanta (Ga.)--
Biography. 3. Atlanta (Ga.)--History--19th century.
4. Atlanta (Ga.)--History--20th century. 5. Georgia--
History, Local.   I. Title.

F294.A853A25 2009   975.8'23104'0922
                              QBI09-600103

V-1.2

"*Paris was very festive. Everyone was dancing on a volcano, but we were all dancing a lot. I had an extraordinary feeling that something was coming to an end—that our world, as we knew it, was fleeing and that we'd never see it again.*"
-- *Eglé de Villelume-Sombreuil Gatins, 1939*

For Fran

Table of Contents

One-armed Grandfather

I initially decided to write this book to find out more about my one-armed, Irish-American grandfather from Atlanta, whom no one in the family ever spoke of. In the end, more than a dozen years later, it had turned into a historical biography of family. I found out more about the French grandmother who married the one-armed man. I found their son, my father, and documented his adventures, which were an exercise in World War II survival and dealing with its post-traumatic aftermath. I found my mother, Colombian in temperament, but very French when it came to manners. And just maybe I unearthed a bit about myself, an all-American mélange, product of many cultures and languages. My forebears said *good day* (in English), *bonjour* (in French), *demat* (in Breton), *latha math* (in Gaelic), *buenos dias* (in Spanish), *Dominus vobiscum* (in Latin) and perhaps even *salaam aleikum* (in the Arabic dialects used in Andalusia).

Readers also should be aware that the Gatins family often had the habit of giving firstborn sons the same first and middle names. To simplify things, here is a reference list of who's who in this particular line:

- Joseph Gatins (1827-1905), my great-great-grandfather. A railroad clerk. Born Killybegs, Ireland, died Atlanta, Georgia.

- Joseph Francis Gatins Sr. (1855-1936), my great-grandfather. Wall Street investor and entrepreneur. Built Georgian Terrace Hotel in Atlanta. Born Atlanta, died New York, New York.

- Joseph Francis Gatins, Jr. (1882-1927), the one-armed grandfather, known as Joe. Sportsman and real estate investor. Born Atlanta, died Atlanta.

- Joseph Francis Gatins III (1915-1983), my father, best known as Francis. World War II veteran and prisoner of war. Born Versailles, France, died Atlanta.

My grandmother, Eglé Gatins, always giving of her love for family, provided a wonderful road map to this reminiscence in the form of a brief oral history tape-recorded in 1976 and then in a much more sanitized, written memoir in 1988. Both recollections touched upon the highlights of her life, sometimes in exquisite, rich detail, and proved a wonderful guide to further research. Unless otherwise noted, all of her direct quotes in this book are from those two sources.

Joseph Gatins, 2009,
at Satolah, Georgia

Chapter 1

Wall Street Operator

The headline on the front page of *The New York Times* of April 24, 1910, was big and bold, its lengthy and detailed article stretching down the entire news page.

GATINS ARRESTED AS BUCKETSHOP MAN

Reputed Backer of Wm. B. Price & Co. Surprised and Distressed When Taken In

KNOWN AS MILLIONAIRE

First Time an Officer's Hand Was Ever Laid on His Shoulder, He Tells Prison Warden

The news had federal authorities listing Joseph F. Gatins Sr. as the "bank-roll man" behind a string of unlawful bucket shops operating across the East Coast, under the banner of the Baltimore-based William B. Price & Co. My great-grandfather was taken to the Tombs that night and briefly lodged in cell 718, according to *The Times* and subsequent news articles in many other papers.

He eventually posted a $5,000 bail bond and remained free for the next few years, which other articles of the day make clear were dedicated to fighting the charges.

Because of a typographical error, which listed his last name as Gaskins, he initially had eluded the federal dragnet that corralled some 29 other alleged co-conspirators. Federal officers eventually caught up to him at a swanky New York apartment at 71 Central Park West, where, as *The Times* put it, he'd been living with his family in "quiet luxury." He was re-indicted under the right name. He was 45 years old at the time. Newspapers in Washington, where the case was to be prosecuted, also had a field day with the bucket shop cases, and it became obvious federal authorities were feeding the press of the day. *The Washington Star*, (in an article of April 23, 1910), described Gatins as "reputed both here and in the South, where he has been a prominent figure, to be worth something like $10,000,000." (That $10 million would be worth more than $228 million today.) *The Washington Post* the next day had him posting his bail in cash, a proceeding during which he appeared to "take his apprehension to heart." He appeared "decidedly agitated during the examination," the newspaper said.

Various newspapers up and down the East Coast then followed the conspiracy case through a tortuous legal chain of events in which the defendants and their lawyers, in their first trial in Washington, managed to have the case thrown out on grounds that the new federal Bucket Shop Law of 1909 violated their constitutional rights. The government appealed that ruling, however, and secured a reversal of the decision from the U.S. Court of Appeals for the District of Columbia in November of 1911, which ordered a retrial.

What was a bucket shop anyway? My old journalistic instincts were piqued. Bucket shops essentially were private and fraudulent stock gambling establishments, which thrived in the days when Wall Street operated with little or no regulation. At the height of the Gilded Age, the term bucket shop referred to an unregulated form of gambling on the daily ups and downs of the stock market—on margin. The book *Trade Like Jesse Livermore*, described them this way: "A bucket shop was a place where one could play the market on 10 percent margin. Its atmosphere was more like an off track betting parlor than a broker's office. The stock ticker spewed out the trades as they happened on the exchange, and the prices were recorded on the chalkboard. The rules were simple: Put up your 10 percent in cash, place a bet by buying a stock and receive a printed receipt for your purchase. Then sit back and watch the action. As soon as you lost 10 percent of the value of the stock, the house swooped in and took your money. Conversely, if the stock went up, you could cash in your ticket at will. The house won almost all of the time. It was usually a sucker play—with the customers being the suckers. They were simply bad stock pickers."

Webster's business dictionaries simply explain bucket shops as "fraudulent operations" in which orders to buy and sell are accepted but no execution takes place. "Instead, operators expect to profit when customers close out their position at a loss. The term [bucket shop] comes from the days when saloons sold small amounts of liquor in buckets. Brokers then spent a lot of time in bars." My brother Martin heard it this way: The bars and drinking establishments where the stock gambling took place often "dropped a bucket" on the bars at the end of the trading day to signal the end of the gaming until the next day. The house, according to contemporary reports, usually was the winner because bucket shops often operated with two connections to Wall Street, a "fast wire," and a "slow wire," much as depicted in the 1973 movie, *The Sting*. Customers were referred to the slow telegraph results, while bucket shop operators, with a 15-minute head start on stock trades, were able to shut out bets that would have been unprofitable to the house. The practice was so widespread that the federal government and Congress had enacted a new law in 1909 making bucket shops illegal. And it was obvious that the feds were going to try to make an example of my great-grandfather and the others caught in their dragnet.

The conspiracy case, not insubstantial, had originated on April 2, 1910 with special federal agents assigned to the Justice Department (precursors to agents of the FBI) raiding interstate bucket shop operations in Washington, New York, Philadelphia, Baltimore, Jersey City, Cincinnati and St. Louis, armed with warrants for arrest of 29 brokers and one telegraph operator. The investigative dragnet, of about 10 weeks duration, was based on wiretapping hundreds of brokerage messages that proved, or so the news reports asserted, that none of the bucket shops were placing *bona fide* securities trades. Eventually, the indictments were enlarged to take in Western Union, seemingly as part of the general trust busting, pro-business-regulation ways of Presidents Theodore Roosevelt and his successor, William Howard Taft and, especially, Taft's attorney general, George W. Wickersham. The political mood of the country at the time was to try to rein in its robber barons.

The news accounts make plain the bucket shop case defendants thought they had done nothing wrong. "This is only a play of the big fellows on the stock exchange to divert attention from themselves," one defendant declared upon his arrest. The case faded from public view after the appeals court decision and Great-Grandfather Gatins is hardly mentioned again in the mass media in connection with bucket shops until he and several other defendants finally pleaded guilty and quietly paid a $9,000 fine, as recorded in a one-paragraph article in *The Wall Street*

Journal of May 12, 1913. They thus avoided the two years of imprisonment also possible under the federal bucket shop conspiracy statute.

I never knew my great grandfather, but I'll admit to being fascinated at finding the arrest article and then trying to find out more of his life in New York. Born in Atlanta, it had been relatively simple to track his climb from a modest boarding house during the Reconstruction era of the Deep South to more substantial quarters of the Gilded Age. If he had something of a shadowy reputation as a wheeler-dealer and stock trader in New York, he publicly had been regarded as a respected investor, builder and entrepreneur in Atlanta. Interestingly, especially to me as a former newspaperman, the three main daily newspapers in Atlanta where my great-grandfather got his start in business, apparently never followed the case involving one of their prominent native sons. They carried an early version of the bucket shop indictments—the "stock gambling" case, they called it—mentioning only a certain Joseph Gaskins of Baltimore. But neither *The Atlanta Constitution* nor *The Atlanta Journal* nor *The Atlanta Georgian & News* followed the case after the "bankroll man" had been properly identified. It was as if they did not want to mention the courtroom travails of a hometown boy who had made good in the financial world of New York. The criminal case against one of Atlanta's native sons would have been hard to miss, given the extensive coverage it received in the major papers on the East Coast. Nevertheless, for whatever reason, they never publicly put two and two together while other, larger media outlets from Washington to New York provided extensive coverage of the bucket shop stories.

Almost simultaneous to the bucket shop developments, my great-grandfather had successfully furthered his other business interests, especially those in real estate in Atlanta, where he apparently maintained an unscathed business reputation. In particular, he had acquired valuable Atlanta property at the corner of Peachtree Street and Ponce de Leon Avenue, upon which he built the Georgian Terrace Hotel in 1910-11. He introduced it to the general public with a spectacular grand opening in 1912. The Terrace, one of the hottest properties in Atlanta in the early decades of the 20th Century, proved a cash cow and maintained the Gatins family for years and generations to come. That legacy was assured in February 1912, when Great-Grandfather Gatins formally placed the hotel property into a trust for the benefit of his three children. This also appears to have had the secondary benefit of insulating the property from the possibility of any bucket shop-related seizure by the U.S. government. *The Atlanta Constitution*, which carried an article about the trust's establishment, noted at the time that Gatins' ties to Atlanta had "laid the foundation of the fortune he has amassed in the east."

The hotel property helped rank my great-grandfather and my grandfather among the largest real estate investors in the southern capital on the eve of the First World War. The extent of that family real estate fortune at the turn of the last century was re-captured in Franklin M. Garrett's massive history of Atlanta, based on an inventory published by Forest and George Adair in 1914. My great-grandfather and grandfather are shown to have jointly held real estate appraised at $550,950, making them the 14th largest land investors in the town at that time. That half million dollars of land and improvements would be appraised in excess of $11.7 million in 2007 dollars. The appraisal sum also probably underestimates the true overall value of the holdings, as the Terrace was publicly estimated to be worth over $1 million two years previous.

That same year (1914), my great-grandfather is listed in the local city directory for Atlanta with an occupation simply listed as "Capitalist"—several light years from his first real job as a modest railroad clerk. No doubt this unusual job listing refers more to his business of raising and lending money and doing deals on Wall Street than to anything political. Other prominent businessmen in Georgia used the same job description at the time. By that time, he was well on his way to putting away large amounts of cash with the U.S. Trust bank in New York and using those sums to leverage more, often by making private loans to friends in the business world. One such loan was made to the Georgia Power Co., then a small electricity generating enterprise, which was hard pressed at the turn of the 20th Century to complete a series of hydroelectric dams and generating stations in the far reaches of mountainous north Georgia along the Tallulah River in Rabun County. That power was needed to run the new trolley cars that had started criss-crossing Atlanta. This loan, confirmed by a source close to the family, was worth approximately $50,000 (about ten times that much in today's dollars) and paid back with interest, according to the files of the Atlanta lawyer who handled the paperwork. At the same time, he kept on making his name on Wall Street as an astute stock speculator, often by making money from others' losses, that is by selling stock "short," according to one of his granddaughters. In that regard, he was no different from today's hedge fund operators and day traders.

I was very intrigued to discover this entrepreneur in the family tree and unearthing what details could be found. What an interesting character, I thought. Back when I was in the news business, assigned to cover a statehouse, we called mining of public records "doing black book." In this case, I was pleasantly surprised to find how rich a vein of family history was there to be mined. My great-grandfather obviously had lived a full life in interesting times.

One chronicler of the day noted that a good bit of Wall Street speculation occurred in after-hours negotiating that took place around the large square bar of The Waldorf Hotel, which opened in 1897, later called the Waldorf-Astoria. There at the bar "one often saw 'Joe' Gatins, an Atlanta millionaire, who was rumored to be a heavy operator in the cotton market," records a book about this era. According to that author, he was in fine company. Perhaps the most famous patron of the bar was J. Pierpont Morgan, the great financier, surrounded by politicians, wildcatters and stock speculators of every stripe who often gathered there after the New York Stock Exchange closed. From 5 to 8 p.m., in particular, it was as if the whole of Wall Street had moved uptown for a continuing stock exchange session, with "men betting on how stocks would perform the next day. In one discreet corner a ticker kept clicking off news. Here market pools were often formed. Here were to be found men who were willing to bet on anything, and to any amount, financiers and market operators, with names that gained newspaper front pages every day or so, clustered about the tables, or joined in the maggot-like surge that squirmed for a foothold on the substantial brass rail that ran along the bottom of the counter." There, they quaffed potent cocktails with fanciful, long-forgotten names like the "Baby Titty"—composed of equal parts anisette, Crème Yvette, and whipped cream, topped with a red cherry.

"A deal would start by one man's reading the news one way, and another in another fashion. One would come in the office feeling decidedly bearish. Another would talk bullish. The bear would decide he wanted to get rid of a lot of steel [stock], or something else he had on hand. The bull would take him up. They would watch the ticker, agree on the price at a certain point, and, bingo! with the exception of the stock exchange proceeding, the deal was made. Then, head to the bar to help make American history. Men staked fortunes there; they formed pools; they plotted to corner markets," that chronicler said.

My great-grandfather died 10 years before I was born, but this bucket shop financier—and his estate—were to play an important role in my own grandfather's life and make it possible to live a lifestyle that brought him into contact with international society, and make for an improbable union with Eglé, a young woman in Paris. He simply put his children and grandchildren on easy street. And eventually, like a hand reaching out from the graves at Oakland Cemetery in Atlanta, the long reach of his legacy would link grandmother and her only child, my father, back to Atlanta.

Chapter 2

Partying at the Ritz

What might a young, international playboy and sportsman with plenty of money do for fun in his free time in the advent to World War I? Well, why not head to Paris for a party like so many others? Thus did my grandfather, Joseph F. Gatins, Jr. become part of the crowd of Americans descending on the French capital during the summer of 1914.

Despite the acrid scent of oncoming war, there was hardly a better place for international socializing and merriment that summer than Paris' famed Hotel Ritz, a favorite watering hole of world travelers. It had opened its doors to almost instantaneous acclaim in 1898, and done so well that it virtually doubled in size by 1913. This was the luxurious retreat for the very rich (and the would-be rich) of America, where Rothschilds rubbed elbows with Morgans, where Goulds and Vanderbilts were mainstay visitors and where countless others came to do a little business under the observant eye of a youthful writer, Marcel Proust. It also was the place to be for New York financiers of somewhat lesser renown, brokers and bankers and Wall Street financiers who provided the necessary lubricant of international commerce. One of these men, investor James C. Brady, owner of an expansive horse stable in New Jersey, always seemed to travel with an entourage. One member of the Brady crowd at the Ritz that summer was a young real estate investor and horseman from Atlanta and New York, a well-traveled and well-heeled 32-year-old international sportsman and aficionado of French history, Joseph Francis Gatins, Jr. He was a member of that class of idle rich spawned from America's Gilded Age, largely living off of his father's considerable fortune, well-traveled in Europe and the Far East, and still an eligible bachelor.

As things were done in that era, he was properly introduced to a lovely and intelligent French girl 10 years his junior, Eglé Marie de Villelume-Sombreuil, who eventually became my grandmother. By chance, she had enough experience and *savoir-faire* to speak passable English. They were attracted to each other. "He was the handsomest man I had ever met," Eglé recalled many years later. "He was very handsome. He was short, nice-looking. He was very intelligent, very well read and had studied in England. I met him at a big party at the Ritz. And very quickly, we were engaged."

"He pleased me very much. He had beautiful blue eyes," Eglé recalled. But she also felt sorry for her fiancé. "He had lost one arm. That was probably one of the reasons I married him."

I discovered two versions of how my grandfather lost his right arm. The first had him taking a tumble while running on a set of stairs as a youth of 16 and losing his arm from that accident. The second, which seems more plausible, had him receiving a smallpox vaccination before his arm was set in a cast, and the vaccination spot becoming so infected underneath the cast that it necessitated amputation.

His recollection of meeting Eglé is not recorded for posterity but the available record suggests clearly that he was very much intrigued by Eglé and her connections to a rich French history. As early as July 1914, he'd sent a cable to Atlanta to announce his intentions, which were duly recorded in a brief article in *The Atlanta Constitution* of July 10. "Joseph Gatins, Jr., wins bride in Paris," the headline said. The article went on to relate that Gatins Jr., "one of the most prominent young men socially and otherwise" in Atlanta, was soon to wed Eglé, daughter of the countess de Sombreuil of Paris, "one of the most aristocratic of French families."

"His bride-to-be is a descendant of a family which for years has been prominent in French history," the article concluded, giving clear indication of Joe's interest in his love. The article also reflected the fascination the Atlanta papers had with this continuing family story. In contrast to the seemingly studied silence with which it had greeted my great-grandfather's legal troubles in Washington and New York, Atlanta's newspapers had a heyday covering and eventually chronicling the social lives of Grandmother and Grandfather and, eventually, their progeny. *The Journal's* social pages and later, those of *The Atlanta Constitution*, made it a habit to chronicle many of the comings and goings of the new couple, and, much later, that of their son, Joseph Francis Gatins III, my father, and then those of his children. In many cases, the early coverage dwelt almost *ad nauseam* on Grandmother Eglé's connection to French nobility, and that of her late father, the Count of Villelume-Sombreuil. Accordingly, many of the articles erroneously referred to Eglé as "the countess," although under the Napoleonic French Code, such titles only transfer to the male line and apply to the women only if they were married to the noble himself. Nevertheless, the post-wedding headline from a *Journal* article was, "Marriage of Mr. Joseph Gatins and Comtesse de Sombreuil in Paris." That was just the beginning of a long newspaper love affair with the Gatins family, which apparently fascinated Atlanta society and its society columnists.

My grandmother was a direct descendant of one of France's best-known families, several of whose members, unreconstructed Royalists, were guillotined during the French Revolution. Another, René de Madec, became a minor French historical figure for his exploits as a French corsair in India during the late 1700s. A sailor from Quimper in Brittany, he'd gotten his start on the high seas in the slave trade to Santo Domingo, then translated that experience into what he hoped would be more lucrative efforts as a privateer in India, sanctioned by the French government.

At any rate, whatever the reasons for their mutual attraction, Grandfather Gatins was interested enough in Mademoiselle de Villelume-Sombreuil to pursue a whirlwind Paris courtship that culminated in marriage but a few months later. It was a period of fancy dress balls, parties and fabulous gourmet food all coming together to mark the end of the *Belle Époque*. Like the scent of the sea that previews hurricanes, even hundreds of miles inland, the odor of rich French perfume and gunpowder was mixing in the air France breathed that summer. Haute couture had women wearing impossibly intricate, large hats and fanciful evening gowns, with tight bodices and generous amounts of tulle and lace, which were soon to be traded in for the more sensible frocks of wartime. Restaurants like the *Tour d'Argent* were still making a theatrical production of gourmet food, selling pressed and numbered "*Canards au Sang.*" The spring of 1914 was a fidgety time for all of France, anxious and prideful as it girded for inevitable war against the hated Krauts. The entire country was itching to extract revenge for the crippling defeat at the hands of the German forces at Sedan and the loss of the territories of Alsace and Lorraine in 1870. It was poised to take on the Kaiser. Whether Socialist or Royalist, whether drinking Veuve Cliquot or common *mousseux*, nothing less than victory, won with flair and *panache*, would do to erase the long and highly divisive national nightmare occasioned by the Dreyfus Affair. (The Dreyfus controversy had roiled and divided French society during the period 1894-1900 after a Jewish French Army captain, Alfred Dreyfus, was wrongfully accused of being a spy for Germany. The affair thoroughly divided the French into two camps, those who supported Dreyfus (Dreyfusards) and those against (anti-Dreyfusards). It also exposed a virulent and long-standing French anti-Semitism that only worsened in the period during and between the two world wars). But rather than focus on dark matters and warlike threats and controversies, all of

Paris strutted and fanned its tail feathers that spring in anticipation of a glorious summer. It seemed as if the entire known world, and its upper crust in particular, descended on the French capital for the season.

And if there were any misgivings about the oncoming alliance between a young demure woman from a family that was French to the bone and a clan of brash Irish-American immigrants from far-off Atlanta and New York, these seemed to be erased by parties galore at the Hotel Ritz and outings to the Bois de Boulogne. Eglé and Joe seemingly were swept up in the martial fervor accompanying the start of the First World War. There was no engagement period to speak of and theirs was not a textbook wedding made for the social pages. No wedding-day photographs exist today, no engagement or wedding ring. There was "no question of wearing a white dress," the bride recalled decades later, as the war officially had been declared in France less than five days before the ceremony. "I thus received the benediction in a blue suit," my grandmother said.

Nor is it known if Eglé's widowed mother and her current suitor, a Swiss banker named Henri Fischer, attended or not, although my grandparents were married in the same church her mother been married in the first time, the parish of St. Philippe du Roule. (Eglé's birth father had shot himself to death in 1912.) "She [my mother] thought it was crazy!" Grandmother Eglé recalled in a 1976 interview. "All my family, the Bretons especially, wrote that, 'you married an American, it's nearly [as bad] as an English.'"

Crazy or not, Eglé, it also seems clear, might have been proceeding with the hurried marriage out of a sense of social propriety—and to clear the re-marriage decks for her own mother's designs with Fischer. The Villelume-Sombreuil family formally had been introduced to Fischer as a possible match for Eglé on a transatlantic boat ride to or from New York around 1912. Fischer, though, found himself transfixed by the mother more than the daughter. As family relations have handed the story down to current generations of Gatins descendants, French society would have looked askance at the mother remarrying before her adult daughter made her own match, a situation solved by the appearance of a well-heeled American. So, it seems our grandmother might have married the Irish-American stranger who precipitously came into her life out of some sense of self-sacrifice for her own mother's happiness. Plus, she really loved the United States, having lived in New York for several years as a teenager.

The extended Gatins family in New York and Atlanta, meanwhile, did not attend the wedding in Paris, "being prevented from crossing (over to Europe) by the unsettled conditions," as a contemporary article from *The Atlanta Journal* put it. In their stead, the bride and groom each brought two witnesses to the mayor's office of the 8th Arrondissement, where French law required that a civil marriage ceremony also be held (on August 5, 1914, the same day as the church marriage). Grandfather Gatins brought two acquaintances as witnesses, probably friends from New York or drinking buddies from the Ritz: Harris Williams, a 25-year-old industrialist, and Charles Loeb, 21, a lawyer admitted before the Supreme Court of the State of New York. Grandmother Eglé was flanked by Régis Masson de Torcy, 65, a veteran of the War of 1870 against the Germans, and Charles Henri Lefrancois, 49, a veteran French cavalry officer. The wedding certificate reflects that there was no pre-nuptial contract. Rather than travel abroad for a honeymoon, the couple moved temporarily into the sumptuous Hotel Ritz as all Europe rushed headlong to armed conflict. By their wedding day, August 5, 1914, the assembled armies of Belgium, France, Germany, Russia and England all had been mobilized, poised for the inexorable war that both sides, especially France and Germany, had been expecting for months. As history well records, the immediate excuse for world war was the assassination of Austrian Archduke Franz Ferdinand by Serbian nationalists in Sarajevo on June 28 of that year. By July 30, both Russia and Austria had mobilized. Two days later, Germany did the same, and its army breached Luxembourg's border at Trois Vierges on its way to helpless, neutral Belgium.

Barbara Tuchman's fascinating chronicle records it thus: "At Armenonville, rendezvous of the *haut-monde* in the Bois de Boulogne, tea dancing suddenly stopped when the manager stepped forward, silenced the orchestra and announced: "Mobilization has been ordered. It begins at midnight. Play the Marseillaise."" Much of France went to war that summer as if marching to the beat of a full-dress parade, according to Tuchman. "French soldiers in red trousers and big-shirted dark blue coats, buttoned back at the corners," marched from Paris with song on their lips. "Cavalry regiments of cuirassiers with glistening metal breastplates and long black horsehair tails hanging down from their helmets were conscious of no anachronism." Eglé, while in the midst of marriage preparations, also was swept up by this flurry of proud, martial display, as her younger brother, Charles de Villelume-Sombreuil, nicknamed Charlic, was shipped out with his unit, the 27th Regiment of Dragoons (i.e., cavalrymen riding to war on horseback) on August 2, only three days before the wedding. Recollection of that movement was writ large in Eglé's memory, almost as large as the unit's pathetic return to Paris less than a month later.

"One evening, in Paris ... my mother got a telephone call from a woman who told her, 'I've got the café in front of the Dragoons' quarters. If you want to see them tonight, I'll save you a table.' We rushed to Versailles. The colonel

13

had received orders to leave clandestinely and at night, so as to not frighten the populace. He was an extraordinary man. His response: 'I don't give a damn. I'll probably be killed in a little bit and I want to make a real show of my departure.'

"They left, the band beating at the front with a fanfare of the most martial music, all the Dragoons with their splendid helmets, their rifles slung at their shoulders and their lance in their hands. It was a very beautiful show, and very moving. Everybody came to the windows. It was gorgeous. Oh, they were beautiful! When I think of it, tears still come to my eyes."

Contemporary photos of such martial parade spectacles suggest the Dragoons were woefully unprepared for the carnage that awaited them. Their parade helmets, shiny brass topped by a horsehair plume, seemed derived from the time of the Roman legions. Their metal breastplates, equally shiny and resplendent, appeared more for show than protection. In these pictures, not a one carried a sidearm, much less a rifle. Their main weapon: A personal *épée*. Contrast that march-to-war spectacle with that of the unit's return less than a month later, after the German juggernaut had easily crunched through Belgium and pushed to within 50 miles of Paris.

"Without news of my brother, I was very anxious. One day, a telephone call. Mother was coming to see me at the little restaurant in front of Longchamps. With some difficulty, we found a taxi and soon found ourselves face to face with what was left of the 27th Regiment of Dragoons," Eglé recalled. "The men were tired, their uniforms in tatters, their poor horses all skinny. Those people were in rags. The Dragoons had been forced to fight as infantrymen. Most of their officers had been killed." Just how futile their effort was is captured in this vignette: The Dragoons, on one occasion, had mounted a cavalry charge—against a squadron of German airplanes!

Tuchman describes the travails of another cavalry unit in the 9th Cavalry Division. "The cavalry, once so shiny in polished boots and bright uniforms, now stained and muddy, sway in their saddles, dazed with fatigue.

"'The men's heads hang with weariness,' one witness recalled. 'They only half-see where they are going; they live as if in a dream. At halts the famished and broken-down horses even before unsaddling, plunge at the hay and devour it voraciously. We no longer sleep; we march by night and face the enemy by day.'"

Nonetheless, remnants of Charlie's 27th Regiment were attached to the troops still garrisoned in Paris and sent back to the front by taxi to try to stop the Germans on the Marne River. As Tuchman points out, the desperate counter-offensive on the Marne River was made possible only by the commandeering of 600 taxis in Paris, each making two round trips to the front, carrying five soldiers each time. "They only stayed a few days to get some food and then they returned to the trenches. There never again was any question of marshalling the cavalry," my grandmother said.

By the time the Marne counter-offensive took hold, "It was time to go home," Joseph F. Gatins Jr. told his young new bride. The couple had already been forced to move out of the Hotel Ritz, which turned its first floor into a military hospital in late August 1914, and then closed by September. After staying some few days at the Ritz after their wedding, the Gatinses moved to another hotel on Avenue Montaigne, then for a few weeks to Great Britain before departing for good for the United States. By that time the newlyweds were already bumping into the harsh reality that proved to be their union. Just how difficult that marriage proved to be is graphically, if incompletely, related in Eglé's oral history and memoir, and also in the long memories of those who knew them in Atlanta in the early days of their marriage. In today's parlance, they would be a textbook example of a dysfunctional couple whose tensions and hurts eventually could not be masked by veneers of civility and social standing. For myself, uncovering these facts was not altogether pleasant, but it explained much of what was to come later. Dysfunction has coursed through Gatins family genes. The fruit of this research was not quite as sweet as discovering that my great-grandfather was a swashbuckling deal maker on Wall Street.

Chapter 3

"I Don't Want You"

❦ ❦ ❦

My Gatins grandfather and grandmother initially approached their new lives in the United States as any normal newlyweds, disembarking in New York in early October 1914. Eglé was introduced to the rest of the Gatins family, which included the new groom's parents (the bucket shop and Wall Street financier and his wife Kate), his brother Ben (a pugnacious, polo-playing bon-vivant) and his sister Mary ("a beautiful young lady who had married an old judge who worked with her father, and from whom she was separated"). The clan received her warmly.

"The Gatinses were so affectionate. Mrs. Gatins was wonderful and so was Mr. Gatins," Eglé said of her new in-laws, although her husband's parents would have preferred and had expected an expansive wedding ceremony and reception. The nuptials had perforce been very small, Eglé said, because of the war and because "I'd seen Charlic and his regiment leaving." But Gatins family regrets at not having had a society-style wedding apparently were more than offset by learning that Eglé shared their religious faith. "The Gatinses were very much Catholic," she recalled. "So, one of the things that pleased them was when they learned I was Catholic." Before Vatican II, the Roman Catholic Church was characterized by rigidity: Mandatory attendance at Sunday mass and Holy Days, repeated confession of all sin, communion, no meat on Fridays, fasting (for adults) at Lent and a richly textured, superstitious belief in the healing and protective powers of scapulars, rosaries, religious medals, prayer cards, indulgences, votive offerings, multiple angels, saints and the Holy Ghost. In America, these precepts were codified in a slim, didactic volume called the "Baltimore Catechism," first published in 1891, aimed at placing and keeping one's soul in a state of grace. Eglé, who had helped teach catechism to little children when she was growing up in Brittany, was right at home in that faith.

My grandparents then stayed a "little while" in New York, a bustling business and cultural center of more than two million residents, many of them new immigrants from all over Europe. Manhattan was known to both of them. He had moved there in 1901, even before leaving the University of Georgia and she knew it well enough from the years 1909-11, when, as a 17-year-old, she had steamed past the Statue of Liberty to accompany her mother following the separation of her parents. Her mother, a vivacious and gregarious Parisiènne, had opened a highly successful millinery store at the corner of East 30th Street and 5th Avenue, which sold dresses and hats to that era's fashion mavens. Mother and daughter (and, briefly, brother Charlie) had lived nearby at 523 West 31st, not far from what was then a new Penn Station.

The new couple then joined James C. Brady, the New York moneyman who had counted Joseph F. Gatins Jr. in his entourage in Paris the previous summer, and his wife, Victoria Perry, at Gladstone, their property at Monmouth Beach, New Jersey. There are two versions of what happened next. Eglé recorded the first, a raw version of events, on audiotape in 1976. That recollection bluntly presages the distress and rejection she was to experience from a bad-tempered, whiskey-besotted husband. The second, more sanitized version was captured in her written memoir about 12 years later.

Here's the first: "We went to see Jim Brady and then Joe got very drunk one day and left for Atlanta. He did not agree with his friend Jim Brady and so he said, 'I'm going back to Atlanta. I don't want you. Stay wherever you want, stay with my mother if you want—you get along very well. Stay with my aunt.' And I stayed with my mother-in-law in New York, who was very sweet."

Here is the second version, well-sanitized: "Joe was in a hurry to return to Atlanta, but my mother-in-law wanted to keep me [in New York] for a family reunion. He thus left alone. I rejoined him several days later."

What Eglé never spoke of at all is that her new husband probably behaved horribly during the first flush of this new marriage, so horribly that it was common currency in Atlanta decades later than he'd been "unfaithful to his wife on their honeymoon." I was astounded when I first heard this story, disbelieving, ashamed and angry that a grandfather might have behaved so. This was truly repellant, priapic behavior. Did Eglé have any inkling of this monstrous moral turpitude? If she did, she never talked about it. Her oral and written recollections tend more to describe the life of a dutiful, loyal and concerned wife. While still in the New York area, she had received a telephone call in which it was suggested she had better come to Atlanta quickly. Her husband had gone on such a bender that he'd been hospitalized. "I learned that he was really sick and in a clinic," she said.

Yet, the worry and concern over her husband's state seemingly was offset by her first experience of the deep South, an experience that foreshadowed a long love affair with Atlanta and its people and the many women friends she made there, if not with the man who had brought her to this brave new world. Outwardly, her new home could not have been more different than Paris: Its population approached a mere 155,000 compared to the French capital's three million-plus residents; recorded Paris history began in the 3rd Century A.D., while Atlanta did not exist as a metropolis before the 1800s. Yet, the social milieu she moved within was remarkably similar: Society in both cities was consumed with maintaining appearances of propriety and class and, for Eglé in particular, putting on a brave public face.

"It was a 22-hour trip in those marvelous Pullmans," she recalled. "Upon waking up in the morning, I was won over by the feeling of the South, the cotton fields, the Negroes coming home from work with a song on their lips." If she was cruelly disappointed upon her arrival at Atlanta's old Terminal Station "to not find my husband there," she simultaneously found herself embraced by the upper crust of a little railroad crossroads state capital down in the middle of nowhere, whose denizens then, as today, appreciated a class act.

Grandmother was met at the station and picked up by two of her husband's aunts, Julia Gatins Murphy, nicknamed "Dearie," and Mamie Gatins, a spinster, who brought her to her apartment at the Georgian Terrace Hotel in a big Packard. "I had never seen such a long car in all my life," Eglé said. The Georgian Terrace had been built in 1910-12 by her father-in-law, the Wall Street financier whose fortune sustained his children and eventually, his grandson. *The Atlanta Journal* turned her arrival in town into a fanciful tale. Here's the contemporary headline and article:

JOS. GATINS JR. HERE; COUNTESS-WIFE HELPS TO NURSE HIM

The countess Eglé de Sombreuil, wife of Joseph Gatins Jr., is at the bedside of her husband in the Georgian Terrace Thursday helping to nurse him through a sudden illness that has alarmed his friends.

(Continued...)

19

The Countess, who was one of the best-known figures in the social life of Paris before she became the Atlanta man's bride, hurriedly packed a grip and cut short her stay at the palatial home of James C. Brady in Monmouth Beach, N.J. to be with her husband. She has been at his bedside constantly since her arrival Wednesday and has turned down scores of pressing invitations from Atlanta society eager to honor her.

The countess has expressed herself as extremely pleased with Atlanta, and surprised and delighted with its metropolitan character. Even if it were not for the illness of her husband, she would be indulging in little social gayety, as she is consumed with anxiety over the fate of her brother, Captain Sombreuil, who has been reported killed in the battle of the Aisne.

As it turned out, Charlic had not been killed, only taken prisoner. As it also turned out, Eglé was forced into accepting one social engagement immediately upon arrival in Atlanta, the memory of which was indelibly imprinted upon her psyche. "They [the two sisters, Dearie and Mamie] had gotten me a reservation in a nice apartment [at the Georgian Terrace Hotel]—you know that apartment, the one with the round turret where we all lived—full of flowers. I told them that as soon as I'd taken a bath, I would go see Joe. They wanted to drive me but I told them I could manage to find a taxi to go see him. Dearie then told me, 'You must meet Atlanta society. We'll come get you at 5 o'clock to bring you to the *Thé Dansant* at the Driving Club. They know Joe, it doesn't matter. But they must see you.'" (The Piedmont Driving Club officially had been established only 20 years previous, but had already attracted much of Atlanta society to its membership rolls by 1914.)

"I explained that this could wait until Joe felt better, but they insisted: 'No, you must come. So, I then participated in the most ridiculous scene of all my life. Dearie, holding me by the arm, took me around to most of the tables, saying as follows: 'I present you my niece, the countess.' I tried to tell her that in France women only receive such titles from their husbands, after their marriage. But there was nothing doing. 'Your father was a count, thus you're a countess.'" She also was assigned an escort, a friend of her husband's named Joe Brown Connelly.

"He was the nicest thing." Many others also asked her to dance, "but I told them with my country at war, I don't feel much like dancing. If I live to be a hundred years old, I'll never forget the *Thé Dansant*."

She begged off having dinner with the aunts and then was dropped off at the Terrace, where she was visited by two of her husband's intimate friends, Albert and Edna Thornton. "I loved them the minute I met them," Eglé recalled. "They remained great friends until their deaths." Her husband was discharged from the clinic the next day and began to introduce his bride to his many friends, as life returned to some semblance of normalcy.

It was in many ways a life of ease and grandeur, much as she would have had in France had her father not committed suicide, and brought down the stigma of disapproval on the Villelume-Sombreuil family from both society and members of its rigid Catholic faith. In Atlanta, Eglé learned to drive a car, a small Model T Ford. She took her first golf lessons at the Druid Hills Country Club, which, in keeping with the racial tenor of the times, Grandmother recalled as having its greens maintained by gangs of convicts hobbled by ball and chain. She had a small dog and walked it around the Georgian Terrace neighborhood. The upper crust of Atlanta would drive up and down Peachtree Street, greeting friends and neighbors who lived on that still-fabled avenue. Families and friends would call on each other, sometimes unannounced, on Sunday afternoons, leaving embossed calling cards if no one answered the door. In Atlanta, use of these cards entailed an elaborate, unwritten subtext of polite messages, depending on which corner of the card was turned down in which specific way.

"Atlanta was a charming place, very much … Southern, you know, from the Sacred Heart [Church] to the Georgian Terrace, lovely homes there. You'd see all your friends rocking on their porches … and up above 14th Street, further up Peachtree, there was nothing. It was really in the country to go to Paces Ferry Road. You really thought you were going to the end of the world. And everybody knew each other. At the Driving Club, there was nobody you didn't know. It's not the same thing nowadays," she said in the 1976 interview.

The Gatinses often were invited to sumptuous lunches at the home of Julia "Dearie" Gatins Murphy and John Edgar Murphy, the latter already well on his way to becoming one of Atlanta's most respected banker-broker-businessmen. As Eglé recalled, he was the founding president of Lowry Bank, which eventually became the First National Bank of Atlanta. "They lived in a pretty house on Peachtree surrounded by a magnificent garden lining 13th and 14th Streets," Eglé recalled. "Invitations to their Sunday brunch were much sought after—and they fed you in abundance, with four or five vegetables.

"Joe and I were often invited," she remembered. "They had excellent Negro servants. Their cook was one of the best in town. The chauffeur and the butler were simply perfect. And there was a certain 'first maid,' Laura, who ruled the roost. Sometimes the lunches were so huge that they'd be held in the ballroom on the top floor!" The only wrinkle to such opulence and hospitality came in the form of Laura's annoying habit of "inundating you with her vaporizer. For those like me who did not like perfume, it was really disagreeable." But the lunches were memorable, and colored her initial experience in Atlanta. "They'd give those delicious lunches with the side vegetables. I adored Atlanta."

At the same time, there is no mention anywhere in Grandmother's memoir or her oral history of the homegrown Dreyfus-like affair that roiled Atlanta and all of America in 1915. This entailed the mob lynching of the Jewish business executive Leo Frank. (Georgia holds the dubious distinction of being the state whose citizens, mostly white, illegally lynched the second-highest number of persons, mostly black, in the post-Civil War era—458 all told. The last such lynching occurred in 1946.)

In like fashion, Eglé never makes any mention of the "big fire" that gutted 300 acres of Atlanta real estate in 1917 and destroyed almost 2,000 homes between downtown and Ponce de Leon Avenue, near where the new couple lived at the time. The conflagration only was checked when fire crews used dynamite to blow the blaze back. Her mention of current events appears strictly limited to matters related to the World War, rather than social issues, which seems strange to me in retrospect. Why was she so oblivious to what was going on around her?

As a new bride, Eglé appeared to prefer remembering what good times did occur, as with her fond recollection of Baltimore, where the young couple moved in early 1915, probably as early as January. Joe had gotten a job as an oil-and-gas investment advisor with Alex. Brown & Sons, a brokerage house in Maryland, according to family lore but that cannot be substantiated today. He pursued one of his favorite hobbies, horseback riding, joining the exclusive Elkridge Fox Hunting Club of Baltimore County. Despite having lost his right arm, my grandfather had learned to ride and turned into an accomplished steeplechase rider, a sport he pursued in New York and on Long Island and almost certainly at his friend Jim Brady's expansive horse stables in New Jersey and, for several years before his marriage, in the hunt country of Melton-Mowbray, England. The couple was quickly absorbed and lionized by Baltimore society, it seems, but they were not above playing a bit of social one-upsmanship with Baltimore society, many of whom dated their antecedents to America's pre-Revolutionary era.

"One day, during a dinner, when all the these people were telling tales about how they arrived to America on the Mayflower, Joe told them: 'My family came from Ireland during the potato famine, but my wife's people date back to the Crusades!' This really impressed the [Baltimore] people, most of whom didn't really know what it meant." Eglé remembered this period in Baltimore as the most peaceful and enjoyable period of her brief, conjugal life.

Chapter 4

"Life Was Intolerable"

Grandmother Eglé's lovely, peaceful interlude in Baltimore did not last long.

"Our pleasant life lasted until spring [of 1915]," she recalled. "But one day, Joe insulted his boss, who showed him the door. I was pregnant. Joe decided that his child must be born in France—a huge error. We thus left for France." The real reasons for my grandfather's decision to have his child born in France remain vague. There are no records to indicate what he was thinking at the time or why he wished his first child to be born in a country that was so deeply mired in the trench carnage of World War I. The United States was still about two years away from joining the conflict, and the loss of his right arm made it impossible for Joe to play any military role. His decision to have the baby born in France was most likely linked to his obvious desire to forge and maintain links to the French side of the family and the nobility that he and Atlanta society thought came with it. This decision later became a significant citizenship issue for their son, both during and after World War II. But in 1915, the main order of business was to have a healthy baby born in France, which occurred on October 8. Eglé gave birth at home, in a temporary residence at 32 rue du Peintre Lebrun, in Versailles, at four in the morning. In attendance was a midwife, Camille Chevalier, who attested to his birth, "the father being absent." Where was the new father? Bending his elbow.

"I once asked Grandmother if she had known that Mr. Gatins was an alcoholic before marrying," her granddaughter and namesake, Eglé Gatins Weiland, said. "She recalled that at our father's birth she sent a message to the barman at the Ritz asking that he inform her husband that she had given him a son—so she found out pretty quickly!" In fact, it seems clear that Grandmother learned of her husband's problems with strong drink early in the marriage, given that he'd gotten "so drunk" at the Brady home in New Jersey and been hospitalized after a drinking binge in Atlanta in 1914. Years later, Eglé recalled what it was like to live with an inebriate, as drunks were called in the early days of the 20th Century in America: "He was quite a gay blade ... and a drunkard. When he didn't drink, he was charming. For many people, when they're not drunk, they're charming." But in 1915, the new wife and mother, having given her husband a son born in France, was apparently more ready to see his charms than his faults.

The couple remained in France for several months, as French and German forces continued to battle each other to a draw in the butchery of the trenches. Joseph Francis Gatins III was baptized on January 15, 1916, at the St. Philippe du Roule parish where his parents were married. The couple returned to the States in February 1916, after a terrible winter steamboat crossing from Bordeaux, to try to make a go of the marriage.

My father, nicknamed *Mitou*, (the "little one," in French), had a nurse from France to attend to his every need, a young and striking Alsatian named Cecile, who quickly learned to speak English. Faded album photos show Francis playing in sandboxes, attending kindergarten at Washington Seminary, swinging his mother's golf clubs and reading children's books while sitting in the rocking chairs of the Georgian Terrace Hotel. The new family first had moved into the Terrace and soon thereafter to a nearby rented home at 583 Peachtree Street where, in between the new father's drinking bouts, it appears the young couple and the new baby sought to establish themselves as a normal family. Eglé learned to keep house, with the aid of household help borrowed from the Georgian Terrace, of which her husband was already a part owner.

Eglé also put her native French to use, teaching American infantry officers rudimentary French phrases after the United States joined the war against Germany on April 6, 1917. At the request of the commanding general at Camp Gordon, a vast U.S. Army training camp established just outside Atlanta, Grandmother, several society friends, "and several other officers' wives whom I do not remember," taught them "ready-made French phrases." The women, according to a news clip from *The Atlanta Journal*, had banded together as "most enthusiastic workers in the National League for Woman's Service" to also teach French to nursing students who would care for wounded French soldiers. Camp Gordon was erected in Chamblee, on the large field that is now the Peachtree-Dekalb Airport. "A certain number of these soldiers told me after the war that this had been a most useful service," Eglé recalled.

The couple's life in Atlanta had both highs and lows. For no reason anyone in the family can fathom today, Joe was failing to support her financially (and probably cheating on her), despite being one of the richest men in Atlanta, a third-generation descendant of one of "Atlanta's pioneers," as its founding fathers liked to call themselves. My grandfather apparently had no need to be gainfully employed, presumably relying on his father and whatever income was being generated by the Georgian Terrace Hotel for spending money. There is evidence that his work life was brief, indeed. There is also a hint that he chafed at not being able to go to war with other American soldiers who, better than a million strong, turned the tide against the Hun in Europe. He sought a commission as a lieutenant in April 1917, to work as a French interpreter, but the effort came to naught. Little more than a year later, November 11, 1918, that big war was over. Eglé, meanwhile, was lionized in the local society pages and assumed an outwardly stoic attitude.

The Atlanta Journal, as before her marriage, could not stay away, recording her return to Atlanta in a spread of March 12, 1916, which included a photo of Eglé holding her infant son and an accompanying cut line:

MRS. JOSEPH GATINS JR.
AND JOSEPH F. GATINS 3RD.

Mrs. Gatins has recently returned with her little son from Europe, and arrived in Atlanta last week to join Mr. Gatins at the Georgian Terrace, where they will be at home for several months. Mrs. Gatins, who was the Countess Eglé de Sombreuil of Paris, before her marriage, is a petite brunette with marked vivacity and charm of manner and she will be one of the most interesting of the many attractive visitors whose presence will add greatly to the social features of opera week. Master Gatins is a grandson of Mr. Joseph Gatins of New York and a nephew of Mrs. John E. Murphy of this city.

My grandmother tried to keep the home fires burning and often found herself and her young son surrounded by other members of the Gatins family, including Great-Grandfather Gatins Sr., who frequently came down from New York to visit Atlanta, and "who adored his grandson," as she recalled it. Still, all was not well at home, despite the active social life and loving attention from family. "Joe had begun to drink a lot. We'd put him in disintoxification houses. Life was intolerable," grandmother said. She also suggested years later that her husband was drinking up the proceeds of his father's generosity, and failing to support his wife and child in the manner she believed right and proper.

Treating alcoholics, or inebriates as they were commonly called then, was an uncertain and inexact science (and to a large extent, still is today). That much of America had a drinking problem was common knowledge—early America had been on a binge! "Between 1790 and 1830, America fundamentally altered its pattern of alcohol consumption," increasing the per-capita consumption from 2.5 gallons per year to more than 4.5 gallons. Various temperance movements and reform clubs sprang up in the 1800s and early 1900s, accompanied by a plethora of "inebriate asylums," particularly for those who were well off. One such asylum, The Kefley Institute of Greensboro, North Carolina, carried advertisements in *The Atlanta Constitution* as late as 1920, "for the treatment of whiskey and drug addiction, the tobacco habit and nerve exhaustion. Thirty years successful operation, correspondence confidential." A staggering number of "miracle cures," patent medicine hangover remedies, such as "gold treatments" and mail-order alcoholism cures like the Hay-Litchfield Antidote and Knight's Tonic appeared at the same time. Many of these were advertised in the popular press of the day. A partial list of early 20th Century home cures included Alcoban, Alcola, Alcodyne, Aurmino, Dr. Haines Golden Specific for the Cure of Alcoholism, Frank's Cure for Inebriety, Pandora's Thirty-Two, the St. James Society Cure, Father Matthew Remedy and Oxien's compound, advertised as follows: "Cures Drunkards, and Makes Weak Women Walk."

Whatever was tried in my grandfather's case did not work and life apparently became so difficult that Grandmother took the unusual step for one of her class, and especially one so steeped in the precepts of Catholicism, to formally declare separation from her husband (by at least March 26, 1920) and then to sue for a civil divorce less than two weeks later. (Catholics only recognized church-sanctioned marriage annulment, not civil divorce. Those who did secure a civil divorce faced automatic excommunication from the church and became ineligible to receive any of the Catholic sacraments.) The divorce court file cannot be found today at the Fulton County Courthouse in Atlanta and Eglé kept the divorce filing a secret from the rest of her family. Her grandchildren never heard her speak of it, and her son kept mum if he knew about it. But research evidenced that she did file for a divorce on April 7, 1920, according to the court clerk's docket book that makes this suit a public record. However, it provides no evidence that any depositions were taken nor does it list specific reason for the suit, or that the divorce was ever granted. *The Fulton County Daily Report*, a legal newspaper in Atlanta that routinely recorded every new Superior Court filing in Atlanta, including divorces, only notes that Eglé's case (No. 44864) was "not docketed." What is clear is that Eglé believed the home situation to be so out of control that she decided to leave her husband—just as her mother had left hers—and to do so somewhat publicly with the divorce filing. At the time, she was a slim and angular brunette, as depicted in a somewhat sultry newspaper photo, a glamour shot, published in *The Atlanta Constitution* just a year earlier. She was just 27.

I am proud of my grandmother for the fortitude she showed in taking the steps necessary to protect herself and her son in the face of an unholy situation. She later explained her decision to leave her husband in unmistakably blunt terms. The decision to take herself and her four-year-old son to France arose "because my husband did not and does not support my child and myself. As I have no fortune of my own, it was impossible for me to live in the United States and in view of the rate of exchange my parents did not wish to provide for my living in the United States."

Along with these frank declarations, sworn to by Eglé in a 1926 U.S. passport application affidavit, a tentative, bi-continental visitation schedule was suggested. Her intention was to "spend about six months in the U.S. every 18 months and my husband comes over to see his son and I for about 4 months between my visits." She reiterated that, "it is not by choice that I reside in France but by necessity, as above explained and [I] would much prefer living in the United States if my husband provided for my support."

The application file suggests that Eglé had attempted reconciliation with her husband during January to April, 1923, coming back to the States for a brief period, but she did not dwell on this time in any detail in her memoir or oral history. "I made an effort to come back to Atlanta but things weren't getting any better. I then came back to France for good," she said. Eglé, Joe and *Mitou*, then seven years old, apparently spent at least part of the three-month visit in Asheville, North Carolina. Her photo album for the period includes a picture of her husband and his son, marked, "Asheville 1923," standing outside the original Battery Park Hotel, which once overlooked the north side of the resort city. (The photograph depicts a wan, one-armed man next to his son, who is forcing a small smile). My brother Martin also recalls her telling of hiking in the Appalachian Mountains that surround the town, going from rough mountain hut to hut on overnight hiking-and-camping treks.

Although exact details are lost to time, Eglé's friends in France were aware of

29

the inner turmoil she had found in Atlanta. One, Claudette de Silguy, told family members she understood that "Eglé suffered terribly."

The American Consul reviewing the passport application also saw little hope of reconciliation after questioning Eglé. "The applicant has frankly admitted, when questioned, that she has no intention of residing permanently in the United States, nor of rejoining her husband from whom, she states, she may obtain a divorce."

By then, Grandmother had a pretty good idea of the reality underpinning her unhappy union. "I used to tell him, 'you never married me because you loved me, but because I had something to do with the French Revolution,'" she recalled in her oral history. "He loved it—he was a specialist of the Revolution."

By then, too, Grandfather was dying a slow death, battered by alcohol abuse and a case of pulmonary tuberculosis. The TB might explain the brief visit to Asheville, whose mountain air and temperate climate had spawned a variety of rest homes for tuberculars. Originally diagnosed in 1921, the year after Grandmother's abrupt separation and filing for divorce, it took six long years for the then-fatal and virtually untreatable disease to run its course. Even at death's door, he spurned his French bride and their son and there is no indication that he contributed in any way to their support. My father had just made his First Communion in Paris, in May of 1927, under the watchful eye of the Jesuits at his school on rue Franklin. "His father had died but a few days before in Atlanta. I had proposed to bring him his son, but he'd refused," Eglé said.

The separation and her husband's untimely death then ushered in something of a period of freedom and growth for the newly widowed Eglé. She lived an intellectually stimulating life at a spacious home at 150 Champs d'Elysées, a *salon* populated by an unusual extended family agglomeration. Under the same roof were her young son, her adult brother, her mother and new stepfather, Henri Fischer, the Swiss banker. While technically in mourning—she clung to widowhood's black clothes for decades thereafter—the period 1920-39 proved to be a most rewarding period in her life before the dislocation and perfect storm that evolved into World War II.

Chapter 5

Burden of Family

Eglé was the product of an interesting, but by modern standards, very quirky, French family. Her mother, under dispensation of Catholic canon law and in keeping with accepted French custom of the 19th Century, had been married off to her uncle. Her father, Charles Jules, Comte de Villelume-Sombreuil, was born in Paris, August 26, 1861, the fifth child of a family of six, descendant of noble lineage dating to an early Crusader and heir to an ultra-Royalist line of predecessors, several of whom had been guillotined in the turmoil of the French Revolution. At age 28, he was married for the first time to a widow twice his age, 57-year-old Eglé Ney de la Moskova. That wedding took place in China, where he was posted as a diplomat attached to the French government's foreign desk. Eglé Ney, duchess of Persigny by her first marriage, died a year later. Less than a year after that, young Charles consummated a second marriage with his niece from Brittany, Jeanne Marie de Madec, 23, herself the descendant of French nobility, secured when a forebear, René de Madec, made a name for himself and the French crown as a privateer in India. Her husband was 30. As family oral history has it, Jeanne de Madec forced her uncle-husband to quit the foreign service, which he loved, "because she didn't like the idea of having to be nice to other wives." She also forced him to move to Brittany.

"She was a very pretty woman, very headstrong and very independent," Eglé said of her mother, but not so strong-willed as to defy her own prideful mother. "My mother was really very much in love with a truly handsome man, charming and rich," Eglé recalled in her 1988 oral history. "But he was just an accountant. And my grandmother, arrogant and proud, never permitted her to marry him." Instead, she was foisted off on her uncle.

Eglé was born less than a year after that, October 15, 1892, in a hunting lodge at Crotoy, a beachfront resort in Normandy. She was named after her father's first wife. Eglé also is the name of a minor nymph of Greek mythology.

This sort of endogamy may seem strange today, very incestuous. It still strikes me as very odd, "but it may not have been as unusual in those days," according to my sister Eglé Gatins Weiland. The union was, however, definitely and noticeably bizarre for the young Eglé and her brother Charlic, who routinely would hear their mother call their father "my uncle."

Initially, the strangeness of her parents' marriage did not affect young Eglé and her growing love for her Celtic homeland, where she spent the first 12 years of her life. The Villelume-Sombreuils made their home at a family property on Kergœl-Kaher, a rocky, waterfront property in the Rade de Brest. The weather there, she said, benefited from a maritime climate, "tempered by the Gulf Stream, which permitted the most beautiful flowers and fruit of the world to blossom: Roses, carnations, blue hydrangeas, strawberries, and all manner of fruit. Fishermen would bring us fresh catch. There was also a lobster aquaculture pond just below our grounds. As a result, we often ate lobster—so much so that the help, when hired, would tell us: 'No lobster more than twice a week. We want meat!'

"In 1895, I had a little brother, Charles [nicknamed Charlic].

"I thus was brought up until I was 12 in that dream world where fairies, elves and goblins were held in such high esteem. I firmly believed in their existence, just like our nanny from Brittany, like all the people there." Her 1988 memoir makes plain that she still believed in them at age 28. "In 1920, my mother and stepfather were touring Brittany. The chauffeur didn't believe in all those stories. But one night, when we were returning from a visit, he crossed a field of heather and broom to shorten his trip. The servants had all told him, 'One should not disturb the goblins—one should not go that way.' The car just stopped. We were desperate when, luckily, a farmer came by in a cart and willingly took us to my aunt's house. The chauffeur was severely chastised by the local help, who had told him: 'Don't bother the goblins.'"

It pleases me no end that Grandmother retained a touch of Celtic paganism, given the dogmatic Catholicism of her time. I imagine it would have been impossible for her to ignore the strong presence that prehistoric, Stone-age Celts imprinted on the landscape of Brittany. When I visited the peninsula, the land was still dotted with dolmen burial chambers and stone menhirs, some of them arranged as if on parade, others, huge stone slabs better than 30 feet tall. Local heritage museums contain all kinds of stone tools, from rough adzes to highly polished knives. Only later, did Romanesque churches also begin to dot the landscape. Even as late as 2004, there was still talk of the supernatural in Brittany, including references to "magnetizers" said to have the power to cure evil and exorcise the Devil.

I have a feeling the Celtic lore of her youth partially explains why she bound herself in 1914 to a first-generation Irish-American with his own Celtic and Irish antecedents and his own superstitions. The family's oral tradition suggests, for example, that he believed it awful bad luck to place a hat on a bed! Of course, Eglé simultaneously was indoctrinated into the very strait-laced Catholicism of the day. The men of Brittany, most of whom had completed their compulsory military service, knew how to speak French, "most of the women, not at all. The catechism was taught to local children in Breton, a form of Celtic language with its own sounds, alphabet and written form. And to set the good example, I had to help," Eglé said.

Catholic ritual was everywhere, almost part of the air they breathed, according to Eglé, with additional religious instruction, in her case, provided by nuns at the school. There were "magnificent processions," she said, with men and women dressed in colorful embroidered costumes, contrasting the "severe countryside, with its little low farmhouses and the hedges demarking the fields. This countryside … was very religious," she said. "I remember when the priest from the village would bring the last sacraments or communion to the farmhouses, an old raincoat covering his vestments and the altar boy in red, also covered by a raincoat, ringing his little bell. When the priest went by, we would genuflect in the mud."

There was also time for childhood play. Little Eglé and her brother learned to "swim" off the rocky beach in front of their home. She'd wear long bloomers, "up to the neck and down to the knee. The coachman would tie us off with a belt and let us dog paddle. It wasn't classic, but we managed very well in the water." In September of each year, the family would take an annual beach trip to Brignogan, also in Brittany. Eglé first visited that beach in 1907, when there were but five houses surrounding the picturesque bay.

If there was any concern about the inbreeding of her family, it was manifested only in the concern that Eglé was so tiny and short that her father "took her to a specialist. The doctor performed treatments where she was suspended by the neck with weights on her feet," according to her granddaughter Eglé. 'It didn't work!" Grandmother claimed to be 5 foot, 3 inches tall in a 1926 passport application, but she was well under 5 feet tall at the time of her death, and suffering from an accelerating case of osteoporosis that bent her almost double.

She and Charlie had their own garden where they grew cabbages and raised rabbits, which they then sold back to the family's cook. She took German as a foreign language at the local primary school, but also picked up some English from some English girls she met playing tennis in the beachfront resort town of Dinard. Later, her father found her an English tutor, but she never mastered English grammar. "That's why I write English so badly," she said.

The family also entertained. Almost every Sunday, there was a large lunch, open to friends from Brest and Navy officers arriving in horse drawn carriages. The house was large, heated in winter by a "big stove in the center of the house" and a big fire in all the other rooms. "One man had to do the lamps and the fire every day," Eglé remembered. "And they had so much linen, they did not wash it but twice a year. In the country, they'd change everything every three weeks to a month, and then once a week when there were guests. There was a washhouse and a big tub. The linen smelled so good."

Once a year, though, the Villelume-Sombreuil family closed its doors to the outside world. On July 14, Bastille Day, the French national holiday, they closed their shutters and the children were not allowed to see Bastille Day fireworks because of the family's royalist antecedents and archconservative political leanings. French kings had ennobled both families, Villelume-Sombreuil and Madec.

On her father's side, Eglé traced her ancestry to Mademoiselle Maurille de Sombreuil, who to this day lives in France's collective unconscious as the brave girl who, minutes before she and her father and brother were to be guillotined, supposedly downed a glass of red wine mixed with blood, crying, "*Vive la Nation,*" in vain attempt to save her father from beheading. This attempt secured a reprieve for the family, but only briefly. Father and son were beheaded in early 1794, and data collected in French archives conclusively proves that she did not down a bloody drink. Mlle. de Sombreuil later married a childhood friend, Charles de Villelume, whose own family had attained nobility during one of the first Crusades to the Holy Land. On her mother's side, Grandmother traced the lineage to René de Madec, a sailor from Quimper in Brittany, who made his name for France first on the high seas in the Caribbean slave trade and then as a privateer and soldier of fortune in India, fighting mostly against the British in that far-off land for 30 years (1750-1779). Upon his return, King Louis XVIII made him a viscount.

Such lineage and a relatively normal early childhood could not insulate Eglé from family reality, though. "My father, accustomed to his brilliant first wife ... found mother a bit spiritless. She had not yet turned into the vivacious woman whom no one could resist," Eglé related. "They were never happy together." Her parents decided to live separate and apart, as the Roman Catholic Church did not recognize divorce. "In a way, we had a rather sad life, because my mother and father got separated," Grandmother remembered. "So, for the children, it's very sad. We'd go and spend three months with my mother and then come back to the country. So, that made for a rather sad life, you know. I was seven, I think."

Her mother moved to Paris, where she maintained two apartments—"the only place she ever loved." Her father stayed in Brittany, which he apparently loathed. "Father said: 'She made me buy a place in Brittany that I hate—and she goes back to Paris.' He would have liked to live in the center of France, where 'the shooting [hunting] was very good.'" While her father brooded in Brittany, her mother lived the life of a socialite in Paris, attending fancy-dress balls, going to the theater and cutting no small swath through a wide circle of international acquaintances and the many women friends she had made growing up in Paris. Eglé recalls her mother as headstrong and strong-willed, with a reputation as a mischievous child at the Convent of the Sacré Coeur on rue de Varennes (today, the Musée Rodin): "I'm the niece of one of your good nuns, so you'll never be able to kick me out!" The nuns became the butt of many jokes that otherwise would have occasioned serious discipline, such as replacing the holy water in church fonts with ink, or tying the nuns' veils together.

Bouncing back and forth from Brittany to Paris came to an end when Eglé turned 12 and her father, whom she liked better than her domineering mother, moved to Versailles. Grandmother cherished her adolescence in the town that once housed the French royal court. "I played tennis and continued my education," Eglé remembered. Versailles had big avenues and alleyways "and I was allowed to bicycle by myself." She also recalls civil unrest during that period in Versailles, when the secular French government moved to take over church properties, including the Trianon. "It was a terrible period," Eglé said. "The government wanted to take over the Church's goods and properties and was taking inventory. Those good Catholics took to defending their rights and there were some real fights over this."

The back-and-forth from one household to the other also took on an international flavor in 1909—Eglé was then 16 or 17—when her mother unexpectedly moved to New York. "To prove her mettle, my mother left for the United States and opened, in New York, a store for women's dresses and hats, which was wildly successful," Eglé recalled. "I went with her and really enjoyed myself."

Like many members of the Gatins family who came after her, Grandmother was to maintain her connections to both France and the States in ensuing decades, but without ever settling into a home that she could really call her own until the last few years of her life, almost 80 years after that first visit to Manhattan. The Gatins family, while officially and finally taking root on United States soil some five generations later, has never fully given up the intercontinental meanderings that characterized Eglé's own transatlantic travels.

Charlic joined them in New York, but only stayed three months, returning to Versailles to join the 27th Regiment of Dragoons, which was then already preparing for the world conflict that was to come two years later.

Eglé and her mother also steamed back to Paris for summer vacations. On one such trip, apparently in 1912, Eglé was to be introduced to a potential suitor, a very-well connected Swiss banker based in New York, Henri Hans Fischer, then about 27 years old. But Fischer succumbed to the charms of the 44-year-old mother and eventually married her instead of Eglé, in 1916. My grandmother, however, seemed to keep a candle burning for her one-time potential suitor, who, in the collective memory of her grandchildren, was swept away by the wiles of her own mother. Photographs of Jeanne de Madec de Villelume-Sombreuil at that time present her as a striking, bosomy woman with a tilted, engaging mouth. Fischer, somewhat bland looking, sports a bushy mustache. His wedding aspirations were simplified after August 29, 1912, when Grandmother Eglé's own father, Charles Jules, Count de Villelume-Sombreuil, committed suicide at Versailles.

Did he shoot himself? "Yes, that was awful," Eglé recalled in her oral history. "Yes, more or less he was depressed and that made a terrible impression on me as you can imagine." But recollection of this terrible family development is totally sanitized in her written, 1988 memoir: "My father died in 1912. We buried him at the Picpus Cemetery [in Paris], where the victims of the [French] revolution have tombs." Suicide has not ingrained itself in subsequent Gatins genes, but it is certain the concern was never far from grandmother's thinking. Her father's suicide, and the stigma attached to it by French society and the Catholic Church, also might explain why Eglé could then so quickly ally herself with a one-armed American gentleman less than two years later. He was a ticket to respectability, but Eglé and Joe seemed to have only two things in common: Superstitious adherence to Celtic lore and Catholic doctrine, and common interest in matters of French history. It was only in retrospect that both of them could be viewed as battered souls looking for safe haven.

Irish-American Bloodlines: Joseph F. Gatins Sr. (1855-1936) and his wife Kate Thomas Gatins (1855-1937).

French Bloodlines: (Clockwise, from top left) René de Madec (1736-1784) and his wife, Marie-Anne de Madec; Jeanne-Marie de Madec and her husband, Charles Jules de Villelume-Sombreuil (1861-1912).

Fancy Dress: Jeanne de Madec de Villelume-Sombreuil (1868-1957).

Young lady:
Eglé de Villelume-Sombreuil
was a pretty girl and grew to be a
striking beauty as a young woman.

Cavalry Dragoon: Eglé's younger brother,
Charles de Villelume-Sombreuil (1895-1963),
served in a French cavalry unit during World War I.

Star-crossed lovers: Eglé de Villelume-Sombreuil (1892–1990) and Joseph F. Gatins Jr. (1882–1927) both looked remarkably peaceful and innocent at age 19, when these photos were taken.

New generations: (Clockwise from top left) A new generation arises. Joseph Francis Gatins III (1915-1983), is held as an infant in France by his great-grandmother, Marie-Anne Michelle de Villelume-Sombreuil (1847-1926), while his mother, Eglé (right), and grandmother Jeanne de Villelume-Sombreuil looked on approvingly. Joseph F. Gatins, Jr., the one-armed man, holds his new infant son, Francis. Francis played in a sandbox with his two cousins, Hope (center) and Dorothy Gatins, and later in the Washington Seminary kindergarten schoolyard in Atlanta.

Atlanta to Asheville: Francis Gatins grew up and rode a scooter in Atlanta at the Georgian Terrace Hotel, where he rocked in the rocking chairs. In 1923, he and his mother met his father at the Battery Park Hotel in Asheville, N.C., the next-to-last time Francis ever was to see his father.

Chapter 6

Killybegs to Buckhead

❧ ❧ ❧

Grandfather and Grandmother Gatins each brought a rich, but very different, texture to their improbable union. Eglé was the inheritor of a noble and fabled French family history, but her fortune and good family name had been tarnished and significantly diminished by her father's suicide. Joe was a nobody from nowhere by comparison, scion of a family whose last name had not existed 75 years before, from a little state capital of the Deep South that had not itself existed eight decades years before the marriage. He was, however, heir to a very large pile of new money and property rapidly accumulated in two preceding generations of thrift, hard work and his own multimillionaire father's knack for capitalizing on the freewheeling, robber-baron-like financial dealings of the Gilded Age. But arrival of the Gatinses in the New World was humble, indeed.

This particular branch of the Gatins family originated as the McGettigan clan of Killybegs, a small, commercial fishing village in County Donegal, on the craggy and stormy northwestern-most coast of Ireland. This territory was so barren and rough and wild that local people viewed some of its rocky features as a gate to purgatory. The Gatins clan still occasionally used the name McGettigan after its members arrived in Atlanta in the late 1840s, but no one in my family knew of the McGettigan connection until almost 150 years later. My brother Martin, detained overnight by British military authorities after mouthing off in a pub in Dublin, decided he needed a friend in Ireland and found a Joe Gatins listed in the telephone book. That Gatins, indeed a very distant relative, was supervisor of Glenveagh National Park in County Donegal, in the Catholic area of Ireland. He surprised Martin with the tale of our McGettigan origins. Old records of the Church of the Immaculate Conception in Atlanta also reflect the McGettigan connection, including a baptismal certificate from January 15, 1855, for "Joseph McGettigan (Gattins), son of Joseph McGettigan (Gattins) and Bridget Cullen, his wife, witnessed by John McGettigan (Gattins) and Ann Cullen." It seems it took several decades for the Gatins name to settle on one spelling. Subsequent baptism, marriage and confirmation records variously used the spellings Gaitins, Gatens as well as Gattins, before eventually settling on today's spelling, Gatins, pronounced "gay-tinz." (It also should be remembered that all records of the day were written out by hand, sometimes in uncertain penmanship, and prone to misspelling.)

Three McGettigan-Gatins brothers, James, John and Joseph (the latter, my great-great grandfather) came to the United States in the mid-1840s as part of the huge Diaspora that brought so many Irish families to the new world as the crippling potato famine decimated Ireland. John and Joseph moved to and remained in Atlanta, marrying two sisters who also immigrated from County Donegal, Ann and Bridget Cullen, respectively. James returned to Killybegs after their father died. No cogent reason for the name change has survived, but some members of the extended McGettigan-Gatins clans today believe that the McGettigans began changing to the made-up Gatins name back in Killybegs so as to not sound too Celtic or Gaelic and thus better their chances of gainful employment from the hated British.

These Irish immigrants, the second such wave to wash upon American shores, especially in the Deep South, were often viewed as barely a notch above the enslaved peoples from Africa and the Caribbean who had preceded them to this new world. Poor, often penniless, hungry, ill-clothed, and tied to a religion that babbled in a foreign tongue at church (Latin), the Irish found themselves shunted to the most menial of jobs, digging ditches and canals or carving railroad tunnels out of hard granite mountains. Sometimes, they were paid in trade—raw moonshine whiskey rather than cash—but those with an aptitude for reading, writing and figuring often bootstrapped themselves from the red clay of Georgia into less back-breaking careers.

John and Joseph Gatins and their descendants, particularly my financier great-grandfather and his children, seemed to quickly outgrow Irish antecedents to become part of the meteoric ascent that Atlanta, with a knack for self-promotion and self-aggrandizement, still evidences today. The extended family emerged from Celtic immigrant beginnings to hobnobbing with Atlanta society in Buckhead and with high international society at the Hotel Ritz in Paris in three generations.

The first Joseph Gatins in this particular line of new Irish-Americans arrived in Atlanta by 1849. Once there, he worked for the next 50 years as a clerk and freight manager for the Central of Georgia Railroad, located in the Atlanta freight depot. The depot building, still standing today, is so close to the Georgia state Capitol that it is now often used as a party venue for politicians and lobbyists. A noted Atlanta historian commented that this first Gatins in Atlanta was a founder of the Immaculate Conception Church—and often was referred to as one of Atlanta's original "pioneers."

Indeed, Atlanta had literally been carved out of wilderness and Indian Territory in 1837, little more than a decade before Joseph Gatins got there. The town originated as Standing Peachtree, a trading post on the Chattahoochee River that served as a dividing line between Creek and Cherokee Indian territories. Originally dubbed Canebrake and Thrasherville by white European settlers, traders and explorers, the advent of the railroads in the area saw it renamed in quick succession Whitehall, Terminus, Atalanta, Marthasville and, finally, Atlanta, in 1845. It did not become Georgia's capital city until after the Civil War.

In those early days, it was a rough-and-tumble kind of place, not yet buffed to the polish and veneer that it sought from inception and still aspires to today. Immigrants, merchants, adventurers and frontiersmen all made for Atlanta and the riches anticipated by the coming railroad lines. By 1851, the town was sponsoring civic barbecues, digging public wells and putting down a suspected "insurrection of Negroes," as it was termed in one early history.

The state of Atlanta politics during that era is reflected in the names of the two political parties contesting municipal elections—the "Moral Party" and the "Free and Rowdy Party." As one historian records it, the small trading and rail outpost had "over 40 drinking saloons in town, to say nothing of the groceries dealing in ardent spirits, and they all did a land office business." Pigs freely roamed the streets until 1854 and "houses of ill-fame abounded in such locales as the infamous Murrel's Row and in the so-called 'Snake Nation.'" Murrel's Row was located on the north side of Decatur Street, between Peachtree and North Pryor Streets, "famed for its disreputable characters who gathered there for cockfights, to drink and gamble," and "who rarely condescended to bid deference to the better element."

The noted Atlanta historian, the late Franklin M. Garrett, described it as "tough town" in its early days and as one whose city fathers, all white, also wrestled with various matters relating to its large black population, both slave and free. Following the so-called "insurrection of Negroes" in 1851, which culminated in the arrest of nine black residents, the city's white fathers adopted a variety of measures aimed at controlling its antebellum black population. In 1856, the city denied the petition of a Negro to open an ice cream parlor, deeming it unwise; forbade Negroes to assemble at night after certain hours; heard complaints from free whites about free blacks and "slave mechanics" working against free white labor (in 1858).

While slaves were bought and sold and traded in Atlanta, historians also point out that Atlanta, unlike the rest of the South and Georgia's black belt (where enslaved peoples often outnumbered their white owners), was not possessed by decades of slave-owning tradition nor, consequently, as much of the race-fueled rage that was to culminate in the Civil War (1861-1865). Of Atlanta's 10,000 residents at that time, about one-fifth were slaves, less than the percentages often recorded in Georgia's plantation counties.

History records that many Irish immigrants made common cause with their fellow Irish Catholics in seeking to avoid having to take sides in the oncoming fight for secession, but take sides they did, as in the case of the Gatins brothers, Joseph and John. John Gatins, his obituary strongly suggests, was with the Confederate side. "At the outbreak of the civil war, he was appointed to the commissary department of the Confederate Army," the obituary said. Great-great Grandfather Joseph Gatins' sympathies probably lay with the other side, and likely would have remained cloaked in the shrouds of long-forgotten history, except for the tireless research provided by Dr. Thomas G. Dyer of the University of Georgia. Dr. Dyer is the author of *Secret Yankees: The Union Circle in Confederate Atlanta*, a seminal and unique review of Union sympathizers and spies operating in Atlanta during the Civil War. A central thesis of that book is that many residents alternated allegiance between Confederate and Union forces, depending on which side seemed to be winning the conflict at any given time. Only after the bloody war ended did many residents' true beliefs emerge, as many Union sympathizers sought official recompense for goods lost or taken by force by the forces dressed in blue. Such petitions were lodged with a congressionally appointed review board called the United States Court of Claims. The claims were made under oath, bolstered by affidavits from friends and neighbors also under oath, and tacked up on the Fulton County Courthouse doors for all to see. These postings, as Dr. Dyer views the practice, would have been tantamount to a most public declaration of one's leanings during the conflict.

In the case of Joseph Gatins, his sympathies lay in helping two Irish friends, James and John Lynch, who sought reimbursement from the Court of Claims for the loss of 108 bales of cotton seized by Union forces during the war.

"The reason that I know so much about this cotton that I have testified to is that I was Clerk in Capt. Hade's department at the time the cotton was taken [during the Union occupation of Atlanta in September, 1864]," Gatins declared. Capt. Hade, according to the Gatins affidavit and the Dyer book, served as the

Union Army's assistant quartermaster in Atlanta at that time. Joseph Gatins also was quick to note that he had "never given any voluntary aid to the rebellion," but had given some needy Confederate soldiers something to eat. "I gave it to them for humanities [sic] sake."

In his deposition, Gatins dates his arrival in Atlanta to 1849, and notes that he was a naturalized American citizen who took seriously his naturalization oath to uphold the U.S. Constitution. But little more is known of his activities during the tumult, or of the several years he apparently spent in Savannah immediately following the end of the Civil War. Nor is it known if his wife and oldest son, later to be known as Joseph Francis Gatins Sr., were actually still in Atlanta when Union Gen. William Tecumseh Sherman and his Yankee forces took the town.

Dr. Dyer believes that Irish immigrants in particular made it a point to try to avoid military service on grounds that it was not their fight and "resolutely refused to take up arms for the Confederacy and spent the war years trying to carry on business as usual while devising ways to stay out of Confederate service." Such methods, historians suggest, included service in volunteer fire brigades or "home defense" fraternal groups, such as the "Irish Volunteers," whose members were exempt from duty in Atlanta. My great-great grandfather Joseph Gatins was a member of these Irish Volunteers. To me, the actions of this ancestor seem like the protective camouflage of a chameleon: He made the best guess as to which color, Gray or Blue, ultimately would triumph. He chose Blue, the color of the Yankee uniforms. What is a bit surprising (and intriguing) in looking back at the family history is how much Grey colored the lives of subsequent generations of Gatins men, down to my own childhood in Atlanta.

It wouldn't have been such a bad idea to surface as a Union man after Sherman came to town in 1864. As Garrett points out in his exhaustive survey of Atlanta history, "those citizens of Union sympathies suddenly loomed into importance. Not a few of their Confederate neighbors sought them out and requested them to use their influence to secure protection of their property. In no instance were such requests refused. The Union people were as uneasy as anyone else and showed a disposition to keep on the best possible terms with their fellow-townsmen."

The Irish Catholics of Atlanta, led by Father Thomas O'Reilly, also took care of their own, ensuring that the church they had founded, the Church of the Immaculate Conception, was spared the torch as Sherman and his troops began their infamous, destructive march toward Savannah. Father O'Reilly, the pastor at the time, had ministered to both Union and Confederate soldiers in field hospitals during Atlanta's siege and is said to have told Sherman's staff that they would face massive desertion from the many Catholic soldiers in the Union forces if they fired the church. The church indeed was spared but much of Atlanta lay in ashes afterwards, with its key infrastructure, the railroads, in shambles. Union troops, after levering and uprooting miles of railroad track, made a habit of creating "Sherman's neckties" of the iron rails, heating them red hot and then twisting them so they never could be used again. As the Dyer history elucidates, some Union families stayed in Atlanta, while others, like that of Joseph Gatins, surfaced in Savannah.

He was no stranger to Savannah, probably having passed through the port town on his way to Atlanta, and having returned there to claim his bride, Bridget Cullen, in 1853. The young couple stayed for a time in Savannah after the Civil War, during 1868-69, living on Jones Street, only a few blocks away from what likely was his job at the Central of Georgia rail yards in that city. The young couple experienced tragedy. Catholic diocesan records in Savannah record the death of two of their young children: On October 25, 1868, that of Thomas, a four-week-old infant baptized on September 27; and on March 17, 1869, that of eight-year-old Mary Theresa, born in Atlanta at the eve of the Civil War. She is buried in Lot 35 of Section D of the Catholic Cemetery in Savannah.

During that period on the Georgia coast, Joseph also took up his civic duty to vote in the first post-war elections and swore, in yet another affidavit filed originally in Chatham County [Savannah], that he had remained loyal to the Union side during the conflict. Such affidavits were required by Union forces during the Reconstruction period and marked the first time that Negroes allowed to vote in the state. The pre-printed affidavits affirmed that those who signed them had not "been disenfranchised for participation in any rebellion or civil war against the United States…. nor engaged in any insurrection or rebellion against the United States, or given aid or comfort to the enemies thereof …" Joseph Gatins filled in the blanks and signed the affidavit on April 8, 1868. His brother John, despite his Confederate leanings, took the same oath in Atlanta on October 15 of the preceding year. Both, early on, had become naturalized U.S. citizens and were obviously ready to uphold their civic duty to vote.

By the mid-1870s, both these strands of Gatinses were in Atlanta for good. Joseph and Bridget raised a family in the ever-expanding Georgia capital, where a fervid pace of growth took hold after Reconstruction. One of their sons, Joseph Francis Gatins, Sr., my great-grandfather, capitalized on this rapid expansion and experienced the signal business success that eventually led him to Wall Street.

Chapter 7

Peachtree to Wall Street

My great-grandfather Gatins got his start in Atlanta and retained his ties there for his entire career, even after transferring much of his business and interests and immediate family to New York. Born in 1855, just before the Civil War, his working life began while living at home with an early job in his teen years as a "leash boy," presumably a description for an archaic job involving walking dogs. He opened what was probably his first bank account around age 16, on September 28, 1871, according to deposit records of the Freedmen's Savings and Trust Co. This institution, commonly called the Freedman's Bank, was set up in 1865 after the Civil War, primarily for the benefit of former slaves, African-American military personnel and impoverished whites.

Five years later, coming of age in the middle of the post-Civil War Reconstruction Era, this Joseph Gatins was working under his father as a mail clerk for the Central of Georgia Railroad in Atlanta. Contemporary records for 1874 list his father, the Irish immigrant, as being in charge of Central of Georgia's freight depot. Both are shown to be living in a boarding house at 52 Gilmer Street. (The city directories of the time did not list wives.) From there, young Joseph got into banking, transportation, cotton and cotton futures, money lending, construction, real estate, securities and hotel industries. Astutely using the virtually unregulated, profit-driven ethic of the Gilded Age, he did so well that three generations of subsequent Gatinses essentially lived off his fortune and largesse.

Nonetheless, the weave of the tapestry that characterizes this long and successful business career is sketchy. For a man in business all his life, only one letter remains, from 1936, just months before his death at the age of 80. Family members apparently did not safeguard any of his personal correspondence, and kept only one photograph, which depicts him as a fair-haired, serious-looking businessman wearing a coat and tie and a very starched collar.

Except for the bucket shop controversy and the news articles that detailed it, the outline of his climb to success is mentioned only today in musty and tattered city directories in Atlanta and New York, and in passing in various published histories. (City directories were published in the United States well before the advent of modern telecommunications and telephone numbers, and included alphabetical listings of city residents, their addresses and often a brief listing of their occupations.)

- In 1880, he was a railroad mail clerk with the Central of Georgia Railroad, boarding with his father at 109 East Hunter Street in Atlanta.

- By 1890, the Atlanta City Directory lists him as cashier for the banking subsidiary of the Central of Georgia, living at 182 Washington Street.

- In 1895, he holds the same position, again living at 109 East Hunter. (The Central Railroad operations, already controlled by outside interests, were sold at foreclosure on August 25, 1895.)

- In 1896, the Atlanta city directory lists him as president of both the Empire Glass and Decoration Co. and the Merchants Transfer Co., located at 47 North Broad, with a home on Washington Street, No. 218. The Merchants Transfer company is believed to be a drayage firm, whose heavy, horse-drawn carts would have been used to transport lumber, cotton bales and heavy goods around town.

- In 1897, he was involved in a private loan business at 47 Walton Street and still lived at 218 Washington.

- By 1899, he's moved uptown to 308 Peachtree Street and lists himself as working with his brother-in-law, the well-respected Atlanta businessman, John Edgar Murphy, in the stock and bond brokerage house of Paine & Murphy, at 2 South Pryor Street. Murphy had married Joseph's younger sister, Julia.

- Around 1900-1901, Gatins moved to Manhattan, where the New York City directory lists him as president of an unnamed firm at 61 Broadway. Other sources suggest that he traveled widely, especially in Europe, during this decade.

- From 1901-1902 until 1904-1905, he's still president of that mysterious Broadway firm, living in an apartment house at 71 Central Park West.

- Around 1905-06, he surfaces as president of his own enterprise, identified as Gatins Fireproof Construction Co., located at 542 East 119th Street with his oldest son, my grandfather, Joseph F. Gatins, Jr., listed as the firm's treasurer. The fireproof construction concern continued until 1910. New York and neighboring New Jersey addresses were listed as primary residences until his death in 1936.

The scant available details of Great-Grandfather's personal life suggest all was not roses for the family. In 1881, he had married a Southern belle and debutante, of Huntsville, Alabama, and Washington, D.C., Kate Thomas. Their union was unusual in that they eventually lived separate lives. It also was marked by tragedy. Of their five children, only two lived past the age of 50, Ben and Mary.

Their first-born, a daughter, died in childhood. A son, Saunders, died of causes unknown at the age of 17, in 1897. My grandfather, Joseph F. Gatins, Jr., Eglé's husband, was to die of tuberculosis—and, it seems obvious, acute alcoholism—in 1927, aged 44.

(My great-grandfather's own brother, John L. Gatins, had died in questionable circumstances in a Turkish bathhouse in Atlanta on August 6, 1904, at the age of 35. John's death, while never spoken of by later generations of Gatinses, burned brightly, and briefly, in Atlanta's collective consciousness. Indeed, it was hard to miss the news the next day as it occupied a huge part of the front pages of the Sunday, August 7, 1904, editions of both *The Atlanta Constitution* and *The Atlanta Journal.*

"Fall In Bath House Kills John L. Gatins," read the headline on the *Constitution's* article. The *Journal* headline screamed across the entire top of the newspaper:

"John Gatins Falls to Death—Slips in Bath House and Crashes Against a Corner of a Marble Washstand—Skull Was Fractured Over Left Temple—Death Came in a Few Minutes After Injury—Was Prominent and Well Known Man."

Unsaid and unwritten, but clear between the lines, was that foul play was suspected, though major efforts simultaneously were being made to quiet any untoward news. A coroner's inquest was held the same night of the deadly mishap, with the official cause of death for the nude man quickly being listed as "a fall from being overheated." Two Negro bathhouse attendants were detained and questioned briefly before being released from custody. And that was it. There were no Turkish bathhouse follow-up articles in the Atlanta papers.)

According to one of his granddaughters, Hope Simpson, this Joseph Gatins was himself a "difficult man," more interested in racing and playing the ponies and hanging out with Irish business cronies in Manhattan than a home life with his wife Kate. He obviously did not want his wife underfoot. The inveterate broker-gambler had sent her to live with son Ben's family in Rumson, New Jersey, while he stayed in New York, residing in various hotels.

"He was a difficult man," Simpson said. "He just dumped Grandmother on Mother. I never saw Grandmother and Grandfather Gatins living together. He shunted Grandmother off to live with us! Granddaddy lived in New York—came out quite a bit for Sunday lunches."

Simpson added: "Granddaddy came down on Sundays by train and when he and Grandmother met it was as if they just did not know who the other was—no affection or even a 'glad to see you.'"

Kate Thomas Gatins found solace in her faith. "She was a convert and her church was her whole outside life," Simpson said. That left Great-Grandfather Gatins free to do what he did best—play with money—both on and off Wall Street. He died at the Fairfax Hotel in Manhattan in 1936 at the age of 80. "He was a keen sportsman, particularly interested in racing," according to brief obituary in *The New York Times*. "Veteran Wall Street operator," *The Wall Street Journal* noted in its one-sentence obituary.

Conversely, he was well remembered in the city that gave him his start. A former business partner, Thomas Paine, eulogized him as a "prince of a good fellow, a beloved friend and devoted companion" whose passing has "cast a gloom over every Atlantan that ever knew him." The newspapers in Atlanta memorialized him as a "pioneer Atlanta businessman and civic leader" and builder of the Georgian Terrace, one who had "saved his money and made wise investments." That was about as close as the Atlanta news media ever came to mentioning the bucket shop origins of his fortune. He'd been at the right place at the right time, fortuitous enough to stay out of jail when the long arm of federal agents and a posse of newspaper reporters came knocking at his door, and flush enough to see his eldest son, the international sportsman, off to Paris in 1914.

Manhattan to Paris

Although he never accomplished half as much in business as his own father, my grandfather Joseph F. Gatins, Jr., obviously benefited from the legacy of the family name and fortune, and was perhaps better remembered in passing than when he was living. When he died in May of 1927, he was viewed as an established pillar of Atlanta society, with multiple international connections. "Prominent sportsman and traveler," the obituary on the front page of *The Atlanta Journal* read. "Part-owner of the Georgian Terrace Hotel. Mr. Gatins was a well-known figure in society and sporting circles in England, France and many parts of this country. He lived for a time in Melton-Mowbray, England, where he was an amateur sportsman of note. He was married in 1914 to the Comtesse Eglé de Villelume-Sombreuil, a member of one of the leading French families, who survives him." (Of course, there was no mention of the sad truth, that Grandmother and Grandfather had been separated since 1920. And only passing mention of "one son," my father.)

The obituary went on to list his schooling and club affiliations: Public schools in Atlanta, graduating from Boys High School and later attending the University of Georgia, followed by post-graduate studies at Yale University. He was a member of the Capital City and Piedmont Driving Clubs in Atlanta, the University and Yale Clubs in New York, and the Elkridge Fox Hunting Club of Baltimore. The accompanying photo depicts him looking stonily into the camera, wearing a black fedora. The picture is cropped so viewers could not tell that he had lost his right arm.

It seems Atlanta really wanted to give him a send-off. I can easily imagine Atlanta society packing Sacred Heart Church for the funeral, as the town often does for its "bad boys." He had eight pallbearers, including several well-regarded public figures like Edward H. Inman, an investor and Princeton graduate who was to become an Atlanta city councilman; James Alexander, a banker; Gus Ryan, a fellow sportsman and "noted fancier of bird dogs," who was also secretary of the local baseball team, subsequently known as the Atlanta Crackers.

My grandfather appears to have belonged to all the right organizations at the University of Georgia, too, which he attended as an "elective student" during the period 1898-1901. Such students only had to pay for "incidental expenses and use of the library," $15 per year. They did not have to attend classes or work for grades, but were allowed to graduate and in every aspect of campus life, treated as students. Tuition was free at a university that was "open to all white males from any state." Gatins was a member of the Phi Kappa Literary Society, the SAE fraternity, the Cotillion Committee and the Irish Club. He's also listed as the "growler" of what sounds like a secret drinking society, the "Tiger Club." Its motto: "T'is better to have loved and lost than never to have loved at all."

The University of Georgia yearbook, published by the University's fraternities (women were not yet allowed to attend the University of Georgia, so there were no sororities) emphasized a rich fraternity life, characterized by a "bewildering succession of rushes, dinners and [fundraising charity] drives." Eight fraternity chapters, each with "mystic little emblems," had smoking, reading and sleeping rooms as well as a "number of bizarre decorations, each with its tale of some wild prank."

The pin for the SAE fraternity, which Grandfather belonged to, was diamond-shaped, depicting a Minerva with a lion crouching at her feet. The group prided itself on producing gentlemen, particularly Southern gentlemen. At the outbreak of the Civil War, 369 of the fraternity's members took up arms for the Confederacy. Only eight ended up fighting with the Union forces. (It cannot be overestimated how tied the University was to the dreams of the old Confederacy, as was society in general. The 1901 issue of the Pandora yearbook, the year before my grandfather left Athens, depicts a disparaging woodcut of a pickaninny toting a bucket and bag. The cut line beneath it was, "NIGGER.")

Apparently as a graduation present, Joe set sail for Germany about a month after finishing his studies in Athens, for what almost surely was a grand tour of Europe before he took up his course audits at Yale and a new life in New York. Following graduation from the University of Georgia in 1901, my grandfather spent several years at Yale, where he took courses at the Law School during 1902-1904. During both years, he was classified as a first year student. From there, New York city directories suggest that he moved in with his father at 71 Central Park West, and joined a family business enterprise only identified as the Gatins Fireproof Construction Co., for which he is listed as treasurer. He held that post from 1905 until 1908, continuing to live with his father at the same address until 1910, the directories suggest, with a bit of international travel sandwiched in between. Boat passenger lists maintained by the National Archives show him landing in San Francisco from Hong Kong, for example, on January 31, 1908.

He then apparently moved back to Atlanta, residing initially at "The Marlborough" at 436 Peachtree Street in 1910-11, and served as the vice-president of an office supply house, Mower-Hobart Co. In 1912, city directories for the Georgia capital show, he moved into the brand new Georgian Terrace Hotel, which his father had just finished building.

The city directories for 1913-14 show him occupying an office in the 3rd National Bank Building, the last suggestion of his being employed in any way, before he headed to Paris, where he was to meet and court my grandmother.

At his death, there was no mention of Killybegs, McGettigans and humble origins. The Gatins family by then had settled on just one way to spell its last name, and appeared light years removed from its Irish roots.

Chapter 9

Salons and Suffragists

In Paris, Grandmother Eglé found relative freedom and rich reward, intellectually and spiritually, in the two decades between the world wars. Denied in love, battered by unholy matrimony and unable to afford staying in Atlanta with her only son, she had formally filed for divorce, and left her one-armed, womanizing husband, Joseph F. Gatins Jr., in 1920. Brief attempts at reconciliation in the States (1923), and in France (1924), had failed. By 1927, she was a young widow back in her native France, wearing the black dresses and plain black overcoats she was to wear for decades hence, her husband having succumbed to the double curse of tuberculosis and hard drink. But she kept his name.

Eglé and her son, Joseph F. Gatins III, had moved into a residence with a decidedly fancy address, 150, avenue des Champs d'Elysées, with her mother, her stepfather, the Swiss banker Henri Fischer, and her brother Charlic, a World War I cavalry veteran, former German prisoner of war and confirmed bachelor. She also found a second spiritual home—the first being the Roman Catholic Church—in the Salon Society that flourished in Paris between the world wars. "My life was truly pleasant. I moved in a very intellectual *milieu*," she said. Her memoirs also make mention of following feminist and suffragist matters, linked particularly to Edmée de la Rochefoucauld "with whom I busied myself over feminist questions, which truly absorbed me. I wanted equality for women."

Indeed, although she never talked of it, she had taken the unusual step to further her own liberation even before my grandfather's death by filing a divorce case against him in 1920, back in Atlanta, and it seems clear to me that the accompanying separation from her husband was likely for good cause. As she said years later, life with him was intolerable.

The Rochefoucaulds maintained a salon, which Eglé recalled as flourishing especially in the lead up to the Second World War. They eventually became Eglé's neighbors, residing in an *hôtel particulier* at No. 8, Place des Etats-Unis, in Paris' upscale 16th arrondissement, or neighborhood, about midway between two well-known Parisian landmarks, l'Etoile and the Trocadéro, directly across the Seine River from the famous Eiffel Tower. Eglé and the Villelume-Sombreuil-Fischer household had eventually moved to an expansive apartment that took up the entire second floor of No. 17 on the same square. It was there, at the Rochefoucauld salon, that she met a wide cross-section of Paris *intelligentsia*.

"Paul Valery was so deep, and he'd play with his grandchildren on the carpet. Paul Claudel, I knew him in America. He was very pompous," she said. "They were intimate friends of the de la Rochefoucaulds, where we met quite a few people." Edmée de la Rochefoucauld was a writer and author of a biography of Valéry, often writing under the pseudonym of Gilbert Mauge. Her involvement in suffragist and feminist issues was largely as the editor of the journal, *Lucien national pour le vote des femmes*, and she traveled the world on behalf of women's issues and rights. Yet, however passionate Eglé and Edmée might have been about women's issues, suffragist history suggests that their struggle appeared less vigorous and determined than the one fought by their sisters in the United States and England. These women staged acts of civil disobedience, street demonstrations, and hunger strikes in jail. By contrast, a French suffragist who chained herself to a bench in the National Assembly was quick to point out that her chains were decorated to match the scarf she was wearing. Edmée admonished fellow feminists in the 1930s not to "dispense with the modesty which becomes our sex." French women did not get the right to vote until 1944, while American women who had been working to secure it since the middle of the 19th century finally were granted the right in 1920, with passage of the 19th Amendment to the U.S. Constitution.

Eglé's photo albums suggest that she also was a great friend during this period with Germaine Roger, a Paris socialite, wife of Baron Pol Roger. Like many on this list of salon-goers, Eglé also traveled in the circle of American expatriates known as the Lost Generation, the motley collection of American wanderers, hard-drinking writers, publishers and adventurers seeking something other than what the United States had to offer.

"In Paris between the two wars, it was marvelous," said Grandmother, who had just turned 30 years old in 1922. "Especially from the 1920s to 1929-30—and the Americans were kings of the place. It was the day of Hemingway and Sylvia Beach and all those people—and Gertrude Stein, [whom] I never liked." Eglé had met Stein through "her great friend, Denise Azam, a Jewish convert to Catholicism who was a writer, art collector and fellow parishioner."

"We used to go see Sylvia Beach because she banked with Hanzi Fischer,"

Eglé said. "She had a bookstore and I saw Hemingway there several times." Sylvia Beach's bookstore, Shakespeare and Company, is writ large in the history of 20th Century English literature. This English-language literary outpost and lending library served as the home-away-from-home to young writers and students from the U.S.A. and as a springboard for experimental poets and writers, including Hemingway, who was just then starting out as a serious novelist and short story writer. Beach's major literary coup was to successfully get James Joyce's somewhat impenetrable *Ulysses* published and then quietly smuggled around the world and sold to a literary public in need of wordy escape.

The Shakespeare and Company bookstore eventually moved across the street on the rue Odéon from La Maison des Amis des Livres, run by Adriènne Monnier, whose clients would drop in at the Shakespeare and vice-versa. Meeting Monnier proved fortuitous to Beach in other ways. The pair fell in love and remained a couple for most of the rest of their lives. They lived quietly and discreetly in contrast to the greater flamboyance and openness that was to characterize gay and lesbian politics in the late 20th Century. Paris in the Twenties seemed tolerant of lesbians, particularly Americans, as it seemed to add yet another *frisson* of excitement to the international capital's cachet. The lifestyle also went hand in glove with the literary bent of Salon Society, according to one of Beach's biographers, Noel Riley Fitch.

The most famous salon of the period, Fitch noted, was presided over by a bisexual beauty from Cincinnati, Natalie Clifford Barney, who lived for seduction—and her weekly literary gathering. "She presided over the most famous salon in Paris—the only salon in the 18th century sense of the word. Every Friday the famous and eccentric were drawn to her exotic, Persian-decorated rue Jacob rooms.

"In her garden stood a little temple of Eros, where she and her women friends danced by the moonlight," Fitch wrote. "But during the Friday afternoons of tea and cakes and ices, reputations were launched, diminished or broken. No alcohol was served by the soft-shoed Chinese servants, but the chocolate cake was from Colombin's and was the best in Paris … Valéry, who was always welcomed as a 'brilliant talker,' attended for the 'tinkle of teacups and the chatter,' which, he confessed to Sylvia, he found 'beneficial after his work.' Samuel Putnam would love the heady atmosphere—the 'grace, the wit, the dignified abandon …' William Carlos Williams would remember only the lesbian women dancing together."

Fitch recounts that Barney, who rode horseback in the Bois de Boulogne every morning, "was openly bisexual," a lover of beautiful women and one whom talented men found irresistible. She was described as wealthy, self-indulgent, charming and attractive, with blond coloring and white clothes. "As [Gertrude] Stein collected art, so Barney collected dazzling people." Whether Barney and Beach also collected a somewhat liberated Eglé along this path is a matter of pure conjecture. What is sure is that their paths probably could have intersected from time to time, since Hemingway's readings often were held at the Shakespeare and Company bookstore.

Eglé in her memoirs talks more of the intellectual side of things and what turned out to be a most rewarding and consuming volunteer activity: Doing charity work for the Red Cross. "We had what we called sections for the workers and I headed one of the 20 [Red Cross offices] we had in Paris," she recalled in a later interview. "The work was varied because it took me into all paths of life of the sick, needy and the poor. I worked day and night to raise money for the poor. How? I just asked people to give it to me and they did."

As for the intellectuals in her life, she felt especially attracted to an old and distant cousin, Pièrre Teilhard de Chardin, a Jesuit priest and now well-regarded paleontologist, whose works were spurned by the Vatican and his Jesuit hierarchy at the time. "He was famous for his paleontological research and he'd tell me: 'Don't read my books. Keep on believing, like a good girl from Brittany, in goblins and fairies.' The Jesuits treated him really shabbily," Eglé said in her memoirs. "They fired him. They made him leave Paris, defrocked him and shipped him to New York, where he died. No one attended his funeral. But when he became famous worldwide, they made him their great man. I've always resented the Jezzies because of that. He was a remarkable man. What he did not know was not worth knowing. He was very amusing. He was charming—so nice, quite open. He always called me 'my little cousin.'" (Eglé and Teilhard de Chardin were distantly related on the Villelume side of the family.)

De Chardin (1881-1955) was one of the more interesting luminaries who populated Eglé's world. He has been described as a "visionary French Jesuit, paleontologist, biologist, philosopher" who spent the bulk of his life trying to integrate religious and Christian theology with theories of evolution. "To this end, he suggested that the Earth in its evolutionary unfolding, was growing a new organ of consciousness, called the *noosphere*." But the Catholic Church at the time would have none of this business of aligning Darwin and Jesus!

While the City of Light and its literary ferment sustained Eglé intellectually, her mother and stepfather, Henri Fischer, apparently were more than ready to take care of her and her son financially. Fischer had come to the States in 1923 on a rescue mission to bring her back from Atlanta on a transatlantic steamer from her next-to-last attempt at reconciliation with her estranged husband.

In Paris, she essentially exchanged one dependency for another, though the second gave her considerably more freedom. She had a stout roof over her head, servants at the ready, vacation trips, particularly as her son grew older, to resorts in Vichy and St. Jean de Luz and the Atlantic shore. The Fischer–Villelume–Sombreuil–Gatins household also took long summer vacations in Switzerland, especially to the Engadine mountain chain surrounding the resort towns of St. Moritz and Pontrésina. The family agglomeration customarily stayed in Pontrésina, and enjoyed many Alpine treks and mountain climbs, some technical enough that the group hooked itself up to long ropes for safety, stuffing their hats with paper to guard against falling stones.

At the same time, Eglé never, to anyone's public knowledge, linked herself romantically to any man after Joe Gatins, even after the final separation in 1923 and widowhood in 1927, at the age of 35. She clung to all-black widow's weeds for years afterward and, according to some reports, well into the 1950s. My brothers and sisters, in trying to find anything out about her love life, recall that Grandmother reported having various suitors after her husband's death, including an unnamed hopeful who knocked on her door the night before he was supposed to marry another woman. Eglé turned him down, though. He wasn't very handsome and had no wealth to speak of, she said!

There is some small evidence, though she never spoke of it during the later years of her life, that Eglé was deeply attracted to the man she would never have and could never have, the poet-banker, Henri Fischer. He'd originally been introduced to her as a potential suitor, but fell sway to the charms of her mother and married her instead. Grandmother waxes warmly about Fischer in her oral history, as warmly as for anyone mentioned in her recollections: "Mr. Fischer was years younger than my mother. He was from Winterthur. Mr. Fischer loved music, poetry, art—he used to write very nice poetry, and like all the Swiss, he spoke French, German, English, Italian. You know, all those Swiss are extraordinary. His main business? Banking! Banking, banking, banking. He worked for a Swiss bank and the Swiss bank then sent him to New York and then he started with Bankers' Trust, as a vice-president. He loved that—he loved it." Of all the thousands of personal letters and papers that Eglé could have saved over the years, only a slim file of Fischer's poems survives, marked "Hanzi," his nickname. Whether these were originally delivered to his wife Jeanne de Madec, or to Grandmother, she is the one who saved them for perpetuity.

Chapter 10

Coming of Age

While he was to see his father only once again in his life, young Joseph Francis Gatins III, known as Francis, appeared to find a relatively stable home life after his mother brought him back to Paris in 1923. He went to primary school, first in a Jesuit academy, subsequently in a private *lycée*, and found new French friends to replace the ones he'd left behind in Atlanta. Resilient as most young children, he transferred memory of his own father to that of two new father figures in the extended family household that became his home: his step-grand-father, Henri Fischer, the international banker, and his uncle Charlie, the World War I cavalry veteran. He recalled a strict upbringing aimed at turning him into a proper gentleman. He never addressed his mother as mom, mother or *maman*, but in the more formal *Madame, ma mère.* Formal table manners were taught in rigorous fashion: To keep his elbows off the dining room table, for example, he had to hold two knives underneath his arms as he ate. Uncle Charlie taught him the exacting art of peeling grapes with a sharp silver knife and the cutting of cheeses to a point.

"Francis first attended school with the Jesuits, on rue Franklin, where he took his First Communion in May of 1927," Eglé said. His father had died a few days earlier in Atlanta. "I had suggested that we bring him his son, but he had refused," she said. Soon thereafter, Eglé said, "Francis was having a harder and harder time getting along with the Jesuits, so I pulled him out of that school. I then placed him in a remarkable private school, run by Monsieur de Tannenberg. He made many good friends [there] and was urged to concentrate on the study of literature." (There is no primary source regarding young Francis' disagreements with the Jesuits, but family tradition holds that he asked too many persnickety questions about the existence of God and about Catholic doctrine regarding Jesus' place in the Holy Trinity. As my sister Eglé, says, "I'm sure there were other reasons.")

Among his good friends at the Tannenberg school were Philippe Manset, heir to a Bordeaux wine fortune, who remained among his best friends for the rest of his life; Marc de Heckeeren, and Samuel Arrellano, a Mexican whose older sister Carmen was the object of the first serious infatuation of his teen-age life. Francis had a talent for schooling and learning. His report card for the 1932-33 school year, when he had just turned 17, positively glowed, reflecting that he was top in his class in history. "Good student. Cultivated spirit. Real intelligent. Very serious and a hard worker. Could take a brilliant final exam." The photo attached to the report card booklet depicts him at what inarguably was his handsomest, dressed in a neat tie and light-colored double-breasted suit, hair brushed straight back, head turned in half-profile to show the prominent Gatins nose to advantage. It is easy to see why women were so attracted to him.

He also had plenty of time for diversion, vacations, and old-fashioned hell raising. For fun, he and Philippe Manset would cull the daily obituaries in *Le Figaro* (a daily newspaper in Paris) and pick the ones they believed would have the best food and drink after the funeral services and burial. Dressed formally, they would walk up to the surviving widows, whether they knew the family or not, and mumble nonsensical phrases that sounded comforting. "*Marron-dinde, madame, marron-dinde, madame,*" they would say: Literally translated, "brown-turkey, madam, brown turkey." Francis loved to tell that story around the dinner table decades later. Another youthful escapade might never have come to light except that he and some friends got caught in late-night revelry and youthful debauchery the night of his 16th birthday, October 8, 1931. Francis and his cohorts started off innocently enough with an ample buffet of champagne and oysters. Monsieur Fischer believed young gentlemen should have a good time, and had sent them to a fine Parisian restaurant—the crustacean bill and wine on him. The birthday bunch then moved to another restaurant for dinner, which Eglé had won in a raffle at their Catholic Church parish. After dinner, the well-oiled crew moved to the Club 122, a high-class bordello at 122 rue de Rivoli, where everyone presumably had his way before crawling home early the next morning.

There the matter would have remained, tucked away in personal memories, except that one of Francis' friends spilled the beans upon being caught by his parents coming home in the wee hours. This led to a most irate telephone call to Eglé from the boy's mother the next morning. Grandmother was not happy, but her mother, Madame Fischer, "actually encouraged visits to Club 122." The Club 122 tale, told and retold many times around the Gatins dining room table assumed a locker-room luster and expanded to almost mythic proportion in the minds of Francis' children. During the time between the wars, Club 122 also became a favorite watering hole for the occasional friend visiting Paris from Atlanta, one of whom regaled both families' children with tales of coming home knee-walking drunk at dawn with Francis from an interlude at the club sometime in 1936.

Family photo albums kept by Eglé depict more sedate pastimes: A vacation trip to the beach resort of Dinard in Brittany (1923); riding a bicycle and a donkey cart in Brittany (1924); visits to the resort town of St. Jean de Luz, just north of the border with Spain's Basque country (1926) and to Juan-les-Pins (1931); trips to Vichy, where Francis and his mother visited for periodic cures. (Vichy has been a favored health destination dating to the time of Julius Caesar, who built the first "resort" there. Many believe the water has healing properties and associate its taste to that of Alka-Seltzer.) The albums include pictures of Arellano family members in Paris (1932) and of his best friend Philippe Manset outside the Manset country home in Argeville, just south of Paris.

Although never mentioned in Grandmother's memoirs, or by Francis in later years, the albums also suggest that Joseph F. Gatins, Jr. made attempts to see his son from time to time. In July 1923, Francis poses stiffly alongside his father on the Brittany beach of Dinard. The last visit, in June of 1924, at the beach resort town of Biarritz on the Spanish border, depicts eight-year-old Francis standing next to the man who was his father, apparently as part of the off-and-on visitation schedule Eglé had once tried to arrange. The Atlanta playboy and international traveler at that point had already been diagnosed with a case of pulmonary tuberculosis some three years prior. Except for his prominent nose peeking out from underneath his hat brim, the father has the dull, hollowed-out, pale look of a man whose lungs were diseased and whose liver was shot from decades of hard drink. The son poses very stiffly alongside. That was the last time they were to see each other.

Henri Fischer figures prominently in the photo albums. He was, after all, supporting the entire extended Fischer, Gatins and Villelume-Sombreuil family. That support, it seems clear, placed Eglé and Francis in the very upper strata of French society, one so rarified that there is not one mention in Grandmother's memoirs or oral history of the Great Depression that consumed the world during 1929-31. According to anecdotal family reports, Fischer lost his position with the Bankers Trust office in Paris after the Depression, but apparently had secreted enough funds in Switzerland to keep up the trips and appearances. His *forte* as an international banker had been to successfully market bonds, known as Jung Bonds, after the man who created them, which were used to finance Germany's reconstruction after World War I.

The only change in circumstance brought on by the huge economic downturn that was the Great Depression was that the household moved from its showy home on the Champs d'Élysées to the avenue d'Iena (by 1931) and then to No. 17, Place des États-Unis (by around 1935), both also located in the 16th arrondissement, then a neighborhood of mostly well-appointed private homes and apartments. Today, many of those homes have been converted into business offices. (The old home on the *Champs d'Elysées* is now a foreign currency exchange bank for tourists.) The home at No. 17 was a most comfortable, high-ceilinged apartment, which took up the entire second floor of that address, which itself took up the entire west side of that square. It was filled with heavy, antique furniture from the Louis XIV and Louis XVI periods and seemed even bigger than it was because a large mirror hung at each end of the long living room area.

Just how wealthy was Fischer? No records survive. But he was most generous with his disposable income over the years, of that the family is sure. His gifts were designed to attract attention, and do so even now. He gave Francis a solid, 18-carat gold cigarette case on his 21st birthday. He gave his stepdaughter Eglé a jeweled watch. The platinum and diamond watch, with silk strap and gold buckle, was made by Cartier in 1917 and, according to Eglé, was given her as a "consolation-type prize" for Fischer's having chosen her mother as a bride instead of her. Grandmother never wore the watch, however, even on the most formal of occasions and Francis, in later years, only used the slim cigarette case, exquisitely shaped to fit the curve of the body in a jacket's breast pocket, when it was time to put on the dog. "*Faut épater les bourgeois,*" he often would say on these occasions. As one well versed in the ways and mores of the hyper-rich in France, he knew one must "dazzle the bourgeoisie." It was a truly arresting piece of gold work. Years later, this cigarette case sometimes ended up in my own tuxedo pocket in the rare instances that black tie was called for and I used it to wow politicians on my news beat. I had learned my father's lessons well.

Fischer's presence and, to a lesser extent, Charlic's, also served to insulate Francis from the grim reality of his grandfather's suicide. In fact, he was not told about it until after he turned 21. Daddy never spoke of this. It is not possible to know how he felt about this tragic event.

Grandmother's photo albums reflect repeated vacation trips to Switzerland, especially to the resort town of Pontrésina, a slightly more rustic and simple place than the much flashier and society-conscious neighboring resort of St. Moritz. There are pictures of Fischer with a tame steinbock (a type of mountain goat) coming up to a patio table, of fellow mountain climbers (many of them Swiss relatives of Fischer) and many panoramic shots of the spectacular Engadine mountain chain that surrounds the small town of Pontrésina.

Francis had a keen appreciation for the narrow valley and the spectacular, permanently snow-covered mountains that surround the town. His love for this particular place showed decades later when he took his wife and three oldest children there for a quick visit in the mid-1950s. The peaks around the town reach to more than 8,000 feet and it is easy to understand why Francis and his family returned there time after time for spiritual and physical renewal. I was fortunate enough to return there in the late 1980s, and found my memories of this place were pretty much as accurate as my experience from the 1950s. The mountain trails leading to high-elevation lakes were as remembered, raked clear every day by the Swiss. Hot tea was still served in glasses rather than ceramic cups; the hot chocolate just as frothy and sweet. Overall, that trip evoked a very sweet memory of a special time with my father. It felt very comforting to be walking the footsteps of my early youth, at a time of true innocence, to be walking in the same shoes as my father as a young man.

As for mountain climbing, Francis found it a lot of fun. Fischer, Eglé, Francis and one or two others, including a local guide, would tie long ropes around their waists and simply start walking uphill past the tree line and onto the permanent snow-and-ice cap. (Madame Fischer apparently was not a mountain climber.) They trekked in heavy, hob-nailed boots and long woolen socks, eventually climbing rock faces hand over hand. There was a hint of danger, and on one occasion Grandmother grabbed and held onto Fischer to prevent his falling into a rock crevice. At certain altitudes, they'd find Alpine huts that provided hot tea, hot toddies and a bunk. At those heights, Francis would recall many years later, one did not need Cognac to get high—a lot of sugar and hot tea did the trick. On one celebrated occasion, well remembered by Fischer's Swiss cousins, Francis accomplished a solo climb of Piz Bernina, a technically difficult mountain above Pontrésina, whose summit reaches 13,284 feet. My father during this period and well into the 1940s also belonged to the Alpine climbing club in Paris, experience he subsequently was to put to further use in the French army.

Meanwhile, there were still studies to be completed. By 1935-36, after taking the *bachot*, that is, the baccalaureate exam required of all French students, he was listed as tops in his class in philosophy and science. "Has totally satisfied me," the Tannenberg headmaster said in the report card booklet. Young Francis, by then 21 years old, received his official "graduation diploma" on January 10, 1936. This was the equivalent of a secondary school teaching certificate, with a double major in philosophy and history. Had world events not intervened, Francis might have ended up working in academia or in a research library. His life-long best friend, Philippe Manset, was of the opinion that Francis was ideally suited to the world of academic research, ferreting out obscure facts. Instead, he returned briefly to Atlanta, where he cruised the party circuit as a most eligible bachelor, then spent a few months at Cambridge University where he is alleged to have pursued studies in economics but appears to have majored in partying. This was followed by compulsory military service in the French army and then the harsh war that would haunt him for a lifetime and turn him into a permanent prisoner of his own experience.

Paris Boulevards: Francis Gatins walked everywhere in Paris with his mother Eglé in the 1920s (top photo), and posed with a group of friends during this period (bottom).

Germaine Roger: Germaine, a French socialite, was a great friend of Eglé's during the Salon Society era. An unidentified man (smoking a cigarette, above), joined Germaine, Eglé and Francis on a stroll in Paris during the 1920s.

Childhood in Paris: Sylvia (top and bottom left), and her brother Miguel and sister Beatrice, posed for professional photographers, as did Francis in his sailor suit.

Alpine highs: Francis (far left and above) learned to mountain climb in the Engadine Mountains of Switzerland with the help of his step-grandfather, Henri Fischer (left), and later became an accomplished solo alpinist.

cure: Francis and Eglé spent time each summer in the resort town of Vichy (here strolling in 1931).

Military service and alpine bivouac: Francis was drafted into an Alpine pursuit unit (Chasseurs Alpins), with its distinctive berets, to serve out his basic military training in the French Army. Conical tents provided shelter, and hot tea and cigarettes warmed the souls of Francis and fellow soldiers high in the mountains.

Colombian bloodline: (Counterclockwise from bottom left), Martin de German-Ribon (1866-192
met his wife Elvira Valenzuela (1885-1968), in Bogotá before moving permanently to Paris. Their el
daughter Sylvia (1915-1987), eventually was introduced to Francis in the late 1930s. Sparks flew, bu
not before Francis accompanied his mother on a social trip to Atlanta in 1936. They are shown (at
center) in a newspaper photo that recorded their arrival at the railroad station in the Georgia capital

Chapter 11

Atlanta Interlude

New York and Atlanta both called to Eglé and her son in 1936. She decided to take him back for a visit late that year. They had last seen the Georgia capital 13 years earlier during the next-to-last attempt at reconciliation with her husband. Contact with American friends was limited to the occasional greeting cards or letters forwarded to Paris, or an occasional Atlanta visitor summering in Europe and somewhat confusing, periodic letters from lawyers appointed to look after Francis' business affairs in Georgia. Eglé put it this way in her memoirs: "He brilliantly passed his baccalaureate exam and I decided to take him to the United States so he might know something of his land. My father-in-law had died, granting his grandson a certain independence."

My father had just turned 21 and, as a son of a French mother, had not yet been called up for compulsory, two-year military service in the French army. Grainy contemporary newspaper photographs depict him getting off the train in Atlanta, jaunty, nattily dressed, with a pencil-thin mustache, giving his arm to his mother. She is sporting a neat beret. They looked like the nobility much of Atlanta society thought they were. Atlanta was apparently ready to greet them with open arms, especially since Francis had recently become one of the city's most eligible bachelors. The wellspring of the Gatins family fortune, the banker-broker-hotel-builder-and-illegal-bucket-shop-backer, the quintessential Wall Street operator, Joseph F. Gatins Sr., had died a few months prior to the visit, leaving his grandson a one-third ownership of the Georgian Terrace Hotel and, the family believes, generous bank and securities accounts. (His wife, Kate Thomas Gatins, passed away quietly about a year later.)

Mother and son left for the states in December, stopping in New York especially so Grandmother Eglé could show her son "the foolish madness of New Year's Eve in Manhattan." They spent Christmas with Francis' aunt Mary, who had just "taken on her third husband, Howell Jackson, a man much younger than she."

On New Year's Day, they took the train to Atlanta, where "we got a marvelous reception from those I knew," Eglé said. Mother and son were lionized by their many Atlanta friends, old and new, and rediscovered by the ever-watchful chroniclers of the Gatins family at Atlanta's daily newspapers. Eglé had fallen in love with the Deep South and Atlanta in 1914, when she first came to the Georgia capital, and obviously felt at home there. "They are forming the inspiration for numerous informal social affairs," as one of the newspapers said.

It was definitely time to party. On Sunday, January 8, *The Atlanta Constitution* recorded that Francis Gatins, of Paris, France, was the "central figure at the apéritif party at which Mr. and Mrs. Albert E. Thornton were hosts on Sunday at their Paces Ferry Road residence. Mrs. Joseph F. Gatins assisted the hosts in entertaining. Members of the unmarried and married contingents were invited to meet the honor guest." Edna Thornton had become a close companion to Grandmother back when she first landed in Atlanta, and had assisted her in the effort to teach American military officers basic French phrases before being dispatched to World War I in 1917. Five days later, mother and son were back on Paces Ferry (now called West Paces Ferry Road) for a cocktail party at the nearby home of Mr. and Mrs. Robert F. "Baxter" Maddox. The Maddox property, called Woodhaven, later would become the site of a new official residence of the governors of Georgia. Maddox was one of the bankers involved in Francis' finances after he inherited his share of the Georgian Terrace.

Francis undoubtedly also linked up to his young cousin, Katherine Murphy Riley, then residing next door to the Maddoxes on West Paces Ferry, at her 8,000-square-foot Italianate pink stucco home, Villa Juanita. Katherine had inheritd the expansive home in 1935 upon the death of her sister, Julia Murphy Whitehead. It was a house made to order for the wild times of the wild children of the Jazz Age. Katherine was known as a stunning beauty, so striking that she had drawn applause one night when introduced to Parisian society. Villa Juanita was built in 1924 for Julia and her then new husband, Conkey Whitehead, son of J.B. Whitehead Sr., one of the founders of the Coca-Cola Bottling Company. It became Julia's exclusive property after she divorced Conkey in the wake of the 1929 crash (and, according to family lore, because he took up with a German woman he met in Havana). The villa sported elaborate gardens, a gymnasium and indoor basement pool, whose cold, cold waters served as a shocking tonic in the middle of Atlanta's hot, hot summers, and "it was known for its parties."

Laura Maddox, Baxter's daughter, recalled, for example, that she would invite her own friends over to Woodhaven when the Whiteheads had a party. They would sit on their side of the dividing wall between the two properties and "listen to the orchestra music, and often called over to the Whiteheads to make musical requests. Every time we made a request, they would play it immediately, and we'd call back and say 'thank you.'"

Many remember that liquor flowed freely at Villa Juanita, and the parties were somewhat less sedate than suggested in the society pages of the local newspapers.

The Murphy girls, Julia and Katherine, had grown up at Hillcrest, the family home on Peachtree where Eglé recalled having such expansive lunches in 1914. While Villa Juanita with its long, tall, pink stucco boundary wall made a statement on West Paces Ferry, Hillcrest itself was nothing to sneeze at. William Bailey Williford, in his book, *Peachtree Street, Atlanta*, describes it as "elegantly appointed," and "set in a sweeping expanse of emerald green lawn," and especially "noted for its lovely Louis XV drawing room." The third floor of the house was devoted to a ballroom, where the Murphy's "lavish hospitality" often was "enjoyed until a light breakfast was served at dawn." An article in *The Atlanta Constitution* of December 24, 1930, related that the Murphys' had, for the better part of 15 years, thrown a large Christmas Eve party for their friends, many appearing in costume or black tie dress. (Hillcrest sat on property that is now the site of the Colony Square business office complex on Peachtree Street.)

The Murphy daughters' parties were definitely not so tame, though, according to Katherine. Julia's parents, John Murphy and Julia Gatins Murphy, often grew concerned when they did not hear from or see their oldest daughter "for weeks at a time," and would send Katherine to check on her. The parties at Villa Juanita often "lasted for a week or longer—day and night until the champagne ran out," Katherine recalled. Afterward, Conkey and Julia "would sleep for days." One such episode took a different turn. Katherine was chauffeured over to Villa Juanita to check on Julia. As she arrived, a taxi came roaring onto the property. Out jumped Conkey and a friend, one of the Grant boys, who also lived on West Paces Ferry. "An argument ensued with the taxi driver over the fare since they had taken the taxi all the way home from the Kentucky Derby! Katherine then joined Conkey and the guest in popping a bottle of champagne. She found Julia, who joined the party. Eventually, the Murphys had to send someone else over to check on Katherine!"

The visit to Atlanta for Eglé and Francis proved to be brief. World events were coming to a head in Europe and "he decided to return to Paris." Rumblings of war had terrified the family of his friend, Samuel Arrellano, which decided to flee from France and return to Mexico. This meant Francis' relationship with the young Carmen Arrellano came to a natural end, a development that apparently did not displease Eglé. "That proved the end of that sentimental Mexican story, thanks be to God," she said in her memoir.

Threat of impending geopolitical conflict also weighed on Francis. As his mother remembers, Francis at that time "stupidly decided to renounce his American nationality. I was very annoyed, but he told me: 'As an American born in France, I would surely be sent to Japan and it would be worse. I think the German prisoner-of-war camps [would be better].'"

The fatalistic nature of those sentiments proved remarkably prescient in his case. His decision to give military allegiance to France eventually marked him for life. He was soon to be swept into the precursor to war and then the real thing, but not before crossing paths with Sylvia de German-Ribon, a fiery young Colombian woman who was to occupy a good bit of his time in coming years, and eventually to become his wife.

Chapter 12

"Dancing on a Volcano"

Called up for compulsory French military service in October, 1936, Francis had made sure he was detailed to what he thought would be an interesting military unit, the 7th Battalion of the *Chasseurs Alpins*, that is, an Alpine pursuit unit that sported a distinctive beret. An avid skier and Alpinist, he thought this would be more fun than the infantry and that it would remind him of his mountain climbing forays in Switzerland. To his surprise, and perhaps chagrin, he was assigned to be a muleskinner and woodcutter. Mules served as the preferred mode of transportation for this unit, based in Albertville in the French Alps south of Geneva. Francis made the best of his job, he wrote sometime in 1938 to his "teddy bear," Sylvia de German-Ribon. "I am perfectly happy here," he wrote. "I leave at 5:30 in the morning to saddle and care for my mules. By 6:30, I'm cutting wood and bringing it in until dusk. I come back at night exhausted."

Francis used the same letter—which, like so many of his letters, was undated—to report on the welfare of the small teddy bear that Sylvia had given him. "The teddy bear is really worn out and losing its hair from always being in my pockets—but that gives him a wonderful expression," Corporal Gatins said, adding that he would really love to hear from the girl back home.

The "girl back home" was the oldest child of Elvira and the late Martin de German-Ribon, the latter a Colombian civil engineer whose long, colorful international career in Colombia, Peru, Mexico, England and then Paris, had ended in premature death on March 16, 1926, a year before Francis was to lose his own estranged father. Colombian expatriates in Paris, apparently hypersensitive to their colonial roots and not wanting to be viewed as savages by Parisian society, bought expensive homes in the toniest of neighborhoods (the 16th arrondissement). Martin and Elvira introduced the diminutive *de* into their last name "in order to sound more French and high class." The rest of the extended German-Ribon family, in England, had no need for this affectation and never assumed use of the *de* in their name. The German-Ribon family was no less colorful than the Villelume-Sombreuil-Madec-Gatins clan. It had originally settled in Colombia in the early 1700s, sent over by the Spanish crown from its home base in Seville to help govern parts of the new world. The family settled in the Mompox area of Colombia, which was then the cultural, educational and riverine transportation center of the country along the Magdalena River (and now a World Heritage Site, largely because of its rich, colonial/Indian architecture). With other Spanish families, they subsequently took up arms against Spain and fought for the independence of Nuevo Granada (in the early 1800s) with the help of Simon Bolivar. The 19th Century proved to be a period of significant prosperity for the German-Ribons, so much so that they minted their own gold coins in England to use as local currency to buy goods for export. They lived in a magnificent home in Mompox and enjoyed the spoils of their new independence and great wealth. But guerrilla incursions and hopes for a better life prompted the entire German-Ribon family to leave Colombia, first decamping to New York City and eventually moving to London, where they sought out a more European cultural environment.

My German-Ribon grandfather Martin and his siblings grew up in London, where he obtained an engineering degree and secured a position with the international public works engineering firm S. Pearson & Son (a predecessor firm to the global Pearson PLC), and where Sylvia eventually was born.

His wife's family, the Valenzuelas, also of Spanish origin, first came to Nueva Granada, as Colombia was then known, in the mid-1700s, when Don Eloy Valenzuela, a learned botanist, was commissioned by Spain to identify and record the new world's plant life. His relatives settled in and never left Colombia and built their own enormous wealth through the acquisition of land and other businesses, eventually settling in Bogotá, the capital. Elvira, *née* Valenzuela, was born in Colombia, descendant of an arch-Catholic family that encouraged her, as a young teenager, to flagellate her back with stinging nettles. She was attracted by Martin de German-Ribon, who first spied her on a visit to Bogotá in 1913. He was immediately struck by her beauty and obvious international savoir-faire, given that she was reading the French periodical, *La Revue des Deux Mondes*. He proposed almost on the spot but her father would have none of it until substantial proof of Martin's reputation and financial standing could be ascertained. As this turn-of-the-century credit check had to come from bankers in far-off London, it took months for this to be completed. (While the Valenzuelas had remained in Colombia, Bogotá society knew virtually nothing of the German-Ribon family, which had moved to Europe decades earlier). But eventually all was approved, and a lavish wedding was organized.

They were married in Bogotá, walking from the Valenzuela home (next to the present presidential palace in the downtown area of La Candelaria) to the church on a long red carpet laid down for the occasion, about a third of a mile.

The couple moved to London, where Grandfather Martin worked for Pearson following international assignments with that firm in Chile, Peru and Mexico. In that last country, he was assigned as a managing director of the Ferrocarriles de Mexico. In 1913, he was assigned to the Pearson home office in London and in 1916, asked to open Pearson's new office in Paris. He died in 1926 and is remembered as a loving husband, who sent Elvira a love note every workday of his life in Paris, via mail-tube. At her death in 1968, though, Sylvia and her siblings, Beatrice and Miguel, also discovered a collection of love letters he had written to a mistress of long standing, which Elvira somehow had found and kept. "We decided to burn them," Sylvia reported at the time.

After their marriage, Martin and Elvira first lived in London, but soon moved to Paris, both because of the new Pearson office and because they believed Paris would be more fun than London. In Paris, Sylvia was introduced to Francis both through her younger sister Beatrice and through Grandmother Eglé. The former was good friends with, later engaged to, and eventually married, Philippe Manset, Francis' old friend from the days of the lycée. Eglé had taken Sylvia under her wing when she volunteered with the Red Cross chapter for the 16th arrondissement. At the time, Sylvia was single and footloose, having broken her engagement to the Prince de Broglie, descendant of a well-known noble French family, shortly after the news of that engagement had been publicly announced to Paris society and its Roman Catholic communities.

According to Beatrice, the strong-willed, forthright Sylvia had had her head turned by an *"homme d'affaires"*—a lawyer and go-to businessman named Edgar Faure, who subsequently had a long political career in various post-war French governments—who was then handling the estate of the German-Ribon girls' uncle Ernesto. Sylvia was barely entering her twenties, and had just finished her high school baccalaureate studies. De Broglie was significantly older and "she wasn't attracted to him," according to family lore. The break-up occurred the same day the church published the Broglie-German-Ribon marriage banns. A really pretty engagement ring had to be returned. None of this sat well with Sylvia's mother, Elvira, who promptly shipped her off to London for a time to get her to come to her senses. Elvira, as a widow and a Colombian expatriate, was courting social disapproval in the 16th arrondissement with the break-up, and Sylvia herself "became depressed—and even saw a psychoanalyst." The infatuation with Faure did not last either. "Captivated by Sylvia's charm and wit," Faure apparently was willing to break off a relationship with another woman to be with Sylvia. But Elvira, ever conscious of her station as a foreigner in French society, put a stop to the relationship.

According to family oral history, Elvira then sought to intervene on behalf of her headstrong eldest child with her own characteristic bluntness. Where to find a proper match for her girl? Not surprisingly, she turned to a fellow parishioner at church, her good friend Eglé Gatins, and said, "Why don't we get her introduced to your son?" Thus, Sylvia was dispatched, first to work as a Red Cross volunteer with Eglé, and then eventually, in a mutual family arrangement, to be formally introduced to Francis. It seems clear that Sylvia and Francis could have bumped into each other previously in Paris, but most in the family date the beginning of their long relationship to a more-or-less arranged (yet unchaperoned) weekend escape to the Swiss resort town of Gruyères, sometime in 1939, before Francis was actually mobilized for war. What is sure is that the young couple hit it off at Gruyères—yes, the town where they make that famous cheese—and that sparks flew between the two young people who had both lost their fathers just as they were becoming teenagers. Sylvia had been forced to wear the black of mourning clothes for five years after her father died when she was 10, which she resented mightily. She was definitely ready to free herself by her 20s. She had dark curly hair, an engaging gap-toothed smile and a quick and ready wit and, to Francis, a most shapely figure. Decades later, around a dinner table in Atlanta, both my mother and father would laugh and josh about who had been the randiest during that period. "It was you, Francis!" she would say. "No, it was you, absolutely," Francis would counter, slapping the dinner table with his hand. On a vacation trip to Switzerland with their three oldest children in the mid-1950s, Francis and Sylvia made a special stop to show the children Gruyères, where Francis first started falling in love with Sylvia. (That visit got me into hot water with my fourth-grade teacher after our return to Atlanta that year. Along with a bowl of cheese fondue, my parents had shared a beer with us three children that day in Gruyères, which I recall to this day as being very bitter tasting. But I thought it pretty cool that they had offered us a brew. I related that fact in a paper about summer vacation, which shocked Miss Mills, my teacher at the time. "I went to Switzerland this summer with my parents and had a beer." Miss Mills promptly asked my parents for a full explanation.)

The late 1930s also were a period of personal growth for both Sylvia and Francis. With rumors of yet another big war swirling throughout Europe, the two entered into a rather cerebral correspondence, while Francis was forced for the first time to associate with regular, ordinary Frenchmen doing military service. It was nothing like the aristocratic upper class he'd been used to. It was the beginning of a learning experience that essentially would democratize him, and show him there was something more to life than the extraordinarily elitist and snobbish upbringing he had known until then. The military taught him a bit of self-discipline, too, especially after a tough career sergeant threw him into a lock-up one Christmas Day for showing up drunk at assembly the night before.

Sylvia, at the same time, was a student in Paris, studying *beaux-arts* and interior decorating. She had completed her high school baccalaureate studies in in 1935, with a mention of "fair," and an art history course at The Louvre Museum in 1938, with a mention of "very good."

Francis, too, fancied himself something of a student, having spent some six months at Cambridge University's King's College prior to his initial call-up to service. Many years later, he would tell his children how intellectually stimulating that period had been, particularly under the tutelage of the celebrated economist John Maynard Keynes, who was at Cambridge at the time. But there is some evidence that Francis was in England for something other than cerebral stimulation. First, Cambridge has no record of his ever having enrolled as a student at any level. According to one of his daughters, "Daddy was more interested in partying. I remember that Daddy was friends with some Englishman … this particular friend would sleep around with men during the week to earn money so he could party with girlfriends on the weekend." Francis himself was particularly struck by the bedroom savvy of long-legged Australian girls he met at Cambridge, a recollection that still occupied space in his memories some 30 years later, when I returned home from a stint in Vietnam that included a week of R & R in Sydney. "Do those Aussie girls still know how to lift their legs so high?" my father wanted to know.

In 1939, though, Francis' mind was on Sylvia. While she was not all that pretty, he later told close friends, "She has a great figure." He stayed in touch with Sylvia by letter, appealing both to the student and the lover in her, while recuperating from a car accident that occurred while he was on leave at the Fischer family home outside Geneva. Both the hospital and second home were located on Mont Pelerin, the peak overlooking the Lake Geneva resort town of Vevey, headquarters of what many called the "Swiss Riviera."

One Friday morning, in a letter addressed to "my little one," he spoke of fellow patients at the hospital where he'd been taken, all of whom suddenly had Hitler and international affairs on their minds. "It would seem better to do like me, to spend their time thinking of your fine legs, your long fingers, the softness of your skin, the brilliant spontaneity of your look, your charming conversation, your kind heart ....Time seems so long far from you," he wrote.

Another Friday morning, still at Vevey, Francis took a more literary tone, recommending to Sylvia a poetry book that assumed English was much more rhythmical and musical than French. That literary discussion, at the same time, was followed by love-talk, interspersed, inevitably, with reference to the impending military conflict.

"Mother and I await, with undisguised impatience, the general mobilization that would permit us to take the train to Paris, to leave this place, and to do something useful," he concluded in that letter. Gasoline was already being restricted and rationed, making it impossible to drive back to Paris. At the same time, Francis criticized those fellow patients who now appeared more interested in discussing their digestion and sleep habits. "Oh, those disgusting bourgeois!" he concluded.

Grandmother Eglé's take on the situation in 1939 was very similar, mirroring the general unease about impending and virtually inevitable conflict. Francis had finished his compulsory military service on October 11, 1938. "Despite the noise of war, he was going out a lot, and played golf on a regular basis, at Saint-Cloud, with friends and Mr. Fischer," according to Eglé's memoir. "He was very close to Philippe Manset, whom he knew from the days at the Lycée Tannenberg. And he saw a lot of two girls, Sylvia and Beatrice de German-Ribon, the younger of which quickly found herself engaged to Philippe."

"Paris was very festive. Everyone was dancing on a volcano, but we were all dancing a lot," Eglé said. "I recall a fancy dress ball at the Polish embassy—in that magnificent private home on rue de Talleyrand. That night, I had an extraordinary feeling that something was coming to an end—that our world, as we knew it, was fleeing and that we'd never see it again.

"The ambassador's wife .... was waltzing with the German military attaché," Grandmother continued. "Afterward, she told me, 'Oh, you know, if he captures me one day when I go back to Poland, he'd gladly put me up before a firing squad.'"

Available government records suggest that portents of the coming conflict weighed on Francis heavily enough that he reversed himself and tried to claim U.S. citizenship, despite his having served in the French military. This effort, initiated November 10, 1938, proved to be the first salvo in a multiyear bureaucratic fight with the U.S. Department of State over whether Francis could claim to be a U.S. citizen and receive another American passport.

The State Department had granted him a two-month extension of an

American passport, originally granted in 1936, good until February 10, 1939, so he could return briefly to Atlanta. But the State Department subsequently denied him further passports when he and Grandmother Eglé opted to return to France in the spring of 1939. "In view of the fact that you have spent two thirds of your life in France and as the passport above referred to was issued for the sole purpose of enabling you to return to the United States to perform the duties of citizenship which are reciprocal with the right to the protection of this government, the Department is of the opinion that you are not entitled to passport facilities to enable you to resume your residence in France," wrote R.B. Shipley, Chief of the Passport Division at State at the time. Francis, at age 23, had "not demonstrated an intention to reside in the United States and assume the duties and obligations of an American citizen but on the contrary he has manifested his loyalty to France by remaining in that country after attaining his majority and performing military service," Shipley said in a letter of March 23, 1939.

To date, no records have surfaced to show exactly why Francis and Eglé made this brief additional trip to the United States, nor was there any real explanation in the Atlanta news articles that dutifully chronicled their visit. Francis and Eglé were fêted at a dinner party put on by Isabel Tompkins on January 18, 1939. Three weeks later, the Gatinses, mother and son, threw their own cocktail party at the Piedmont Driving Club. The passport file correspondence with Francis' lawyer hints that they might have been in Atlanta to clear some tax matters.

Francis and Eglé had left Paris and arrived in the States on December 21, 1938 and were due to return to France aboard the Ile de France on March 18, 1939. (In fact, they didn't leave until early April, using their French passports). Francis himself wrote Shipley, the State Department's passport official, on April 7, before leaving New York, that he'd had no intention of returning to France to live there permanently "where I have no home, but only to spend the spring in Paris where I planned to be married and come back after that to this country. I quite understand that the Department of State cannot grant me passport facilities and protection when I am still a French citizen, especially with all the trouble that is now going on in Europe," Francis said. "I am entirely willing to repudiate the French nationality."

But world events swept Francis into the vortex of war—as a conscript in the French army—before he was able to marry Sylvia. It took him years more to formally and finally claim U.S. citizenship. The French army mobilized him on September 1, 1939, just in time to endure the "phony war," *la drôle de guerre*, and then endure capture on the western front at the hands of the advancing German forces.

Chapter 13

"War Is Such a Curse"

There was little to no surprise when war finally broke out September 1, 1939, with Germany's *blitzkrieg* attack on Poland. The Gatins and Fischer families, vacationing that summer in Switzerland as they had for the past 18 years, had been expecting it for weeks, as had most of Europe.

It was obvious the Germans were gearing up for ground action. "One night, there was a big dinner in St. Moritz—we were staying in Pontrésina—and some Germans were there," Eglé recalled. "They were very, very nervous. They said, 'We're returning to Germany tomorrow.' The man at the [hotel] desk said, 'All the Germans are leaving—either by car or taking the 6:15 a.m. train.' So, after that, we decided to go, too."

Fischer, his wife, Eglé and eventually, Francis, then moved closer to the French border, to a small town near Lausanne. Mother and son decided to get back to Paris by train. They arrived in Paris at night during a blackout, while the Fischers waited out the early days of the conflict in neutral Switzerland. "We tried to find a taxi, which was impossible, so we took the Métro, which was working very well. The next morning, Francis went to report," Eglé said. That was September 2, 1939.

The allies, France and England (the United States was still assuming a studious neutrality) then waited out *la drôle de guerre*, the "phony war," during which both sides, after Poland was overrun, simply observed each other from their respective borders. The French hunkered below ground in their allegedly impregnable Maginot Line along France's eastern border with Germany, a heavily engineered and interconnected series of underground bunkers and interlocking firing positions.

Francis was detailed initially to a collection company, made up of French citizens not previously assigned to a specific unit. These included many Frenchmen from abroad, including Moroccans, Algerians, expatriate Poles, Jews from all over Europe who had fled to the supposed egalitarian haven of France, and the like. They were barracked in a small military camp in Coulommiers, less than 38 miles east of Paris. He fought off barracks boredom with letters to Sylvia and the company of a few new friends, notably Robert Tancrède, who became a lifelong friend. Eglé would go see them on Sundays, taking packages full of food and busying herself by helping clean her son's quarters.

During the week, she worked as a Red Cross volunteer and gave generously of her time in the government offices of the 16th arrondissement, where she had reported the day after the general mobilization. The district's mayor, a physician and former "Communard," that is, an adherent of the Parisian commune that briefly ran things after France's embarrassing loss to Germany in 1870, was more than glad to have her support. "He said, 'I'm glad to have you—everyone else got the hell out of here,'" Eglé said. In French: "*Ils ont tous foutu le camp.*"

Grandmother continued thus in her memoirs: "Paris was empty. There was plenty to eat, but so few people to buy anything. No servants. Everybody was in Brittany or in the south of France and very shortly we had a lot of work at the *mairie* [literally, the mayor's office] with refugees from Belgium and the north of France.

"We set up soup lines," she recalled. "It was very busy with these people and we were not ready." Orphans and children were organized into groups and packed away to the country by train, detailed to country properties and *châteaux*. My grandmother also remembered being very busy setting up a project for the wives and girlfriends of the men who'd been called to wartime service. She had them sewing shirts and knitting socks that were then sold in the military commissary stores. Eglé spoke elegant volumes regarding her distress at these world developments in a letter to her friend Edna Thornton in Atlanta, which subsequently was reprinted in some detail by the society columnist for *The Atlanta Constitution*, on Nov. 19, 1939.

DISTRESS AND SUFFERING
IN FRANCE DESCRIBED
BY MRS. JOSEPH GATINS

I have been working like a mad woman on relief work. There is so much to do and so much misery. The war is hard on soldiers, but at least they are well fed and well clothed. You cannot imagine the sad life of those poor people who had to leave their homes, because they were too near the line of bombardment. So many children and old people are in this tragic class. And I was made ill from the pathetic plight of my people.

War is such a curse, and twice in 25 years is a little too much. Of course, I am heartbroken with my son and brother gone, but, outside of that, and what I suffer for my country, nothing so far has happened to me.

I shall ever be grateful for any amount raised to help relieve suffering and distress caused by the present war, which I hoped and prayed would be averted.

Eglé ended the letter with a desperate plea to help collect money from a virtual who's who of 21 Atlanta society figures, most of them women friends from her early days in Atlanta, to help the needy French civilians.

Francis, meanwhile, kept up with Sylvia by letter, anxiously waiting for armed conflict—he was still young and idealistic then—while trying to fend off the tedium of military routine.

September 5, 1939
[three days after reporting for duty]

I'm actually trying to catalog my thoughts about the war and my native land. For now, I'm heading to war with faith to defend what we had this spring: Our nightclubs, your dresses, your perfumes, our cigarettes, the champagne we drank. All that seems like good causes to defend, what do you think? Smile, everything is lovely. Yours affectionately.

September 20, 1939

Maybe your sweet letter of September 9 will calm my rage. Imagine, it's been 18 days that I'm here and we're still dressed in civilian clothes!" [He went on to describe the motley crew with him.] There are three types of people: First, the Frenchmen from abroad; then, those who'd lost all their paperwork; and, finally, a bunch of others pulled out of other units. We have three professors from the University of La Loire, a business rep from America (he is fat, effeminate and a Christian Scientist), two missionaries, two business executives, three musicians from the orchestra in Boston, representatives from every French colony, including one from Shanghai, a former champion sprinter, a ski champion, a young man of letters, a French theatrical scene-setter who's spent his entire life in Germany, a business rep from Berlin who spends his time reciting poems, especially by Baudelaire. In this disparate crew, we also have some who are really amusing — those touched in the head. Unfortunately, one of them several days ago had the funny idea of throwing himself out the third-story window and broke his hip. They're getting rid of the rest of 'em. What remains is a veritable mishmash of twisted souls, hunchbacks, those with a limp and every form of alcoholic degeneracy, and all the victims of what the immortal Céline calls "the bleeding heart Jews ..."

Francis in that same letter, almost in passing, makes further reference to an apparent adherence to the rampant anti-Semitism that was common currency in France during that era. The letters make clear that he was no exception to this shameful practice. "I've picked up some good friends, with whom I play bridge all day long, and with whom I practice anti-Semitism," he casually wrote in that same letter to Sylvia.

I was shocked to see evidence of this prejudice, so casually voiced, but such sentiment was widespread among non-Jews in France between the wars, despite France's token adherence to *Liberté, Egalité* and *Fraternité*. Many Gentiles, especially Catholics, resented both Jewish business successes, particularly in the banking world, and also the waves of Jewish immigrants who fled Germany and Austria and all of eastern Europe as Nazi pogroms became common there in the 1930s. Discovering this casual anti-Semitism in my father's past stopped me cold, particularly since neither my siblings nor I ever had an inkling of this disposition, nor had he sought to ingrain us with the same attitude. We exchanged many e-mails over this troubling finding, both to probe our memories and to try to understand what motivated his anti-Jewish sentiments. We all wanted to excuse him, but in the end, we could not. He was a product of his time. French anti-Semitism was everywhere in France, virulent and violent in the years leading up to World War II. French police documented the existence of at least 10 organized anti-Semitic groups in Paris alone in 1939, some of them dating back to the 1890s, some of them linked to anti-Dreyfus organizations. They published broadsheets and pamphlets and tracts to further their cause, with the circulation of the "most renowned" anti-Semitic newspapers, *La Libre Parole* and *Le Petit Journal* exceeding two million readers, according to researcher Paul J. Kingston. His slim volume, *Anti-Semitism in France during the 1930s*, more than adequately conveys a flavor for this torrent of propaganda, the gross caricatures that illustrated it, and the deep-rooted prejudice that spawned it. It explains, to a large degree, how the most rabid members of such groups in France ultimately found common cause with Nazi aims and provided leadership for, and complicity in, the state-sanctioned mass murder that was the Holocaust.

Some of these groups and their members took violent umbrage at seeing Jews in their midst in France and attacked them unmercifully in public. Citing a Paris police report of December 8, 1938, for example, Kingston found that violence "revealed the viciousness of the social manifestations of the prejudice, with the anti-Semites initially provoking Jewish customers in cafés with such obscenities as: 'It smells of Jew in here!' and 'You're nothing but dirty Jews! Get out, we're going to discipline you!'" Sometimes, the assailants used truncheons and pistols. Sometimes, Jews repelled the attackers and fought back in violent street mêlées. Such provocation was particularly aimed at Jews in the 4th, 19th and 20th arrondissements of Paris and occasioned numerous formal complaints from Jewish leaders.

Bernard Lecache, president of the *Ligue Internationale contre l'Antisémitisme*, filed many such complaints as early as 1935, suggesting the mood of the country and of Parisians was dangerously chauvinistic and violent. By September 1938, with the increased likelihood of a new war with Germany, Lecache complained that anti-Semitic provocateurs were seemingly aiming to blame Jews for instigating the coming conflict.

It was in this context that my father could make passing reference to Céline, one of the better-known anti-Semitic writers in France in the years leading to World War II. These references bubbled up like boils in his letters to Sylvia, though much of the correspondence dwelled on the disparate crew of citizen-soldiers that formed his company.

Undated, October-November, 1939.

[Francis regaled Sylvia with descriptions of his fellow soldiers—more of a foreign legion than a traditionally French unit.] In effect, I am now an important man—platoon leader. Here's the list of these fellows: Kujou, Sodowski, Narogny, Matusiak, Lucyak, Pryewozneczach, Murecnie, Machenski, Wastoviak, Bybiec, Babick, Murama, Skypzoc, Sweredsky, Dupont, Przygoda and l' Heureuse. These are all Polish miners from up north, except for two of them, who are French. But I must admit that I don't understand them any better than the Poles. They're nice, but a bit dense — they half throttled a little Jew from Galicia who claimed to be Polish. It's wonderful to be with guys like this—headquarters wouldn't hesitate to get us all killed with men of this sort. It's likely we're headed to the same destiny in three or four months.

The rest of that letter, typically, focused on Sylvia and their time together in Paris during a two-day pass. Francis suggested they think of a ski trip to

Switzerland in December, when he would have a longer leave but he also talked about befriending a fellow soldier, a Gypsy, who taught him how to "fish" for chicken, by baiting a hooked line over a farm wall and pulling the chicken to the other side.

Francis, Tancrède and a handful of other soldiers then were relieved of barracks duty and placed in a small, rented farmhouse in Coulommiers, apparently because they'd been assigned to head up the sports and physical education program for the 1,800 members of the unit. Francis also speaks of trying to get reassigned to a combat unit, perhaps a British army unit. He also pledged himself to Sylvia:

> *Undated, September-October, 1939.*
>
> *I would like you to know, my dear heart, what you mean to me. You are all my life and thoughts (how stupid words are sometimes). I sometimes despair of this war that is separating us—I'd even think of deserting to find you. But at the same time, I'd like to do a really good war to be deserving of you through courage and suffering—to be worthy of you.*

By November 12, 1939, Francis tells Sylvia is openly trying to get reassigned to what he views as a more worthy military unit. Efforts to get help from his uncle Charlic, then on the Maginot line in eastern France, had failed. "It seems to me he could have done this if he'd really tried." Eglé had figured out a way to get her son detailed as an interpreter to a British unit. "But I refused. I'd rather fight with the Savoyards, Bretons, and even Parisians or those from La Creuse—but not with those idiots." There was even talk of trying to get assigned to a French unit in the Middle East. Francis was so ashamed of the soft duty that he refused to write his many friends in America—"I would have to tell them where I am and what I'm doing." Sylvia had sent him a pair of hand-knitted socks, which Francis had given to another soldier who really needed them. (Many of the soldiers were finding that the pay allocations that were supposed to be sent home to wives and parents were not getting there in timely fashion). There was more brave talk, and more allusions to his anti-Semitism. "Finally, let's hope the big fight begins, and that I can find a position in the military." Then, this:

> *A young Jewish man, ... despite his obvious upbringing, made as if he could not understand our anti-Semitic allusions. One day, we jumped on his wife (a small Rumanian girl) and we made her speak against the Jews in front of her husband. He got the hell out of there the next day. Shortly after, we got rid of another compatriot, who was trying to get himself demobilized. In fact, he succeeded. The only real pleasure (other than your letters and the two friends remaining in the farmhouse) is to find one of those many Jews back at the depot barracks and to tell him that I've got a good tip—that he's going up to the front the next day. You should see their look.*

A rambling letter from the spring of 1940 then announced his arrival in Paris, where Francis had been detailed to help with instruction of new recruits. He mentions he might be reassigned to a unit in the Middle East, or to the 5th Infantry Regiment. Francis thanks her again for the hand-knitted socks she is sending him.

Francis then wrote another letter to Sylvia, probably also from the spring of 1940, from home on the stationery for 17, Place des Etats-Unis, as his girl friend vacationed with her mother at La Chezotte, a four-story, 15th Century redoubt, complete with battlements, which served as the German-Ribon family's country retreat. La Chezotte was in the remote and wild and very rural department of La Creuse, just north of the Auvergne, near the tiny hamlet of Ahun. He reported that Paris was coming back to life after the first evacuation of 1939. Little bistros and bars had reopened. He reported that his mother Eglé was troubling him: She was tired, depressed and had visibly aged. Like any man in love, he asked Sylvia for a photograph of herself.

> *I do hope the war is going to start up for good. I am really tired of being in this depot with all these old-timers, men with a limp, waiting for enemy paratroopers that don't show up very often. Don't consider this war like a crusade. I'm in this not for an idea, a principle or a sentiment, but simply*

(Continued...)

> *to kill as many Germans as possible, including women and children, so that our children, at least, can live in peace. Without hate or passion, I want the destruction of Germany.*

His next two letters brought an end to all the brave talk, beginning with an undated postcard, probably written shortly after being reassigned to the 5th Infantry Regiment. Obviously, for the French and for Francis, the "phony war" had come to an end, as he then relayed to Sylvia in a letter of Wednesday, May 22, 1940.

> *My Teddy Bear: Here is my new address. The regiment has lost about half of its men and materiel. We are reinforcing the regiment. I don't know how long this will last, or if we'll stay in the same place. I'm here with my pals — morale is better than excellent. I think of you. Affectionately.*

> *May 22, 1940.*
>
> *I am going to tell you what I have seen. The first few days, we fed Belgian refugees. It was awful — they'd been shot with a machine gun all along a byway. The children were the most pitiful. Then the village we were in was evacuated. And as our regiment had been forgotten by headquarters in the general confusion, we fed ourselves very well on local resources. I am full from wolfing down chickens and rabbits. For the past week, we've been doing fairly complicated night maneuvers and most uncomfortable camping during the day, while we wait to join the regiment that is being re-assembled in the most celebrated spot of the second war.*
>
> *All along the roads, we go by villages that have been evacuated — and pillaged and ransacked by French troops. Even the churches. It's shameful. After seeing this, one*

(Continued...)

cannot have many illusions about human nature. As for the fighting you've heard of, I've unfortunately seen none. We've only been shelled and shot at a few times. It's pretty impressive the first time ...but one gets used to it.

Today's sad developments seem to present a good lesson. The reserve officers have shown a certain competence, but too often a lack of character and understanding. It's the same in France: There are too many intelligent people, and not enough decision-takers. That deficiency arises in almost all ranks, from the little bourgeois (employees, shopkeepers, workers). I've unfortunately heard it said several times, 'Better be German than be dead.' But our farm laborers, and even the miners from up north, who had some terrible news from their home country, exhibit fierce resistance. We should have engineered a moral revolution before going to war. We should have been more serious rather than taking everything on with a smile. This is almost a 'mea culpa.' All this is a good lesson for me, as I have taken all this in with really too much mirth.

The German advances of May 1940 were indeed unstoppable, taking over, in quick succession, Denmark, Sweden, Belgium, and Holland. France succumbed in less than six weeks to a tank campaign that cost 100,000 Frenchmen their lives—and eventually shipped almost two million Frenchmen to Germany as prisoners of war. The Germans simply went around the Maginot line, pushing what was left of the British Expeditionary Force to Dunkirk and from there to an embarrassing retreat across the channel.

French authorities declared Paris an "open city" on June 14, which meant that the French would not try to defend it. (The notion of an open city, "*une ville ouverte*," refers to the wartime practice of declaring that a city would not be defended, under open or tacit agreement between the enemies, so as to safeguard cultural monuments and civilian population.) Paris experienced a second, pell-mell depopulation as those who still could fled to the countryside at the same time as French political leaders readied for defeat. By June 22, 1940, the French government had fallen and its replacement, led by Maréchal Philippe Pétain, based in Vichy, had signed a humiliating armistice with the occupying German forces.

Francis and members of his platoon, meanwhile, were cooking eggs for supper when his position was overrun. He was taken prisoner on June 14, 1940, the same day Paris opened its doors to Nazi invaders. He was force-marched with thousands of fellow French soldiers across German lines and from there herded into a cattle car to a brave new world of Nazi prisoner of war camps and an uncertain future as a captive. Memories of those days remained indelible in my father's mind. "We didn't stop for six or seven days—nothing to eat and very little water," Francis would recall of that forced prisoner march. "When we finally stopped, I shit out a turd harder than stone." It had not taken very long for my father to abandon pre-war bravado and bluster.

Chapter 14

"These Were Terrible Times"

"These were terrible times," Eglé recalled. Her son Francis and his fellow conscripts from Coulommiers had been sent north, where they were swept up into "the grand, bloody mess. They were not sufficiently equipped. My son was taken prisoner and I did not know where he was." In fact, Eglé did not learn that Francis was still alive until Robert Tancrède, the friend he had made in Coulommiers, went to her home in Paris to report that he was alive and that he'd been taken prisoner. Tancrede himself had been wounded and left for dead.

Francis' exact whereabouts were not officially confirmed until two months after his capture, when Eglé received a postcard notice from the International Committee of the Red Cross. My father had filled out the card, dated August 15, 1940, which confirmed he was being held at Stalag VIII-C. That same day, Eglé's stepfather, Henri Fischer, died.

Her brother Charlic, originally detailed to duty on the Maginot Line, had tried to get to the front near Denon, but he too was taken prisoner by the Germans as Maréchal Pétain signed the armistice with the invaders. France was partitioned into two zones. The German invaders immediately occupied the northern portion, including Paris. Initially, a so-called "free zone" took up the southern portion of France. Charlic, who'd been a German prisoner during the First World War, was freed after about a year as a sop to the French, whose new German masters decided to free the World War I veterans. They were too old to be much of a threat. Charlic was then 45 years old. But Francis was forced stay in Germany, beginning the hard life of the prisoner of war.

Grandmother Eglé at first did her utmost to try to enlist U.S. authorities in Paris and Washington to get him released from the prison camp, vainly claiming that he should have dual U.S.-French citizenship and that he should be released since America was then still neutral. When that rationale didn't work, she did everything in her power to make his incarceration and that of his fellow prisoners from the 16th arrondissement less woeful, leading a very organized effort to send care packages to them.

She had launched a concerted and determined campaign to get American authorities at the highest levels of the U.S. government to help her locate Francis and then get him released, on the grounds that he was a native son of a well-known Atlanta family, part-owner of the equally well-known Georgian Terrace Hotel and, therefore, eligible to at least claim American citizenship. Re-enter the chief of the U.S. Department of State's Passport Division, R.B. Shipley, the same bureaucrat who had denied him a passport as he sought to return to France in 1939. Francis was not an American citizen as far as the United States was concerned, she said. "For your information," Shipley wrote U.S. Sen. Walter F. George, D-Georgia, on August 31, 1940, "it may be stated that an American passport was refused Mr. Gatins to go to France and he presumably returned to France as a French citizen. Under the circumstances, he is not entitled to the formal protection of this government." But Shipley conceded in the same letter that back-channel "informal inquiries" were being made to find him.

Those inquiries, originating from Eglé, eventually involved Edna Thornton, her old friend from Atlanta; Francis's aunt and uncle, Ben Gatins and Mary Gatins Jackson (co-owners, with Francis, of the Georgian Terrace Hotel); those ever-mindful observers of Gatins family doings, *The Atlanta Journal* and *The Atlanta Constitution*; Howell Jackson, Mary's current husband, a former judge based in Middleburg, Virginia; Welborn B. Cody, the Atlanta lawyer who handled both Francis' passport and business affairs; Senator George; Ronald Ransom, then a member of the Federal Reserve System's board of governors and an old acquaintance of Eglé's from her early days in Atlanta; the American Red Cross; the International Red Cross in Geneva; the World Alliance of the Young Men's Christian Associations (which at that time still had some access to authorities in Berlin); the French Embassy in Washington, and the American embassies in Paris and Berlin. The frenzy came to the attention of Adolph A. Berle, Jr., then an assistant secretary of state, who forwarded the dossier to Freeman Matthews, the U.S. *chargé d'affaires* at the American Embassy in Paris. "Ronald Ransom was recently in Atlanta, where he learned that Francis's relatives were anxious to be apprized [sic] of his whereabouts, both for personal reasons and because property interests are involved," Berle wrote Matthews on September 10. "I hope this request will not cause any inconvenience, and I want you to know how grateful I will be for your kind cooperation."

Ransom himself had pointed out in his letters to State and to Eglé herself (one of which was forwarded to her via the U.S. diplomatic pouch), that he remembered Eglé fondly. "I remember most pleasantly the days when you were living at the Georgian Terrace, and we lived on Juniper Street. At that time, my daughter was a little girl, who was always so glad to see you when you were out walking with your dogs," Ransom said.

Cody, the Atlanta lawyer, also weighed in at some length, arguing that Francis was really an American citizen. "Under these circumstances, it seems to me that he deserves the protection of the Federal Government, and that the State Department should make some effort to see that he is released by the German authorities," Cody wrote State on October 1.

Cody and Edna Thornton also enlisted the publicity machine of Atlanta's daily newspapers, which on August 20, 1940, chronicled Francis's capture and the fact that he was then believed to be missing in action. Two subsequent articles, pasted into a scrapbook kept by Sylvia, went to some length to detail Cody's efforts to untangle Francis' citizenship questions and to relate his being found alive.

GATINS IS FOUND
ALIVE IN NAZI
PRISON CAMP

Grandson of Atlanta Pioneer was 'Missing' Since Fall of France

Joseph Francis Gatins III, 25-year-old in the French army and grandson of one of the builders of Atlanta, has been found alive in a German prison camp, according to a cable received here yesterday.

When no word had been received from the young soldier for many weeks after the fall of France, both his mother, who lives in Paris, and relatives in Atlanta believed him dead.

With his mother, the former Eglé de Sombreuil, he spent the winter of 1938-39 at the Georgian Terrace Hotel, which his grandfather built and of which he is part owner.

That last article went on at Biblical length to detail Francis' family ties to Atlanta, describing him as the "grandson of the late Joseph Francis and Kate Thomas Gatins, pioneer citizens of Atlanta, and the son of the late Joseph Francis Gatins Jr. of Atlanta and Paris. He is the nephew of Mrs. Howell Jackson of Middleburg, Virginia, and Ben Gatins, of Atlanta and Rumson, N.J. Atlanta relatives include Mrs. Julian Riley, a cousin." The latter referred to Katherine Murphy Riley, the cousin who probably had partied so hard with my father during his visits to Atlanta in 1936 and 1938-39.

The inexorable push of world events was soon to ensnare America in the world war and when that happened, the Atlanta contingent backed off its efforts. As lawyer Cody pointed out in a wrap-up letter after the war, efforts to secure Francis's release paled at the time. "I believe the State Department had about gotten to the point where they could arrange this [his release] when the United States Lend-Lease Program began to amount to participation in the war and I learned from the State Department that there was little chance of getting his release." Cody wrote. "Shortly after that, we actually did enter the war and no further effort has been made to obtain his release." The Lend-Lease Act, which provided massive amounts of combat materiel to the Allies (England, France, China and the Soviet Union, initially), was signed into law in March of 1941. The U.S. formally declared war on Germany on December 11, 1941, three days after Pearl Harbor and two days after it had declared war on Japan.

As far as Ronald Ransom, was concerned, the matter was closed in December of 1940. "During the latter part of September, I was advised that he had been found and was being held as a prisoner by the Germans," Ransom wrote Berle, the assistant secretary of state on December 16. "Would it be advisable to notify the Embassy so that they will know that the matter is closed so far as the request to locate him is concerned?" All, too, was quiet from Aunt Mary and Uncle Ben.

As for Francis, all the attention from U.S. interests did not measurably help his cause behind the barbed wire compounds of Stalag VIII-C, a 120-acre prison camp near Sagan, Germany (now Zagan, Poland), that, according to various sources, eventually served as a testing ground for Nazi brutality.

Upon arrival at this Stalag, he was promptly interrogated and a well-thumbed address book inspected. "They beat me because, at first, they thought I was something of an American spy," my father told me about 15 years later. "The book was full of names and addresses for all my friends back in the United States, in Atlanta and New York, as well as those in England and France."

Chapter 15

Prisoner of War No. 50-894

Following his capture on June 14, 1940, Joseph Francis Gatins III, member of substantial and upstanding families in both France and the United States, bon-vivant, international party-goer and part-owner of a well-known hotel in Atlanta, landed in the middle of Stalag VIII-C along the Rhine River in Germany after a week-long forced march and an uncomfortable ride in a railroad cattle car. Then a 25-year-old corporal in the French Army, Francis was to spend most of the next three and a half years in a series of prisoner-of-war camps used to incarcerate and punish the thousands of Allied soldiers swallowed up by the maw of the European theater of World War II.

Efforts to piece together the details of his imprisonment into a coherent whole have not been easy. My father told and retold bits and pieces of the tale many times to friends at cocktail parties and to the family at the dinner table, but it never emerged as a whole. Nor did he ever tell anyone, except perhaps his wife and his mother, of the terrible brutalities—torture, in fact—that he endured. When, as his oldest son, I needed a subject for a "show and tell" report in fifth grade in the mid-1950s, he tried to tell me the story for later retelling to my classmates, but left out a good many of the horrifying details that later came to light. Of course, I did not keep any notes on that elementary school report to Miss Rivers' class nor did I have a tape recorder in the mid-1950s to record it for posterity. What I remember most from that report is that during one escape attempt he had pushed out the ceiling tiles in a prisoner bunkhouse to make his escape through an adjacent room. I thought that was so cool. The Germans thought he was a spy. I thought that was cool, too. I was immensely proud that he had escaped.

His French military records are more than sketchy about this period. His German prisoner-of-war records, along with all the others seized and confiscated by American troops in April 1945, were subsequently forwarded to French authorities, who apparently no longer know where they are located. Yet, snippets of information about Francis' days as a prisoner are recorded here and there: With the International Tracing Service of the International Committee of the Red Cross, based in Geneva; in his French military discharge papers; from U.S. State Department affidavits filed after the war, and, most crucially, in the *Kriegsgefangenenpost*, the German prisoner of war correspondence system. My mother kept many of my father's letters, each complete with a return address for his current camp name and location, each hand-cancelled with a German military post office date stamp. Thanks to this most efficient German military bureaucracy and Sylvia's decision to safeguard some 26 letters and postcards written during 1940-43, Francis' descent into an increasingly harsh camp system can be roughly approximated. Today, conditions in the camps also are described in the blossoming memorabilia files, hundreds of personal stories posted on the Internet, a plethora of books and, more bureaucratically, in inspection reports of the prisoner-of-war camps, which are available to the public from the International Committee of the Red Cross.

Every French prisoner of war customarily was permitted to dispatch two postcards and two letters home per month, sometimes fewer, depending on the captors' whims, as well as to receive two packages from home, using self-addressed tags provided by German prison guards. Francis used his correspondence privileges primarily to write Sylvia and to his mother.

Once she knew where to find him, Eglé redoubled her efforts to help him and his fellow prisoners. "I was without any news [of Francis] until August 15, 1940, when I got an answer from the Red Cross in Geneva giving me the name and the number of his Stalag, No. VIII-C ...," she said. "At the same time, we received postal tags permitting us to send care packages. We thus expedited as many packages as we had address tags, full of food and warm clothes, including some boots secured on the black market from Francis' boot maker." Eglé, who had busied herself as a Red Cross volunteer during the phony war by collecting hand-made socks and shirts for resale to her son's unit, turned the prisoner care package business into a growing concern in the 16th arrondissement. "I was very busy both by Red Cross duties and by the 'prisoner package effort,' which the Red Cross had asked me to head. We had 4,000 names on these rolls.

"I had a small number of paid employees and many volunteers who were admirable in their devotion to the task. Those families who could reimburse the package committee did so, the others were covered for free," she recalled. "We also asked those with more expansive means to provide a little extra money, which ensured the mailing costs of those who could not afford them. We never lacked for cash. Certain people from the 16th arrondissement were extremely generous with us."

At the same time, she said, Paris had again largely turned into a ghost town as the Germans easily took over the French capital without a fight. "The Germans took everything," she said, occupying every major municipal building and hotel in Paris.

Francis, meanwhile, sent his first postcard to Sylvia, dated July 15, 1940, postmarked from Stalag VIII-C, addressed to La Chezotte and subsequently forwarded to Biarritz. It contained seven lines of tiny print, terse and stylistically clipped, written in pencil:

> *Sylvia: It's been more than a month that I am a prisoner. I will never get over all of this. I am in good health. I am without news of Mother, not knowing where she is, or whether she is still in Paris. Send me news of you. What a difference this is from our spring. I'm not working yet, and really have the blues. From time to time, a care package would be most welcome. Je vous embrasse tous.*

No other letters survive from Prisoner of War No. 50-894 at Stalag VIII-C in Zagan, Upper Silesia, now part of Poland. I know from my own experience in Vietnam that soldiers far from home, whether prisoner or not, have an absolute need for sanity's sake to maintain connections to home. Whether by letter or care packages or both, they are a true lifeblood and my mother and grandmother were the main donors for these absolutely necessary transfusions for my father.

Francis later suggested he tried to escape for the first time from the 120-acre camp at Zagan by walking off a work detail with a fellow prisoner and temporarily hiding in a barracks latrine. Squirreled away behind a bathroom partition, Francis could see German soldiers in a mirror, brushing their teeth. But they did not see him. The two prisoners then skedaddled out of the camp only to be recaptured a few days later.

Eglé says in her memoirs that Francis had just begun a long series of capture-escape-recapture escapades. This was followed in every case by transfer to a different prison camp and two weeks of solitary confinement. Francis recalled coping with solitary by replaying in his mind, hole by hole, every golf course he'd ever played.

Eglé's recollection was: "He escaped several times and often I did not know where he was. He continued these escapes and I'd get letters telling me, 'I've got nothing to wear—send me some clothes, I can hardly believe the number of clothes we thus lost during this war!" The German military prison bureaucracy also docked him for every piece of clothing lost during the escapes and years later Francis figured he still owed about 150 German marks for lost clothing.

The Stalag System

It took about two months for the German military to formally book Francis and his fellow prisoners from the 5th Infantry Regiment into the brave new world of the German prisoner of war camp system. French prisoners like Daddy, along with men from the French colonies of Morocco, Algeria and Senegal, went to Stalag VIII-C. The site is about 120 miles south-southeast of Berlin and more than 650 miles northwest of Paris, as the crow flies.

The Germans made room for the new French captives by simply moving out all the Polish prisoners who had been imprisoned there after the *blitzkrieg* of 1939. History suggests that the Germans, in contravention of Geneva Convention war protocols, simply deprived the Poles of their prisoner status in June 1940, and transferred them to forced labor camps.

The first French prisoners of war started arriving on the plain of Upper Silesia in May. Francis got there by July 3, 1940. By December, the camp itself housed some 7,500 French prisoners and was responsible for another 37,000 scattered in some 1,300-to-1,500 work details, some as far away as Austria. Most of those workers who stayed in the main camp were detailed to repairing shoes (200 prisoners) and as tailors (some 140 prisoners).

Contemporary Red Cross inspection reports provide a detailed outline of the camp's organization. The prisoners lived in standard, identical bunkhouses, each housing about 375 prisoners stacked into three-decker bunks. Each had electric light and a woodstove for heat. The barracks were made less severe with attendant flower gardens and, in some cases, mosaic tiles. There was an infirmary for the sick, a theater, a monthly prisoner newspaper, a soccer field, a library (largely stocked by the American YMCA) and about a dozen French Catholic priests who said mass daily.

No prison in the world runs without the cooperation of its prisoners, however sullen they might be, and this one was no different. A "man of confidence" (*homme de confiance*, in French), a senior non-commissioned officer acting as a combined prison trustee, liaison contact, postmaster and work supervisor, was chosen as intermediary with the German captors to regulate distribution of care packages (with the help of some 10 prisoners detailed to that task), deliver and track incoming and outgoing mail (after it was censored by the Germans) and try to keep tabs on the many thousands of prisoners scattered in separate work camps in that part of Poland, Austria and nearby Germany. The outside labor battalions, or *Arbeitskommandos*, were detailed to everything from agricultural work on German-owned farms to industry, including "textiles and road-building." Prisoners were paid the equivalent of 18.2 Deutschmarks per month for this labor, most of it redeemable only at camp canteens, which had lemonade and malt beverages for sale and, sometimes, fresh produce such as turnips, onions and lemons.

Stalag VIII-C, at least at the end of 1940, was deemed by the Red Cross to be a healthy and well-ordered prison, "where a high morale reigns due to the camp commandant and his deputy." The Red Cross inspection team was particularly struck by the flourishing artistic enterprise visible throughout the camp, most of it spurred by the efforts of an artist named Michel. The Germans had provided Michel and his cohorts, many of them former students of the Beaux-Arts ateliers in Paris, with paint, canvas, easels and a studio and some freedom to pursue their art in their free time. "One of those painter-decorators told us: 'Our group is so homogeneous, we work so peaceably, that sometimes we have a hard time realizing that we are prisoners.'" According to one Red Cross inspection report for 1940, prisoners at the main camp in Zagan got one hot shower per week, had no complaints about the food, enjoyed weekly soccer matches, were permitted to send one letter and two postcards home per month, and had access to health and dental care. Only 90 prisoners had died during the first year of custody in this camp, which was deemed a small number.

The inspection team did record a few minor complaints: Not enough consecrated wine for the priests to say mass; need for more shoes, underwear and soap; and a desire for greater speed in receiving mail from home. Letters from France were held five to eight days before being turned over to the prisoners, as German censors, who sometimes had to process more than 700 letters per day, excised any detailed information about the war or the occupation back in France. All in all, according to the Red Cross inspection team's summary conclusions, Stalag VIII-C on December 3, 1940, was an "excellent camp," with a remarkable development of artistic enterprise.

This camp grew much less cozy as the war ground on over the next four years. By November 27, 1944, long after Francis was gone, this stalag was responsible for 34,918 prisoners of war, including soldiers from Poland, Yugoslavia, Rumania, Belgium, England, Canada, Australia, New Zealand, South Africa, India and Saudi Arabia, including 26,562 French prisoners. Of this total, only 6,708 were actually housed within the barbed-wire confines of Stalag VIII-C, the others being scattered about nearby towns and locations as forced laborers. Some 4,868 of the French prisoners, it was pointed out in another 19-page, typewritten report from Red Cross inspections, also had been incorporated into the German civilian labor pools under a so-called "transformation" process used by Nazi captors to beef up their much-depleted workforce at home.

Conditions had visibly deteriorated since 1940.

- Barracks bunkhouses were overcrowded, taking in up to 370 prisoners where there was only enough room for 350, in part because 2,000 French prisoners from three different "disciplinary detachments" at Ehrenfost, Blechhammer and Hugolust, had been sent to the main Stalag.

- Heat and light were insufficient. Many windows had been broken and not replaced.

- Bunks were totally deprived of straw mattresses, as there was no straw to be had.

- Barracks roofs leaked, requiring "continuous repair."

- Food rations were declining even as work requirements were increasing.

- Many of the prisoners' clothes were confiscated upon arrival in the camp. Field jackets were lacking.

- Both Germans and other prisoners routinely pilfered prisoner-of-war packages.

- British prisoners from India complained of not receiving curry and betel nuts.

- Latrines were full to overflowing and water pumps failed.

- The infirmary lacked basic supplies.

- The libraries were well stocked, but there was no longer enough room for study halls, theater, music, etc.

- Those on work details were worked hard, sometimes as much as 82 hours per week, sometimes seven days per week, with some so-called "civilian employers" giving themselves the right to punish workers in their factories and assign them additional hours of work. These enterprises included a sugar refinery, a lumberyard and a brick-making factory. Some work details were used to build fortifications and dig trenches for "passive defense" of various factories.

- Prisoners often were subjected to frequent searches, with any food and tobacco forever lost to the prisoners' use.

- Mail was a sometime thing, with mail to and from Tunisia, Algeria and Morocco rare, and no mail at all for prisoners from Corsica.

- Those prisoners deemed to be Communists or hard cases had their packages from home routinely stolen.

The inspection team took up 28 separate complaints with the German camp authorities, most of which were brushed aside. The French prisoners complained of having only one urinal for 1,500 prisoners, forcing them to use the walls of their barracks. "There are sufficient urinals, but the French prisoners are too lazy to go to them," the Germans reportedly responded.

The two Red Cross physicians conducting this inspection concluded that the very existence of the prisoners of war at that time was becoming "more and more painful," given the overcrowding, the searches, and the increasing work requirements. Conditions in this stalag and similar prison camps only deteriorated further as the war churned to its conclusion. Like millions of others, Francis learned to endure the misery of the prisoner's life—and to forge strategies crucial to survival.

Lifelines in Purgatory

Life for the prisoners of war in the stalags was not only a matter of physical survival but also of fighting off boredom as best one could, rolling cigarettes, writing letters, reading books sent from home when not spending many long, waking hours on German work details.

Each one of my father's letters to my mother was written on identical slick, grey-colored paper, 5.5" X 10.5" in size, with 25 pre-printed lines on the inside, and strict warnings from the German censors to stay within the lines and the margins and to write legibly. Written in pencil in tiny, cramped penmanship, each of his letters typically contained about 250 words, far less than he was accustomed to writing Sylvia before the war began. His letters before the war often ran six to eight pages, in equally tiny print. (None of my mother's letters survived the war.) Given the restrictions and censorship, the true news of camp life could only be alluded to in passing, or relayed back to loved ones in France by the occasional prisoner sent back to the homeland for health reasons.

Although the Geneva Conventions in force during World War II technically forbade forced labor by prisoners of war, Francis and thousands of other enlisted men found themselves sent outside the barbed-wire confines of the main camps to work in smaller details or battalions. The Germans called them *Kommandos*, for short.

Francis' letters to Sylvia describe a variety of such outside jobs in a variety of work battalions: He was used as a busboy in German cafés, as a common laborer, occasionally as an underground coal miner and as a farm worker digging beets and potatoes at harvest time. He took the place of German men deemed more useful to the Reich on the eastern and western fronts and he was not alone. By the end of the war, the German war machine had imprisoned more than 1.8 million French soldiers, and between 4 million and 5.7 million from the Soviet Union, according to accepted current estimates.

In addition, the French, in the initial months of the armistice signed with Pétain and his traitorous Vichy government, had voluntarily sent 200,000 skilled "guest workers" to Germany, a number that ballooned to about 650,000 when the volunteer work details were turned into mandatory slave labor. That *Service de Travail Obligatoire* (Mandatory Work Service) was so roundly despised in France by 1944 that it finally led many French men and women to take to the *maquis* and resist the German rule they had meekly accepted in 1940. (*Maquis* is the word for a dense, scrub vegetation found in some parts of France, and adopted by the Resistance as a generic description of the movement against the Germans).

"I worked the month of August moving rock, the month of September as a laborer," Francis wrote Sylvia in a letter of December 22, 1941, postmarked from the 24th Battalion of Stalag II-B, the camp he'd been assigned to after his first escape attempt. "Then, I changed camps and worked in the postal delivery section. Physically, I'm enduring captivity as well as possible. I've only lost unneeded fat and unnecessary hair—which makes me look like a baby bird fallen out of the nest," he continued. "As for morale, it's been harder." He concluded the letter with a special request—that Eglé's next care package, all 11 pounds of it, be composed entirely of Gauloises cigarettes and tobacco, the common currency of any prison or lock-up to this day.

Stalag II-B was located just outside Hammerstein in West Prussia (Pomerania), another sprawling barbed-wire compound originally built to barrack Polish prisoners of war, and which, like Stalag VIII-C, experienced its own descent into brutality and pain as the war came closer to an end. The Francis-to-Sylvia correspondence also mentions periodic stays in prison hospitals, which my father made plain served as an excuse not to work, as well as occasional assignment to "health companies" (*compagnie de santé*), where mandatory physical exercise was much on the schedule.

In a letter of January 30, 1942, also postmarked from Stalag II-B, Francis wanted to make sure that a prisoner buddy had relayed news of his situation in person and alluded, almost in passing, to the harsh reality of camp life. "I got out of the hospital 12 days ago and am now back in the camps," he wrote. "My arm is perfectly set, but severely atrophied. I don't know if it's ever going to be as it was before." It was only after he returned to Paris that the real story of the broken arm came to light. Faced with probable transfer to another stalag, reportedly on an island from which escape would have been difficult, my father, amazingly, opted to have a fellow prisoner break one of his arms so he could be hospitalized, thus delaying any transfer and, he hoped, stopping it entirely. The first attempt failed. The biggest prisoner in the camp was unable to break his arm. A smaller prisoner, but one with some strength, a butcher in civilian life, then took up a wooden cudgel, as Francis placed his arm between two chairs. The smaller man snapped his right arm with one quick, hard strike. As a result, Francis's right arm ended up about two inches shorter than his left, and his handwriting in the letters—he was right-handed—grew noticeably larger. To this day, I cannot imagine the fear that would lead to such self-mutilation. That experience does shed some light on his later, vague allusions to survival sometimes being a brutal business. At other times, though, he would minimize his prisoner experiences with quips, glossing over the horrors and beatings he had endured and which were to mark his psyche forever.

The letters from the period 1941 into early 1942 suggest that the long days away from hearth and home and loved ones were weighing heavily on the 26-year-old prisoner. "I've had a rough time," he wrote Sylvia on March 5, 1942. One of his best friends had escaped and Francis felt lonely and alone. Sylvia had hinted at possible marriage, which pleased Francis enormously, but this letter also referred to his concern for the turmoil that was sure to befall France after the war. "With war continuing and the explosion of hate that will follow, the violence with which social questions will be handled, [as well as] questions of race, revolt from yellow, black and red [peoples], it will be impossible for anyone, for better than 100 years, to avoid the coming disturbance." He also thanked Sylvia for staying in touch. "You cannot know, my little one, how your letter and your photo please me. Pray for me from time to time. God bless you, dearest."

A letter of April 17, still from Stalag II-B, seemed more mundane: "Thus, I spend most of my time smoking your cigarettes, reading your books, writing to you, reading and re-reading your letters..... and dreaming. Don't be surprised if there's a delay, or even a full stop, in my correspondence. But with the spring coming on and my arm getting better, it could be that there will be new and numerous disturbances in my life as a prisoner." Francis apparently was telegraphing yet another escape attempt past the German censors.

Indeed, in the months to come, Francis was to experience increasingly harsh dislocation, which required more than prayers to survive. He escaped from Stalag II-B, attempting to get to Hungary, which was then still a neutral country in the war, and was shipped after his recapture to a more forbidding prison camp, Stalag X-B, at Sanbostel, from which he again escaped. Recaptured yet again, his next letter to Sylvia was postmarked August 6, 1942, from a cruel hellhole of a punishment camp, the notorious Stalag 325 at Rawa-Ruska, in the middle of the Nazi killing and extermination zone on the border between Poland and the Ukraine—birthplace of the Holocaust.

Chapter 16

Eglé's Private Resistance

❧   ❧   ❧

While doing all in her power to keep her son alive by sending him cigarettes, clothes, socks, soap and the like, Eglé also was fighting a private war right under the noses of the German forces occupying Paris. She sneaked escaped prisoners to the then still free south of France, hid papers for Free French forces and aided the budding Resistance as best as she could. Unlike many of her countrymen and the cowardly Vichy government—and not a few collaborators of her own class of society—she had little use for the Nazis and the French puppets who were running what was left of the government, or for the Vichy policy of working hand-in-glove with the Nazis' anti-Semitic extermination programs. She particularly resented the military parade the Germans staged down the Champs d'Elysées every day of the occupation in Paris, so jarring to one who had seen the magnificent victory parades down the same long boulevard after the Allied victory over the *Krauts* in World War I. Brought up to be a French royalist and no friend of the French Revolution, given her Villelume-Sombreuil ancestry, she nonetheless assumed a strong French Republican patriotism during the occupation of Paris.

"In 1942, that was awful, the roundup of Jews in France," she vividly relayed to her granddaughter Sophie in a tape-recorded interview some 34 years later. "All the Jews had to wear the Star of David. First, they could not ride the Métro. Imagine that, poor people. Then, they could not attend the theater, and then they started sending them to concentration camps.

"They took the little children away from their parents and put them in the town halls and never allowed them to see them again despite the Geneva Convention, and Pétain signed that agreement. I hated him for that, and all were sent to camps, where most of them perished, as you know."

Eglé apparently also was a peripheral witness to the most barbaric of the

Jewish roundups in Paris, the unforgettable sweep of the Vel d'Hiv, starting at 4 a.m. on July 16, 1942. German forces, clearly with help of French police, rounded up a total of 12,884 Jews that day, about 75 percent of them women and children. Any child over two years old was eligible for this pogrom. Most of the men immediately were shipped to the French concentration camp at Drancy, while almost 7,000 of the remaining hapless Jews were jammed into the Vélodrome d'Hiver, or Vel d'Hiv, for short, an indoor sports arena in the 15th arrondissement. There was little food and hardly any water. About 100 of the prisoners committed suicide on the spot. Another 100 who tried to flee were shot dead. There was hardly enough room to lie down, and few toilets. Diarrhea and dysentery were rampant, and "a terrible odor infected the place."

"Eglé and the Red Cross went to try to talk the Germans into letting them bring milk for the babies, which the Germans refused," her granddaughter Eglé said some 60 years after the event. "She said that you could hear the babies and children crying. It was so frustrating not to be able to do anything. She would always get emotional and use the expression '*les sales Boches*' (the dirty Krauts), when recalling this story."

Indeed, contemporary accounts paint a terrible picture of what transpired in the five days of the Vel d'Hiv sweep.

"There were no sanitary facilities, no sinks, no toilets. The water had been cut off and we had to fetch drinking water in pitchers to try to stem their thirst," J.M. Mathey-Jenais, a Red Cross nurse, recalled regarding conditions inside the arena. "No food except for a bit a soup ... and not in large enough quantity to feed everyone. It was stuffy, nauseating, with nervous cries and shrieks, children crying and even adults at the end of their rope. Several madmen panicked the crowd. All piled up on each other without mattresses, without sleep." The men, women and children jumbled into the Vel d'Hiv were dispatched to the Drancy concentration camp after five days, with most then shipped in cattle cars sometime thereafter to Auschwitz, where almost all were put to death.

Grandmother Eglé, meanwhile, was more successful in doing what she could to foil German intentions, at the very local level of the Red Cross offices for the 16th arrondissement. (Almost all of the arrondissements in Paris had a similar local Red Cross office, involved in dispatching military care packages to prisoners in far-off Germay and Poland.) In the early years of the occupation, in 1940-41, goodly numbers of escaped French prisoners of war were still fleeing through Paris, trying to get to the south of France, which was then still classified as a "free zone."

"So, we looked for passage and with money we could pass people through there," Eglé recalled. "Thank God, we got some money, and the most important thing was a man in Montmartre who could make phony papers. He could make the best phony papers—you could not tell the difference from the real ones," she said. "That's how I could get so many people out." (Eglé knew Montmartre well because she made a weekly visit to the Basilica of the Sacred Heart, on a hillside in the 18th arrondissement, as a prayer vow for Francis' safe escape.) The escaped prisoners Eglé explained, including several British escapees, were directed to a safe passage near Macon, a small town in Burgundy, about 35 miles north of Lyon, where a Red Cross committee provided them money "after they'd crossed the line," (that is, the boundary between occupied France and the "free zone" in the south of the country). "When the free zone was taken over by the Germans, it became much more difficult, but we managed to do so anyway. We had to watch out, though, because not everyone thought the same way as us, that is to say, they weren't opposed to the Germans," she said.

She also made the best of a difficult situation in the Red Cross offices where she and other workers collected and packed the goods for the prisoner-of-war package program. They would keep on sending packages to prison camps in Germany even when they knew a prisoner was no longer in that camp, "knowing that the food never went to waste." She recalled that German soldiers "would come to us and would ask us if we knew anything about these prisoners. We'd answer that we knew nothing. Some of these soldiers were disagreeable, but in the main, they were minimally polite," she said.

In time, she made contact with a Colonel Alfred Touny who thought "the right way—he was anti-Kraut." Touny, a veteran of the First World War, had been promoted to head of O.C.M. (Organisation Civile et Militaire), one of the key Resistance groups organized to counter German occupying forces particularly in the north and west of France. The group originally was composed of mostly conservative Germanophobes, but later included many Socialists, according to various historic accounts of the group's activities.

One day, he told me, 'If something happens, they'll come for me. Could you keep these papers for me? You would have to turn them over to a man who will use the following password: 'Everything's well in Brittany.' Of course, I told him. As he feared, he was arrested, transferred up north and executed."

Eglé hid the papers under a stack of clean laundry in the Red Cross offices. Col. Touny's contact called her and they made an appointment to turn the papers over on a Saturday. "He showed up with a machine pistol, which terrified me. He put the papers in his briefcase and left." Grandmother Eglé's work in safeguarding Touny's papers, as well as her helping prisoners escape, was recognized after the war as a signal achievement that garnered her the highest award possible for French civilians, the *Legion d'Honneur*.

She also was able to keep the finances of the Red Cross and the welfare activities of the 16th arrondissement during 1939-46 in the black, "reimbursing all advances" made by the administration. Similarly, Eglé's prisoner care package program netted a surplus at the end of the war, which was distributed to needy prisoners.

My grandmother hardly ever spoke of these times afterwards, and did not say much about the French government's special recognition. In fact, there is much more information in the Legion of Honor organization's files than she ever related to her grandchildren, but she was quietly proud of her own resistance and bravery and for the rest of her life she often wore a tiny red rosette in her jacket lapels, signaling to those who understood and recognized this symbol that her wartime activity been a real and true accomplishment. The rosette attracted hardly any attention when she moved to the United States, and received only passing mention when the Atlanta newspapers published an article that re-introduced her to their local readers. On some lapels, she had a tiny red thread sewn into the fabric to hint at the award. And on some very few formal occasions, she would wear the Legion's medal itself.

My father, meanwhile, with a different kind of bravery, soldiered on with his own war of rebellion against the German captors in increasingly difficult circumstances.

Chapter 17

Deaf-Mute Escape to Hamburg

Around June of 1942, after two full years of incarceration, his broken arm now definitely on the mend and a third escape attempt and customary two weeks in solitary, my father was transferred from Stalag II-B to Stalag X-B at Sanbostel, located on cold, swampy ground about 34 miles west-southwest of Hamburg, and still a long 450 miles from Paris.

This camp was reserved for hard cases, escapees and those who refused to work in German forced labor detachments. The prisoners housed there were further punished by being put on half-wages for whatever work they did perform.

It eventually became a notorious death camp for about 50,000 of the more than one million soldiers and civilians held there between 1939 and 1945, who died of hunger, disease or were simply murdered. When Allied forces liberated the camp in April, 1945, they found some 8,000 civilian prisoners housed at Stalag X-B in "utterly horrifying" and appalling conditions—"everywhere the dead and dying sprawled around the slime of human excrement."

Red Cross inspection reports for this camp of August 6 and 21 November, 1942, while terming the stalag in generally decent shape, registered a number of worrisome findings: Hot showers had been cancelled; a typhus infection had broken out; tuberculosis was rampant in some barracks; mail from home, as usual, was not getting to prisoners in timely fashion; the uniforms of the French prisoners, in particular, were rotting and replacements were in very short supply; mattresses were so soiled, and so full of bedbugs, that prisoners were sleeping on the floor of the wooden barracks.

Conditions in the remote *Kommando* work camps attached to Stalag X-B were still more horrific and included routine brutality perpetrated on the prisoners. The August report listed some 19,253 French prisoners, of whom only 3,127 were actually housed in the main camp. Others were scattered across nearby territory, harvesting crops, building roads, cutting timber, working in factories and, given their proximity to the North Sea, working on the docks of Hamburg.

One work detachment and its 2,000 prisoners found itself detailed to loading and unloading ships in an old dockside assembly point where immigrants once bound for the U.S. boarded the ships of the Hamburg-Amerika Line. The prisoners had no shoes, only wooden sabots. "One notes frequent work accidents because the sabots slip on the wet cobblestones," the November Red Cross report noted.

It is not known which detachment Francis might have been assigned to. What is known is that Hamburg and the possibilities it presented for another escape attempt—his fourth—proved a powerful lure to him, as he laconically reported to U.S. consular authorities in Paris in understated fashion some two years later, upon application for a U.S. passport. "I had false identity papers under the name of André Monteil. At that time, I was free just two weeks when I was caught in Hamburg and sent to a concentration camp in Poland."

There are no letters from Stalag X-B to Sylvia that survived the war, nor any details as to how Francis remained free for that two-week period. There is, however, anecdotal evidence suggesting he used the false identity papers to present himself as a deaf and dumb guest worker from France, simply hitchhiking from Sanbostel to Hamburg.

His escape attempts, like the more than 200,000 such escapes attempted by Allied prisoners of war in World War II, served to tie up German forces that otherwise might have been occupied on eastern or western fronts. But most prisoners did not try to get away. According to the records in *World War II in Europe: An Encyclopedia*, the historical record suggests that the number of successful escapes only "possibly number 85,000." This represents 12 percent of the more than seven million Allied prisoners held during the war.

Francis probably got special help from home. That he got crucial aid from his mother to secure the false papers under the name Monteil seems clear. Francis, feigning a sweet tooth, often included a special request in his letters to Sylvia: Please have Mother send some of that wonderful honey from Brittany in the next care package. But it was not the honey he loved so much as the currency and gold coins that Eglé secreted in the honey. Grandmother successfully and surreptitiously larded the tins of honey with gold coins, the key to bribing guards, buying false papers and opening the doors to escape.

"I had some gold. Your father needed some money in Germany," she related in a tape-recorded interview in 1976. "So, we found the best thing was to put the gold in the honey. It was beautiful. We'd also roll paper money in plastic and roll it into the honey, too. I was lucky. If it'd been cigarettes, they [the Germans] would have stolen it. But the honey—they left it alone!" As related many years later, Eglé had the honey tins re-soldered and resealed, and then shipped to Germany in Francis' care packages.

Francis used the gold and cash to buy off German guards and recompense the forgers who manufactured his false papers. Eventually, he used the same scheme for his fifth, and final and successful escape back to France, but that was still some very long, stressful months away.

First, he had to survive that "camp in Poland," the little-known, but deadly Stalag 325, another punishment camp, this one specially reserved for recalcitrant and recidivist French and Belgian prisoners of war, sited adjacent to the small town of Rawa-Ruska, now just across the Polish boundary line in the Ukraine.

Chapter 18

Hell in the Ukraine

I never heard my father specifically refer by name or number to Stalag 325 at Rawa-Ruska. Rather, he would talk of imprisonment "back in Poland," or allude to vague prisoner-of-war memories "in the Ukraine." But those brief references got my attention. Often, they went like this: "So, Sylvia, where was God in the God-damned Ukraine?" This kind of rhetorical question usually bubbled up at the Sunday dinner table—issues of religion and segregation and integration also were common discussion topics—toward the end of long, alcohol-fueled meals with little forewarning from its protagonist. My mother, who'd probably heard it all before, habitually tried to hush him up, in vain.

French and German military records and archives, as best as I could determine, do not contain any formal record of Francis being shipped to Stalag 325. Indeed, there is historical suggestion that the German military and its Nazi hierarchy hoped these prisoners would get lost in a vast prisoner-of-war system. If they died in a forgotten stalag of the eastern front, so much the better. The International Committee of the Red Cross has no record of his being there either. The only actual evidence that he was at Rawa-Ruska is contained on the return addresses of three faded prisoner-of-war letters and one postcard saved by my mother, my grandmother's oral history and memoir, and a very tattered copy of *Gone With the Wind*, stamped with a Nazi censor's imprint for Stalag 325.

The correspondence indicates that he was detained at this special punish-ment camp for French and Belgian prisoners of war in Galicia, which was then nominally part of the *Général Gouvernement* administrative zone carved out of eastern Poland and western Ukraine by the Nazis. The former campsite is located today just across the international boundary, in the Ukraine. Francis' imprison-ment there lasted about four months (July-to-late-November, 1942), based on the dates of his correspondence to Sylvia. This punishment camp, like Stalag X-B, was reserved for the recalcitrant, repeat escapees and those prisoners who refused to work for the Nazi regime. Rawa-Ruska, a small village, and the nearby prison camp, located more than 1,000 miles from Paris, were both made for hard time in one of the Nazis' most notorious corners of hell. This was the bleak geographic area where the Holocaust took root and blossomed into an evil and deadly plant of unparalleled murder and plunder. The French prisoner-of-war punishment camp represents a relatively smallish footnote in the midst of this mayhem, but the effects of what happened to my father there loomed large in his soul for the rest of his life. Modern medicine calls it posttraumatic stress disorder.

The prison camp was originally established in 1941 to house Soviet prisoners captured in the Nazis' early, successful drives into the Soviet Union. About 15,000 Soviet prisoners died of hunger, disease or flat-out murder there, between December 1941 and April 1942. The last of these Soviet prisoners were force-marched to a field about two miles away from the nearby town, shot to death and dumped into common graves. Once exterminated, they were replaced by French prisoners with records of previous escape attempts, suspicion of planning an escape, or general unwillingness to cooperate with their captors' regime. At Rawa-Ruska, they were forced to labor under a harsh work regimen aimed at breaking the will of stubborn and disobedient soldiers who refused to kneel before the Nazi war machine. Indeed, it seems certain the Nazis placed the camp in the *Général Gouvernement* zone specifically because it was not a real country and therefore unrecognized by the international community. Rather, it was a killing zone, probably designed to be immune from the constraints of the Geneva Convention regarding treatment of prisoners of war.

My father and the more than 13,000 French prisoners eventually dumped at Stalag 325 and further dispersed to its dozens of remote work detachments, got a rude awakening even before landing at the Ukraine punishment prison. First, they were confined for two weeks at one of three collection points, most of them housed in stables. They were stripped of shoes, underwear and jackets. Latrines overflowed and they only were allowed 15 minutes of fresh air per day. Then, they were stuffed into cattle cars and shipped to Rawa-Ruska by rail, trips that took days to complete. Sleep was impossible.

Upon arrival, finally, the second and third wave of prisoners were housed in stables still spattered with the blood and brains of the Soviet prisoners who preceded them, along with the remains of dead horses. The first 2,000 French prisoners arrived on April 13, 1942 and were housed in a blockhouse. The stables were for later arrivals. They'd been collected from assembly points across Germany and then shipped by cattle car, 80-110 men to a car built for 50, without straw or blankets, no food and little water for trips that sometimes lasted as long as seven days. Their new home was the sprawling camp on the harsh, sandy plains of Galicia, suffocatingly hot in summer, buffeted by cold Arctic wind in winter, with temperatures sometimes plummeting to well below freezing.

"None of the buildings had running water, light, heat or latrines. There were no mattresses, nor straw, nor blankets. The men slept on the ground or boards stacked three or four high, where there was hardly enough room to sit. Large, open-air pits served as latrines," according to a vivid description collected by a French veterans' organization. "On days when it rained or snowed, the outdoor assembly point where the prisoners were counted was nothing but a mud hole. The soil, the walls and some of the 'sleeping boards' were covered with vermin."

Francis was most likely shipped there after being recaptured in Hamburg, as part of the wave of cattle-car prisoner convoys in July 1942. He, too, was shoeless when he got there. On August 6, he wrote Sylvia, in his typical understated fashion.

> *Your last two letters did not get forwarded. And now on the third anniversary of our wonderful walk in Gruyères, I find myself even farther away from you. But I still have hope that I'll see you again.*
>
> *It's very peaceful in this new camp. The only thing that one might find reproach with is that we're lacking in comfort. Running water, clothes and food are in short supply (and Red Cross care packages are doled out only drop-by-drop). But we're perfectly happy to be clothed in rags, barefoot, living without soap or much water, no razors, and for the better part of my buddies, without much to eat.*
>
> *Morale is better here than in some of the other prison camps, while still far from perfect. I'm a bit disoriented here. While there are many I've seen before, few of them are real friends.*

Francis ended this letter with a cryptic reference to the motto contained on the Villelume-Sombreuil family crest, *Et adhuc spero*—roughly translated "And even now, hope."

The French prisoners shipped to Stalag 325, per German prison camp custom, were parceled out to more than 40 work detachments—some as far as 375 miles away. Some had their tattered uniforms marked with inverted red triangles, which, under the Nazi prison and concentration camp classification system, were reserved for political prisoners. Yellow stars of David were for Jews, pink was the color used to denote homosexuals, green for common criminals, black or brown for Gypsies and purple for Jehovah's Witnesses.

The work details included building roads (the Nazis were hoping to extend their *autobahns* to the newly conquered territory along the Eastern front), crushing rock with sledgehammers (rock in some cases, pulled from headstones in Jewish cemeteries), building and repairing rail lines, cutting timber, and other hard work that left many of the men mere wisps of their former selves, given the reduced food rations they were served. Some reported losing more than 80 pounds. Most of the Rawa-Ruska work teams, as detailed in Red Cross reports, were herded at least six days a week, for 10-hour work days on average, to work for the Nazi industrial war machines: This also included clearing snow off roads and railroads, hauling timber, tending to an airport, working in camp kitchens, repairing shoes and clothes, building rock walls, occasionally waiting tables or washing dishes in local brew-houses, keeping refineries and distilleries functioning, tending to retail shops, digging irrigation trenches, and rather cryptically, working "on railcars, or put to work by the railroad administration of the Reich." In my father's case, the railroad work was to be of a horrific nature.

A Red Cross medical team that inspected the camp in August of that year found its conditions deplorable and listed three dozen significant problems, central among them lack of food and brutality on the part of the guards. That brutality included a tiered schedule of discipline: First, hit the prisoner with the butt of the rifle; second, stab him with a bayonet; third, shoot him. (Although French authorities from the Vichy government had alerted the International Committee of the Red Cross to the new prisoner-of-war camp for French prisoners in March of 1942, the Nazis did not officially confirm its existence until June and then denied a visit to the camp until August.)

During the first week of August 1942, according to the calculation of one of the camp's physicians recorded in the same Red Cross inspection report, the average daily caloric value of the food provided the prisoners was about 1,490 calories. Usually, the minimum intake for an adult male was 2,400 calories. No wonder individual prisoner reports penned after the war also mention the quick dismemberment, processing and cooking of a hapless, skinny nag that dragged itself into camp one day, as well as the butchering of a guard dog belonging to the camp commandant, Rittmeister Fournier.

The prison commandant was nicknamed Tom Mix, after the well-dressed cowboy from the silent movie era, because he had a habit of riding around the camp on a bicycle, threatening prisoners with his sidearm, and shooting it in the air and into various occupied buildings. Fournier wore an SS uniform, not the Wehrmacht army uniform worn by his guards, and spoke perfect French. He cruised the camp with his dog, some sort of mongrel German shepherd. "One day, a buddy got the dog to come into the latrines, and another cut its throat. It is thus that we ate the dog of our tormentor, cooked in water with a bit of whale oil…a feast! Tom Mix spent a long time trying to find his dog, but we hid his muscle and bone in the bottom of our hungry stomachs and he never found it!" Even the Red Cross inspection team found the camp commander slightly beyond the pale. "It seems he sometimes loses his composure. If the prisoners don't assemble fast enough for his taste, he's prone to threatening the prisoners with his revolver," the team disclosed in an August, 1942 report.

Red Cross care packages were of some help once they started arriving, but were in too short supply to provide sustenance for all the prisoners. Raymond Jarny, a Rawa-Ruska veteran who penned a first-hand witness book about his experiences, reported the packages engendered an unholy trading system, in which some prisoners who "had nothing swapped their wedding bands or gold teeth … for a bit of inedible bread or a cigarette." There was a persistent scrambling and scrounging for anything that could be eaten, including the vegetable peelings and kitchen scraps thrown away by the prison guards, which were then cooked by the prisoners in small, make-shift pots over open fires. In one instance, a root cellar abandoned by the guards after they'd finished all the good potatoes once kept there, turned into a hunting ground for prisoners so starved there was little reluctance to pick at the leftover rotten and frozen tubers. "As we uncovered them, [there was] a terrible smell. We were picking up the feet and the arms of dead men, scattered among their bones. The root cellar had been placed on top of a charnel house for several thousand Russians, dead of typhus!"

My father never ate many potatoes after Rawa-Ruska.

By far the greatest problem was lack of water, which dribbled out of just one faucet for the entire punishment camp, and then only for a few hours per day. Prisoners stood in long lines for hours to get a drink of water, often going thirsty because the water was cut off. There were similar long lines for the latrines—particularly when dysentery was rampant—which were set up "Russian-style," that is with a long, stout tree trunk laid over an open trench. The tree was long enough for 20 men to defecate at the same time.

Given the conditions, there was little stomach for prisoner defiance, and when there was, it was beaten back by the brutality of the camp guards or the general weakness experienced by young soldiers put on minimal rations. The weakness of the prisoners also was exacerbated by frequent, lengthy and repetitive physical exercise. Nevertheless, on July 14, 1942, in honor of Bastille Day, the French prisoners staged a full-dress parade through the camp, singing the *Marseillaise* and displaying a French flag, to the dismay of the camp commandant. The prisoners also created a "hymn" for Stalag 325, whose title, "Up-the-Ass," clearly expressed volumes about their feelings. Similar defiance was expressed in a brief, typewritten statement that Daddy kept in his files after the war. Those six-paragraphs described the camp at Rawa-Ruska as a "seminary" for the hard-core and the untamable, whose spirit was "one of resistance and struggle beyond all measure."

Conditions there were so unsanitary and so harsh, due primarily to lack of water, that the Nazis shut it down in January, 1943, transferring the camp's administrative headquarters to a large military barracks in the nearby Ukrainian town of L'viv. "This transfer became necessary due to the fact that it would have been impossible to fix the numerous inconveniences described in the preceding report," two Red Cross physicians, Drs. Wenger and Masset, reported upon visiting the new camp quarters on February 7, 1943. "In fact, the prisoners could not have spent the winter there, without their health being severely threatened." (L'viv, the town in question, is spelled L'viv in Russian; Lwow or L'vov in Polish, and Lemberg, in French, English and German. The town is now located in the Ukraine, but was deemed part of the *Général Gouvernement* territory in 1942-43.)

Eglé said in her memoirs, "The camp was closed by the Red Cross as it was unsanitary." At the same time, close reading of the Red Cross reports for Rawa-Ruska (and most other prisoner compounds where Francis stayed) did not stray far from a set inspection formula that most certainly did not challenge the underlying assumptions for the forced labor camps, only the conditions therein, and then not always very vigorously. In the case of the system in force at Rawa-Ruska, the two physicians seemed to describe the camp exactly as the Germans wished it. "The camp is reserved for prisoners trying to escape and for French and Belgians who by their actions are trying to stir up trouble in the camps of the Reich. The regime of Stalag 325 and its work detachments is considered severe by all prisoners of the Reich, and its seems that mere threat of a transfer to the *Général Gouvernement* has a decidedly salutary effect on prisoner discipline. We consider this camp as a special camp because the winters are so severe, the living quarters so primitive and communications most difficult." That's obviously how the Nazi SS troops and their Ukrainian underlings wanted this particular camp and its 42 slave labor detachments to operate. Red Cross reports make no mention of the Nazis singling out Jewish prisoners for especially harsh treatment, although history makes clear today that was also part of the Rawa-Ruska blueprint.

Camp conditions were so harsh that the Nazis set up a camp-within-the-camp for those prisoners who were pushed over the edge and simply lost their minds. Raymond Jarny details in his book, *The Hell of Rawa-Ruska*, that their Nazi captors some time after All Saints Day, 1942, had built the internal compound for those who were touched in the head, the so-called crazies, or *Verruckt*.

"The 'camp for the madmen,' itself surrounded by barbed wire too, fills up too fast," he reported. "Every once in a while, one of these unfortunates, haunted by the denial of his liberty, is gunned down. Some 500 of these grabbed onto the barbed wire, screaming at the guards, despite our vain efforts to quiet them down or stop them, [and] were assassinated by pistol fire," Jarny continued.

The author suggests some of these "crazies" knew what they were doing, in an effort to be repatriated back to France, but others succumbed to personal despair or "the cruelty of our persecutors" and placed in the enclosure for the *Verruckt*. "They wandered about, inside their barbed wire, abandoned in their wretched holes where they are thrown a few bits of whale fat. From time to time, a bit of water. The majority of them die of confinement, isolation, hunger and thirst. The Germans find their disappearance convenient."

The camp's veterans group in Paris, *Ceux de Rawa-Ruska*, has documented and confirmed the death of 72 French prisoners attached to the camp, but also notes that it is impossible to tell how many never made it back from far-away commando detachments or, perhaps, were shipped straight to the nearby Belzec extermination camp (two cattle car convoys of French prisoners never made it to Rawa-Ruska), or how many were simply killed out in the field. Significantly, Allied prosecutors at the Nuremberg war crimes trials signaled that the bodies of French prisoners had been unearthed there in mass graves. Paul Roser, a former French prisoner testifying at the Nuremberg trials, provided this gripping testimony.

"I should say that our stay at the punishment camp, Rawa-Ruska, involved one thing more awful than anything else we prisoners saw and suffered. We were horrified by what we knew was taking place all about us. The Germans had transformed the area of L'vov-Rawa-Ruska into a kind of immense ghetto. Into that area, where the Jews were already quite numerous, had been brought the Jews from all the countries of Europe. Every day for five months, except for an interruption of about six weeks in August and September 1942, we saw passing about 150 meters from our camp, one, two, and sometimes three convoys, made up of freight cars in which there were crowded men, women and children. One day a voice coming from one of these cars shouted: 'I am from Paris. We are on our way to the slaughter.' Quite frequently, comrades who went outside the camp to go to work found corpses along the railway track. We knew in a vague sort of way at that time that these trains stopped at Belzec, which was located about 17 kilometers from our camp; and at that point they executed these wretched people, by what means I do not know.

"One night in July 1942 we heard shots of submachine guns, throughout the entire night and the moans of women and children. The following morning bands of German soldiers were going through the fields of rye on the very edge of our camp, their bayonets pointed downward, seeking people hiding in the fields. Those of our comrades who went out that day to go to their work told us that they saw corpses everywhere in the town, in the gutters, in the barns, in the houses. Later some of our guards, who had participated in this operation, quite good-humoredly explained to us that 2,000 Jews had been killed that night under the pretext that two SS men had been murdered in the region."

It is my belief that witnessing such horror, or even hearing about it second-hand, might have been as awful for the prisoners as having it perpetrated on them. But given that the mail was censored, Francis made no mention of harsh treatment or deprivation or what he himself witnessed, in his letters to Sylvia, as exhibited in this note from Rawa-Ruska of September 4, 1942.

> *"I'm astounded by this veritable deluge of marriages [four friends of Francis and Sylvia]. I've got the feeling that when I get home, I'll be the only bachelor left among all my friends. I hope, if you're still single, that you'll keep me company for at least three little minutes—nothing more.*
>
> *This business of economic slavery [an apparent reference to Rawa-Ruska work details] does not satisfy me at all. I have no intention of waiting for another year for the end of the war to bring you some flowers. Do write me a nice letter.*

He continued in the same vein in a letter of September 29, but also warned that his correspondence, as in May of that year, when he was apparently in transit from Stalag II-B to Stalag X-B, might be interrupted. "It could be, as in May, that it might be a long time without a letter from me. But you know this will not prevent me from thinking of you," he said.

And Francis seemed almost giddy with pleasure in a postcard from Rawa-

Ruska to Sylvia of October 22, 1942, after receiving a special care package from his girl back home, which included a cured ham that miraculously made it past the censors and pilferers. "What a ham! Oh, Sylvia! This was truly an event worth noting in the history of this war. It is delicious, and created a real sensation. Life is good. Affectionately yours."

Despite the effort at seeming good cheer, Daddy's imprisonment at Rawa-Ruska was to mark him physically, psychically and indelibly, as his children would discover decades later. What he never spoke of in any detail was that he was singled out for special punishment and torture there. In something of a supreme irony, given his anti-Semitic, pre-war practices, he was taken for a Jew by his captors, who burned off his eyelashes. That point was well known to Sylvia and Eglé, but not to his children. My father was perhaps taken for a Jew because of his prominent, hooked nose, but it's more likely "because he was circumcised," according to a confidential source who was one of my father's close woman friends in Atlanta. He'd been circumcised, per American custom. French boys were not circumcised unless they were Jews.

I only learned that something awful had been done to my father's eyes in the early 1970s, when he told me he'd had a hard time letting an ophthalmologist treat his eyes after a storm blew dust and tiny gravel into them—it reminded him too much of what had been done to him. After Francis' death in 1983, a close family friend in Atlanta also divulged to his children that their father had been tortured during the war.

Grandmother Eglé described the torture this way in her memoir: "After his last escape, he was recaptured and sent to a terrible camp at Rawa-Ruska, in Russia. [Georges] Scapini, in charge of [French] prisoners even though he was blind, came out for an inspection. He asked them how they were being treated. Francis answered that a German had burned his eyelashes. 'A good German would not have done that,' Scapini retorted. 'Your friends are not good Germans,' Francis countered. The other prisoners then cried out, 'Hurrah for Francis!'"

(Scapini, a World War I veteran appointed by the puppet Vichy government as an ambassador to the Germans, with prisoner of war issues his particular portfolio, was twice prosecuted after the war for his actions. Ultimately, he was acquitted of all charges on July 28, 1952. He died in Cannes on March 5, 1976, at the age of 82.)

Yet, my father's torture seemed almost incidental compared to the truly terrible forced labor that he and probably some other prisoners were forced to undertake and witness.

Chapter 19

"His Mind Went Crazy"

The six Gatins children from time to time, often at the lunch or dinner table, would ask their father about the prison camp and conditions in the Ukraine since the topic came up often enough to pique curiosity. Francis usually would try to deflect the queries with witty and wry anecdotes, in attempts to amuse his audience. Sometimes, though, truth would burst forth, as his son Martin well remembers.

"He was basically a guard," Martin reported. "At this point in the war the extermination camps are going full swing ... and the French prisoners are considered slave labor. And so his job in the Ukraine is basically ... he's a guard or a processor, emptying the rail cars of the Jews."

I could hardly believe it when I first heard of this mad work in 2001, some 13 years after Daddy had died. This was all news to me. I suppose that I had been away at school when this remembrance cracked into the open like lava flowing from a caldera.

"Absolutely!" Martin said. "He said he would sit there and open the rail cars. These Jews had been packed like sardines, half of them dead, coming from Poland, I remember him telling me. He'd say, 'My job was opening the rail cars.' I remember his screaming that out—it was at dinner one night. It was one of those situations where he stood up from the dinner table and yelled, '*Mes enfants*,' and then Sylvia would try to hush him up. 'Francis, sit down.' And he'd say, 'No, Sylvia, you weren't there unloading the Jews from the railroad cars!' And she'd say, 'Yes, yes, but let's have some dessert.'"

To my knowledge, no historic records have yet come to light that officially document this particularly horrific use of French prisoners. The Rawa-Ruska veterans group in Paris makes no mention of such work and believes most death trains bound for the nearby Belzec extermination camp did not stop at Rawa-Ruska.

Nor have Holocaust and concentration camp history experts and researchers, so far, pinpointed any documented reports of French prisoner-slaves being put to widespread use in this fashion.

But today I do believe my father was used this way, a fact that makes my body recoil with revulsion. What could have driven Nazi captors to manipulate prisoners like that, and what set of evil forces could have prevailed on Francis to take part in this? Perhaps it was the same instinct that drove him to self-mutilation a year earlier when he got his right arm broken. My gut tells me that the guards had to use a powerful extra lure for this type of work detail—a promise of extra rations, or more likely, harsh brandy or vodka. That liquor was available is documented in the Red Cross reports; some prisoners were assigned to work in distilleries and landlords dating to the 18th Century in this region of western Ukraine each had their own brandy distillery, used to enslave and control local peasantry. I know and my brothers and sisters know that our father had a powerful thirst for alcohol during his imprisonment. He had even once vainly tried to convince a prison priest to let him imbibe some sacramental mass wine.

Whatever the reason, the thought of his taking part in these inhuman crimes makes me very queasy. I was not able to accurately document exactly where Francis might have been unloading cattle cars full of hapless Jewish victims, but he and his fellow prisoners were definitely working in and around the blackest of the black holes created by the Nazis—the way stations to the plunder-and-death camps of "Operation Reinhard." This originally secret plan, which entailed extermination of all Jews in Poland and the *Général Gouvernement* administrative zone, was probably named after Reinhard Heydrich, one of the prime architects of the Holocaust. It required widespread use of death camps. It is generally accepted that this massive genocide, or the Final Solution of the Jewish Question, as Nazis and SS Aryans termed it, resulted in the murder of some six million Jews, and the death of a host of other groups deemed undesirable by the Nazis—homosexuals, Gypsies, Poles, Slavs, political dissidents, the mentally and physically disabled, Jehovah's Witnesses—a vicious and deliberate campaign of genocide resulting in the death of nine to 11 million individuals, all told.

The train station at Rawa-Ruska and the larger, nearby town of L'viv, as is well-known to legions of Holocaust historians and scholars, were both used as transshipment points to the notorious extermination camp of Belzec, less than 12.5 miles away from Rawa-Ruska proper.

The French prisoners at Stalag 325 placed Belzec in something they called the Triangle of Death. Within that area, maps clearly mark Rawa-Ruska at the southeastern section of killing zone that included the most barbaric of the concentration-slave-labor-and-death camps. Auschwitz, Belzec, Chelmno, Majdanek, Sobibor, and Treblinka are names forever burned into the collective memory of the very few who survived the Shoah (the Hebrew word for the Holocaust). The death camps were run by the Nazis and specially picked butchers, cruel Ukrainian sympathizers, many of them graduates of an earlier "euthanasia program"—that is, state-sanctioned murder—to eradicate undesirable races and classes. Recent historical research proves that this area was the birthplace of the Holocaust, with special troops (*Einsatzgruppen*), seconded by a hodge-podge of Nazi police and intelligence units, and sometimes regular Wehrmacht forces, all dedicated to exterminating the Jews of eastern Poland and conquered Soviet territory (including the Ukraine) by any means possible. This early slaughter included murder by shooting, burning, clubbing, drowning or burying alive, as well as by grenade or mobile gas vans—an estimated 1.5 million men, women and children who were erased into mass graves even before the death camps were established.

The sheer scale of the additional Holocaust murders in the Triangle of Death camps is staggering.

- Auschwitz. 1.1-1.3 million murders. May 1940—November 1944. (At least 1 million are Jews)
- Belzec. 434,508 murders. March-December 1942.
- Chelmno. At least 152,000 murders (including up to 2,000 Gypsies). December 1941—January 1945.
- Majdanek. Between 95,000 and 130,000 murders, (88,000-110,000 Jews). November 1941—July 1944 including subcamps.
- Sobibor. At least 167,000 murders. May 1942—November 1943.
- Treblinka. Approximately 925,000 murders. July 1942—November 1943.
- Total 2.8 to 3.1 million murders

Out of all these people, only about 120 Polish Jews survived, according to copyrighted information available from the United States Holocaust Memorial Museum, Washington, D.C. The museum's chief historian, Peter Black, provided the updated murder figures. The accompanying plunder also was staggering.

A summary of goods stolen during Operation Reinhard (encompassing just Belzec, Sobibor and Treblinka, and their rail transshipment points), "included money from 48 countries; gold coins from 34 countries; 2,910 kilograms of gold bars; 18,734 kilograms of silver bars; 16,000 diamond carats, and more." The total value was estimated to be 178.7 million Reichmarks, roughly equivalent to $78 million US in 1943—and more than 10 times that amount in today's dollars. That did not include the vast sums known to have been stolen by SS and Ukrainian captors or lost forever in the death trains.

The French prisoners at Rawa-Ruska, like their captors, like the civilians still alive in that special area of hell on earth, knew there was ungodly work going on around them. It was hard to miss. French prisoners detailed to work outside the camp's barbed wire enclosure often became unwilling witnesses to the Holocaust and saw more than they were probably supposed to see. My understanding is that witnessing atrocities can sometimes have as dire an after-effect on individuals as experiencing them, which likely explains my father's distress at remembering and reliving his own memories of this time.

According to some reports, French prisoners witnessed grisly scenes of the pogrom in the nearby Ukrainian city of L'viv. There, Nazi thugs threw infants over a wall so their colleagues could take potshots at the babies on the other side, like a skeet shoot. Just outside the camp—the length of two football fields—stood the town's crematory oven, surmounted, according to one contemporary report, by a "fat, rectangular chimney that smoked night and day. The unfortunate are stuffed into the fire. A black smoke thickens. The smell is unbearable when the wind comes back our way." By some estimates, the civilian population of Rawa-Ruska, most of them Jews, had numbered around 25,000 before the war. By the spring of 1942, it was down to about 9,000 and a year later, to 3,000.

The murderous carnage perpetrated against the Jews was well known to the French prisoners as an inescapable fact of life in the Triangle of Death. Witness this first-hand account from Raymond Jarny, the French prisoner who lived to write the book, *The Hell of Rawa-Ruska*:

"The guards herded us to the railroad station in the town, where I witnessed a terrible scene. The Germans had parked some Jews with their women, their children, the elderly in padlocked cattle cars, immobilized on a siding under a burning sun by day and glacial cold by night, without food or water—for days at a time. We sidled by this sinister wagon train which was carrying, no doubt to the Belzec extermination camp, this supposed race of subhumans (*Untermenschen*), condemned and banished in this rolling sepulcher of the death trains.

"A pitiful woman with a baby in her arms cries out: 'Water for my child.' A German sentry locks and loads his rifle. We're here to unload a carload of red beets. As soon as we begin, we hear heart-rending screams. They're exterminating the Jews, shooting blindly into the cattle cars with machine guns. The image

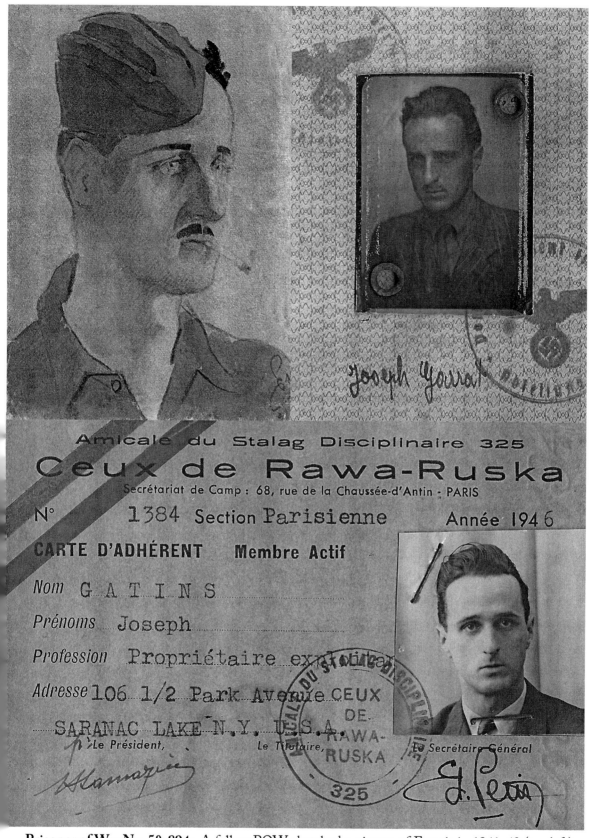

Amicale du Stalag Disciplinaire 325
Ceux de Rawa-Ruska
Secrétariat de Camp : 68, rue de la Chaussée-d'Antin - PARIS

N° 1384 Section Parisienne   Année 1946

CARTE D'ADHÉRENT   **Membre Actif**

Nom GATINS

Prénoms Joseph

Profession Propriétaire exploitant

Adresse 106 1/2 Park Avenue

SARANAC LAKE N.Y. U.S.A.

Le Président,   Le Titulaire,   Le Secrétaire Général

Joseph Gatins

Prisoner of War No. 50-894: A fellow POW sketched a picture of Francis in 1941-42 (top left). A somber looking mug shot was used on the phony ID he used in Berlin, while a still-gaunt looking TB survivor (in 1946) graced the card showing he was a veteran of the Rawa-Ruska POW punishment camp.

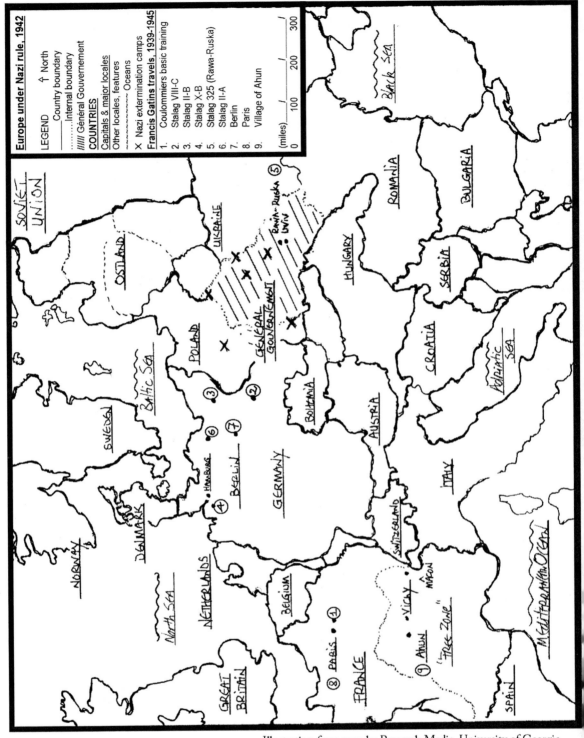

Prisoner way stations: Francis was bounced to five different POW camps before making his final escape (as a French guest worker under an assumed name) from Berlin.

Illustration from map by Research Media, University of Georgia

Europe under Nazi rule, 1942

LEGEND ↑ North
——— Country boundary
.... Internal boundary
|||||| Général Gouvernement
COUNTRIES
Capitals & major locales
Other locales, features
~~~~ Oceans
X Nazi extermination camps

Francis Gatins travels, 1939-1945
1. Coulommiers basic training
2. Stalag VIII-C
3. Stalag II-B
4. Stalag X-B
5. Stalag 325 (Rawa-Ruska)
6. Stalag II-A
7. Berlin
8. Paris
9. Village of Ahun

(miles)
0   100   200   300

Hell in the Ukraine: Some French POWs taken in cattle cars to Rawa-Ruska were housed in a blockhouse while others were stacked three-high in a former barn spattered with blood of Russian prisoners imprisoned there before them.

Wartime wedding: With Paris still under German occupation, Sylvia and Francis wore street clothes for the civil ceremony on Dec. 6, 1943, but got all decked out in formal attire to take their church vows at the parish of St. Pierre de Chaillot two days later.

Wartime honeymoon. The chateau of La Chezotte, tucked away in isolated rural France, served as a combined hideout and honeymoon retreat for Francis and Sylvia and occasional visitors, in this case Paul and Zette de Villelume and their son Gérard. Another visitor, Francis's good friend Robert Tancrède, painted a striking watercolor of the chateau and its moat in 1944.

Wartime survivors: The young couple, much in love, stayed in a cottage in Saranac Lake, N.Y., after Francis survived a deadly bout of tuberculosis in 1945–46.

of this Jewish martyr, holding out her baby in the garret-window of the car to help him breathe for just a few minutes more, has never been driven from my memory."

The railroad freight depot for L'viv's main train station also served as the rail assembly point for cattle cars heading to Belzec. By the time the war was over, perhaps some 500,000 Galician Jews had passed through L'viv on their way to Belzec and other death camps.

My father's own description of the Jews packed into the freight cars echoes contemporary eyewitness accounts of the death trains. "In practice, death and destruction began while the Jews were still in the freight cars rolling toward the death camps. Designed to carry a maximum of 60 or 70 people, including their belongings, the cars were packed with double that number. Deprived of air and water, with no sanitary facilities, forced to spend endless hours traveling or waiting in stations in the packed freight cars, many died en route."

Contemporary accounts also make plain that regular German soldiers and German civilians brought in to settle the *Général Gouvernement* zone knew all about the killing camps. It was impossible to avoid the sickening, sweetish smell of death and the strong odor of burning flesh emanating from Belzec.

While the weight of evidence is pretty clear that the French prisoners were unwilling witnesses to the slaughter, there are also faint hints that they too, like my father, sometimes became unwilling accessories to the Shoah. Father Patrick Desbois, a French priest whose grandfather was a prisoner at the Rawa-Ruska prison camp, suggests this did occur. In one instance, according to Father Desbois, a French prisoner was detailed to a crew sent out to harvest wheat straw. Jewish women, carrying their infants, were used as draft horses to pull the carts. "The German who was guarding them could not stand their crying, so each time [they cried], he'd grab a little one and slam it into the cart. That evening, all that was left was the women, the carts and the straw."

This priest, head of a team of researchers documenting the early Holocaust shooting sprees along the eastern front, also received a Soviet document that suggests the French prisoners from Rawa-Ruska were used to further the extermination of the Jews. According to that evidence, in November 1942, "some French prisoners of war dug a trench about 60 feet long, 26 feet wide and about 13 feet deep." Early in the morning of December 5, 1942, seven truckloads of Jews are brought to their mass grave and executed six at a time by six shooters with machine pistols, the document continued. Children less than two or three years old were not shot, but thrown alive into the grave with their mothers.

Such reports might be viewed as scant evidence by Holocaust researchers and historians, but the overall memory of such actions appeared to define my father and overshadow his overall experience as a prisoner of war. "He didn't talk all that much about it—but he could picture it," his son Martin reported. "Our father was a basket case [over this]. When you asked him a question, he'd say, 'Yes, they were like sardines," Martin said. "They were all dead—frozen—been in there for God knows how many different days.' Those in the rail cars sometimes stopped for days waiting for other trains to be coming and going. He said it was awful. What he saw was abominable."

Martin concluded, "You could tell that the Ukraine affected him—they were packed like sardines. That's basically when his mind went crazy."

Nonetheless, though he was starved, beaten, tortured, and thoroughly psychologically scarred by the Stalag 325 punishment system, Francis survived Rawa-Ruska. Like many prisoners there, he eventually was sent to a "regular" stalag. In his case, that was Stalag II-A near Neubrandenberg, 90 miles north of Berlin, but still some 600-plus miles from home.

Chapter 20

Last Stalag

Francis obviously was itching to tell all about the Rawa-Ruska ordeal to Sylvia, his girl at home, and his mother Eglé once he was transferred to Stalag II-A. "Do I have some things to tell you," he wrote Sylvia in a postscript to a letter of November 28, 1942. He could not, of course, because all letters were censored. As in so many other letters to Sylvia, Francis meandered from topic to topic: A little camp news here, a little commentary about fellow prisoners there, a bit of intellectual musing. There was more about the work details, which were much more mundane than anything experienced in the Ukraine: pulling sugar beets, work in an underground mine, serving Germans as a waiter in a gasthaus. In the latter case, he made plain that a lot of the soup he was serving ended up on the ground or on the clients, but that he was serving it with "style and dignity."

In a letter of March 21, 1943, Sylvia's 28th birthday, he expressed the optimism about the future that often peppered his letters home.

> *Don't worry, my little one. Next year for your birthday, I will personally bring you a garden-full of flowers to make excuses for not having brought you anything these past three years.*
>
> *This is another birthday far from you. With the weather we've got today, that would be depressing—except that I am full of optimism for the future. [Later in the same letter, he talked of the men in his new work detachment:] My new Kommando is fine, the fellow prisoners nice and obliging. But ... they lack character. I don't think France will ever*

(Continued...)

> *get back on its feet after this war.*
>
> *Please excuse this useless babble, but I cannot pen all the pressing matters I want to tell you about. Be good. Pray for me from time to time—I am soon going to truly need those prayers. Best wishes, my Teddy bear. Affectionately yours.*

In fact, Francis had telegraphed in a previous letter that he was impatient to try for another escape, and needed his mother's help to make it happen. "Could you ask *maman* to send me some honey from Brittany," he'd written Sylvia on February 1, 1943. A mere 11 words sandwiched into the body of the 25 lines of tiny, barely legible penmanship, written in faint pencil: That was his way of getting his actual intentions past the censors.

The rest of that letter went off on tangents that presumably were designed to throw off any military censor:

> *After working two Kommando stints, three days each, the first pulling beets, the second as a metalworker, and some 45 days in the camp, I've now been assigned as interpreter and platoon leader of another Kommando. What's really amusing is that I don't speak a word of German. I make myself clear by using large gestures. I'm in a pretty little town on the edge of a lake. I'm responsible for buying food, the accounting and the discipline.*
>
> *Up until now, I thought that slavery was reserved solely for blacks, but I'm finding out that it works the same for whites. Make sure they're fed and they'll work seven days out of seven. I'm surprised by these people [his fellow prisoners]—they don't seem able to live without working and their arms in perpetual motion. I really worry about the 70 guys in this Kommando. I have greater and greater disdain for my half-compatriots, the French, including those in France, my friends, etc...*
>
> *It's been three years since I saw you, but it won't be long now. Affectionately.*

In fact, Francis had been hinting at another escape attempt since the beginning of the year, expressing hope in a letter of January 6 that 1943 would bring him good luck. His fellow prisoners, he said, seemed resigned to their fate and expressed little hope at getting home. "As for me, I do hope that 1943 will bring me a bit of luck; I intend to pursue that chance like mad."

In similar vein, in a letter of December 7 the year before, still incarcerated under the control of Stalag II-A, he wrote that he was… "full of hope and optimism, and feeling pretty good. Maybe someday you will see me arrive back in Paris—what a number of stories I've got to tell you, what a discussion we will have!"

Indeed, Francis proved to be a *débrouillard*, a combination scrounger and problem-solver, who managed by April 1943 to finally untangle himself from the prisoner-of-war system that had been his lot for almost three years.

Chapter 21

Surreal in Berlin

My father's next letter to my mother, dated April 20, 1943, was written on blue-colored, civilian stationery, not official, grey prisoner-of-war correspondence paper. It was half in English, half in French, and obviously not censored. Francis still pined for Sylvia, and now felt less constrained about saying so. "I often try to imagine in waking dreams that you are near me, that you have your hands in my hands, that we talk together—and that I hold you tight in my arms," he wrote.

Seven days later, he hinted that he'd escaped from Stalag II-A's control and asked that she not talk too much about his situation. "Eglé will tell you everything that has happened," he said.

Francis then wrote Sylvia from Berlin on May 17 and spelled out his new circumstances. He was working in the German capital as a house painter under the name of Joseph Garrat, living in private lodgings that were "neither very clean nor very comfortable." But he seemed energized and pleased at this new chance at life. "I've barely arrived here in Berlin and I'm counting the days until I find a way to come see you."Francis described a somewhat surreal scene. "I'm not at all out of sorts thanks to all the friends I have again found here. Berlin is really a very lively city. And these thousands of foreigners, soldiers and workers make for an extraordinary mix. You can tell that my morale is still good. Here is my address: Joseph Garrat, 38 Tasserdorfer Strasse, Berlin."

My father obviously had received and made good use of Eglé's last pot of honey, using the gold coins or cash hidden therein to gain himself a new false set of papers, a *Fredempass*, just as he had done when trying to escape under the name Monteil from Stalag X-B in early 1942. This time, he'd simply walked off a Stalag II-A work detail, and bought himself a train ticket to Berlin using the new false papers. Taking the train, he found, "was a more scientific way of escaping."

Once in Berlin, Francis benefited from the Nazi war machine's near-insatiable demand for labor and the German High Command's decision to establish a formal "transformation" program to turn some French prisoners of war into "guest workers." With many of its men dead or dying on the eastern front after its invasion of the Soviet Union in 1941, Germany first tried to convince French men to voluntarily come to Germany for work, then imposed the involuntary *Relève* system, which sought to repatriate some 50,000 French prisoners in exchange for some 150,000 new workers. Finally, the Reich convinced Vichy to impose the much-despised *Service de Travail Obligatoire*, which netted thousands more French workers. By January 1943, Germany wanted yet another 250,000 French workers, and the Vichy government opted to offer up its prisoners of war instead under the so-called "transformation" program.

Although it was supposed to be an individual decision, entire French prisoner *Kommandos* were often summarily "transformed" into the German civilian workforce, often doing exactly the same job they'd been doing as prisoners, but laboring in civilian clothes instead of uniforms and subject to Gestapo and civilian police discipline instead of military control. Those thus "transformed," perhaps without realizing it, also lost whatever protections from abuse they might have had as prisoners of war subject to the Geneva Conventions, but few exhibited much in the way of moral qualms at this change in status. Almost 225,000 French prisoners voluntarily or involuntarily opted for the "transformation" process by June of 1944, (out of a total at that time of 956,101), and another 220,037 more did so by January of 1945, (of the 920,598 French soldiers then still listed as prisoners). That was in addition to the French civilians, like Joseph Francis Garrat, who had gone to Germany voluntarily or involuntarily to work for Nazi masters.

My father, thus personally "transformed" under a false identity, house painter by day, essentially had the run of the capital by night, often staying up until the wee hours of the morning. He never once was asked by anyone to show his false papers, he later told an Atlanta newspaper columnist, "living practically as he pleased in Berlin" for the next six months. Francis told that interviewer about eight years later that he "was free to eat in restaurants, drop in on nightclubs and go out of town on weekends, since that was when the British usually bombed the city. He came in any time he wanted to, sometimes night-owling until 2 a.m.," Hugh Park, the columnist for *The Atlanta Journal*, wrote. "The Germans were paying him an adequate living wage of approximately 50 Deutschmarks per week. He also had free medical care and was on social security. No one ever asked him for his papers. He could make long distance telephone calls inside the country." He'd found himself a more comfortable apartment as well, the Roy Guesthouse on Krossen uber Luckau.

Said Francis in one of his letters to Sylvia from Berlin: "There wasn't anyone left in Germany, men from 16 to 60 were away at war. The country was being run by foreigners and the very old." In his free time, he often went to the movies, he wrote Sylvia on June 27. "I only understand a few words here and there, but with a little imagination, one can invent a story line, which often is better than the one on film."

But he had little good to say about his fellow Frenchmen and some of the foreign workers who also found themselves in the German capital.

> *One has to see the French of Berlin to know to what depths of decadence we have fallen. They are as dirty as those from the Balkans, full of stupid excuses. Their only good quality is that they're generally good workers. Their thirst for gain makes them take on enormous amounts of overtime. As for the French women—catastrophe—they're dirty as combs, their legs full of crud—one would swear they'd just gotten out of the whorehouse in Guéret [the departmental capital for La Creuse, where Sylvia's mother had her country property].*
>
> *I'm working with some Slavs, which would be fine, if they weren't so untrustworthy. They're not liars, but they don't know how to tell the truth. They spend all their time informing on one another.*

By contrast, he reported getting along quite well with a work crew from Holland. Francis also was the happy recipient of more frequent packages from home, filled with soap, hams, clothes and the ultimate lifeline, the cash and gold secreted in Grandmother Eglé's honey tins from Brittany.

"My dear Mother," he wrote Eglé on June 27, "I've received your magnificent care package of May 28, and two other packages, one with the cap, the other with the butter and the cigarettes. I can't thank you enough. It really made me happy. I found it all Saturday, when I came back to Berlin." (He'd been working during the week on a rural construction site about 50 miles outside Berlin.)

The letters to Eglé and Sylvia also make veiled allusion to their combined efforts to secure a compassionate leave to Paris for the "guest worker" who, with their help, had fabricated a story about a fictitious sick wife named Marie in Paris.

Eglé explained this ploy in detail in her memoir. The gold coins were to be used to "buy oneself a German."

Sylvia had a Colombian cousin who knew a certain German captain who was more than happy to get a few pieces of gold, Eglé said in her memoir. "So, I cooked up an entire little story, telling him that he [Garrat] had to come home, that his wife was gravely ill. I provided the address in Paris of a certain *concierge* whom I was absolutely sure of, on rue du Bouquet de Longchamps. Then I went to see the headquarters for the labor service in Germany, which was housed in the former *Chambre des Députés*. In all my life, I was never so scared. I told them my little story and, trembling, convinced them to send a telegram to the guest worker to get him home."

By September 3, Francis had received the telegram, as well as a false doctor's certificate telling him that Marie, was "gravely ill," after childbirth. "My boss [the painting contractor Adolph Rachow, located at 2 Peterburger Platz] was very kind and he would have wanted me to take off right away," he wrote Eglé on that date, "but I was not able to do so because the visa from the *Kommandatur* wasn't enough—it has to be signed. I don't understand why the paper wasn't complete."

Five days later, on September 8, in his last letter from Berlin, he tells Sylvia he doesn't have much to say.

> *I continue to paint all the attics of Berlin with inflammable product. It's not too difficult, but it ruins your hands. Compassionate leaves are suspended until October 15— catastrophe! But morale is good and I hope this, too, will pass. Let's hope that I will see you again soon. I really need, my Teddy bear, to find my bearings, because I really do not know how to live without you. Very affectionately.*

Eleven days after that letter, with all the false compassionate leave papers finally in order, Francis finally set foot in Paris, stepping down from a Berlin-to-Paris train. He never returned to Germany. French authorities with the Vichy government who were supposed to keep tabs on such workers simply added the Garrat dossier to the list of "French workers on leave in France who had not returned to Germany on their assigned date." The guest worker file for Joseph Garrat simply noted: "Does not respond to summons."

Chapter 22

Wartime Wedding

Paris was still occupied territory in September 1943. The Germans had commandeered some of the most important buildings of the French capital upon taking over three years earlier. The Gestapo was installed on the Avenue Foch, not far from L'Etoile. The German military headquarters in France was located at the Majestic Hotel on Avenue Kléber, a few blocks from Eglé's and Sylvia's homes in the 16th arrondissement. German troops still paraded daily down the Champs d'Elysées, to Eglé's dismay. Despite the privations and rationing that most Parisians were experiencing, much was still for sale on the black market for those who had enough money to pay. From foie gras to champagne, chocolate éclairs to real bread, the French upper crust and foreign nationals like the Colombians who had assumed technical neutrality in the world war could still tend to both need and luxury if they had enough gold or cash. Elvira de German-Ribon, Sylvia's widowed mother, supplemented her purchases with periodic deliveries of produce, cheese and foodstuffs from La Chezotte, her country property in the department of La Creuse. (A department is roughly the equivalent of a county in the United States.)

Even prisoners on the lam like Francis experienced a little taste of freedom. He first stopped at the German-Ribon home to say hello to Sylvia and finally hold her in his arms after three years of privation. Then, he headed two blocks away to his mother's house. Her prisoner-of-war packages often had kept him alive in Germany. Now, Eglé recalled, "he was very nervous, so very afraid of being recaptured." (Although French authorities still listed his alter ego, Joseph Garrat, as being AWOL from his made-up address of 92, Boulevard Garibaldi, there is no indication much attempt was made to find him. They appeared satisfied to simply acknowledge he had not returned to Germany on his assigned date.)

Francis did not want to live at home, so he moved in with a friend, Eglé said. "But even there, he was not at peace. So, he had the idea of renting a room in a little hotel near Place des Etats-Unis, stuffed with ... workers." As Francis later explained to his children, one could hide out, too, in *maisons de passe*, little combined bar-whorehouse establishments that still dotted the French capital. Germans would not bother French men tending to bodily business in these establishments or going to and from them, which also often led Francis to hide in the Métro, taking endless rides from one end of Paris to the other.

Then there was the matter of Sylvia. "He was very much in love with Sylvia," Grandmother recalled. "But as she had already turned him down twice, I was a bit worried. Then finally she showed up one day and told me: 'It's decided. I am going to marry Francis.' Needless to tell you my joy—she had been my friend for years."

Francis essentially had been courting Sylvia since they started dancing on their own pre-war volcano in Gruyères, Switzerland, in the spring of 1939. That flame flickered and endured through more than three long years of uninterrupted separation while he was in the Nazi prison camps and Berlin. I wish some of her correspondence to my father had survived the war, just to see how she sustained him, but it did not. What is evident today is that the thought of love with the blithe spirit that was my father before the war apparently had been kept alive by Sylvia, despite whatever misgivings she might have had about his prospects before the conflict erupted. Sylvia was approaching her 30s at the time, already stretching what was considered in society as the proper age for marrying. She had already turned my father's proposals down several times, after breaking it off with the Count de Broglie and Edgar Faure in her early twenties. A combined horoscope and handwriting analysis that she kept from this period noted that she'd already missed three possible unions, two of which hurt especially hard. "Your heart is going to bleed a bit from hurt and a forced trip coming up soon," that analysis continued. "Expect financial complications in the long term, questions of differing priorities within the family—and trouble over a property." But Francis knew nothing of these doubts. One of the Sylvia letters from Berlin hinted that she had finally said, "Yes, maybe," and was willing to consider a relationship with Francis for the long term. My father had been quick to respond, in a letter of July 5.

> *My very own Teddy bear,*
> *I got your wonderful letter of the 19th. As you can easily guess, it pleased me more than the others. I am so happy that I fear happenstance might take vengeance on me by giving me a hard time. I've become superstitious, and above all my nerves are out of whack. That's why you are exactly right— you will have to relearn about the person I have become.*
> *I don't think I'm more serious—to the contrary—and I think I've probably turned into the opposite of the 'good man' sought under the criteria of your family and friends. In addition, you know that until the complete end of the war, tranquil happiness in France will not be for me.*
> *All I wish to tell you is that I love you. I am absolutely incapable of adding an adverb to that verb, or to tell you that I love you more than before. All I know is that my greatest times of happiness, of fun, are always tied to your presence. A future without you would seem eternal ennui.*

The young couple had a no-frills, pre-nuptial marriage contract drawn up on November 25, but there is no evidence they ever signed it. The document, in a nod to the obnoxious anti-Semitic laws promulgated by the Nazi occupiers and the Vichy government, noted conspicuously that Francis was deemed to be of French nationality "and non-Jewish," while Sylvia was of Colombian nationality "and non-Jewish."

The attendant paperwork also included a long, hand-written affidavit from the Colombian consul in Paris, affirming that Sylvia was a Colombian citizen, born of Colombian mother and father. The file also included a notarized translation of Sylvia's birth certificate from London. (She was born in England because her father was there for business reasons in 1914, and while she was quick to claim her Colombian citizenship in 1939, she had never lived for any length of time in Colombia. Culturally, she was thoroughly French.) Highlighting one's "non-Jewish" origins might seem like bureaucratic overkill but given the harshness of the official, anti-Semitic laws promulgated by Vichy at the behest of the Nazis, and that Sylvia's curly hair and prominent nose could look positively semitic, perhaps not. (The Colombian branch of the German-Ribon family has been able to trace its antecedents to Seville and Andalusia during the Moorish period, but there is no confirmation that the family originated in North Africa, or was Jewish or Moorish. Whatever their true origins, the German-Ribons had become missal-thumping Catholics.) During the war years, Sylvia's brother Miguel was dispatched to Colombia, which was technically neutral in the conflict, to avoid any possible complications with French authorities or German occupiers. He ended up making a permanent home in Bogotá, the Colombian capital.

The genocidal set of French anti-Semitic ordinances, first defining who was a Jew, and aimed at the "economic Aryanization" of Jewish properties and goods, included laws that forbade Jews from working and required them to wear the yellow Star of David. The laws also forbade them to shop, except between the hours of 3 and 4 p.m. In the end, their property was seized and many were shipped, first to concentration camps within France, and then to death camps behind enemy lines. (Many of those French concentration camps had been erected before the war to house Republican sympathizers and Communists fleeing the Spanish civil war of 1936-39.)

Somehow, in the middle of wartime, surrounded by occupying German forces, Francis procured a spectacular looking engagement ring, with a large diamond surrounded by eight smaller, faceted diamonds, set atop a heavy gold band. Elvira, the bride's mother, secured an apostolic benediction from the Pope, forwarded by telegram to the young couple, which was saved in the family files by Sylvia. As required by French law, the couple first was married in a civil ceremony at the mayor's office for the 16th arrondissement on December 6, during which the mayor gave a little speech that was particularly effusive about Francis's escape from German captivity. "We are happy to see you here, sir," the mayor said. "Without giving up, you adhered to the sacred duty of all prisoners of war: To use all means to escape." This was followed by a church wedding at the Roman Catholic parish of Chaillot on the 8th. "The evening of the civil ceremony ... we had a little reception at the house," Eglé recalled. "After the mass, Madame de German-Ribon provided a large, really elegant lunch. I still don't know how she managed to snare all that food," Eglé said. The lunch included a wedding cake—made from bean flour—that was so tasty the hungry guests gobbled it all up before the bride and groom arrived for the reception. Records suggest this was not a small wedding, at Elvira's behest. Uncles Charlie and René de Madec served as Francis' witnesses, while Fernando Sorela y del Corral and Charles de Yturbe, Colombian and Mexican family friends, seconded Sylvia, in front of more than 75 guests and relatives. Everyone wore street clothes—including some amazingly elaborate hats for the women -- for the civil ceremony. But the bride and groom were in most formal attire for the church wedding two days later.

The parallels to Eglé's own wedding to Joseph F. Gatins, Jr. in Paris almost three decades earlier are striking. Both couples experienced a hasty wedding with an engagement period less than three months long. The press of war was in the air, with one major difference—the Germans had not taken Paris in World War I. Both couples honeymooned in luxury hotels in Paris. And as with Eglé and her husband, the news about Francis and Sylvia eventually made it back to the Atlanta newspapers, complete with a glamorous bridal photograph, via the playwright Robert Sherwood, who passed the information to Mary Gatins Jackson (my father's aunt), who gave it to Sally Forth, one of the social page columnists for *The Atlanta Constitution*.

"Joseph Gatins Weds Beauty After Nazi Prison Escape." That fanciful headline was followed by a description of Sylvia's Colombian antecedents and portrayed Francis as "representative of families long identified with the building and progress of the city." While undated, the clip probably was not published in Atlanta until sometime in mid-1944, as Aunt Mary had not received any official word of my father's escape and wedding until a cryptic telegram was delivered to her in early spring from Barcelona, purportedly signed by someone identifying herself as "Carmen Eglé."

"Joe Francis back married December to Sylvia de German-Ribon y Valenzuela Most popular and charming Are delighted STOP Pray and hope you are all well Love to Family and Friends. Carmen Eglé."

The telegram message was cryptic enough that the U.S. Office of Censorship and its Cable and Radio Censor called on Aunt Mary. "Will you be so kind as to furnish this office with the complete explanation of the text, including the location, the full name and identities of the parties mentioned therein," the U.S. censors wanted to know. Aunt Mary turned the matter over to a lawyer for Gatins family interests in Atlanta, who promptly gave a full explanation of Francis's prewar perambulations. "My personal opinion is that this young man has escaped from the German prison camp where he had been held," the lawyer explained.

Sylvia, meanwhile, studiously kept a list of all the wedding gifts she received, a five-page, handwritten compendium of mirrors, silver, china, cigarette boxes and the like. The list included 27,000 French francs. By some family accounts, Sylvia's mother also contributed $100,000 U.S. (about $1.2 million today).

After the church wedding and reception, the newlyweds repaired to the Lancaster Hotel, where they spent several days and nights honeymooning in the intimate, 11-suite hotel just off the Champs d'Elysées, which also was occupied by "numerous Germans" at the time, as Eglé recalled. The newlyweds dined on their wedding night at Maxim's, the legendary gourmet restaurant on the rue

Royale, again surrounded by German officers, as one family friend recalled the story. In fact, the German authorities probably knew that an escaped prisoner of war had gotten married that day—but simply could not be bothered to look into the situation. Both Eglé and Francis recalled years afterward that it was common knowledge in the local bistro outside the Chaillot parish church that the Gatins-de German-Ribon wedding involved an escaped prisoner of war. My German-Ribon grandmother's butler, in fact, had overheard German troops talking about it as they had a drink the day of the wedding. "I was very nervous," Eglé said.

Within days, though, the young lovers flew the dangerous Paris coop, having somehow secured a travel pass that permitted them to cross the old demarcation line between occupied France and the "Southern Zone," formerly the "Free Zone." The Germans had established this administrative boundary when they essentially cut France in two at the time of the humiliating surrender in 1940. (In November, 1942, Germans invaded and took over the southern part of France, too.) At the old demarcation line, about 75 miles from their destination, they found bicycles, strapped on their suitcases and half-rode and half-walked on to the German-Ribon's country property, La Chezotte, a comfortable castle-keep tucked away outside the tiny, remote village of Ahun, in the department of la Creuse, a true, rural backwater lost in the middle of "*la France profonde*." The village encompassed a church, a baker, butcher, café and post office and not much more, with a population that even today barely exceeds 1,500 souls. The castle redoubt seemed a perfect hideout, isolated in one of the least populated and most remote of France's *départments*. With little more than 201,000 population in 1940, it had little industry to speak of, just a few coalmines and stone quarries and a reputation for excellent stonemasons, many of whom had fled to Paris for employment. One of its few claims to fame was that Aubusson, the famous tapestry center, was located within its borders. As many Frenchmen found, and as my parents were counting on, it was so remote that it was tailor-made for hiding out in *le maquis*, its wild backcountry forests and harsh scrublands, peat bogs, and vast expanses of centuries-old pines, firs, beech, birch, oak and chestnut trees, tall ferns, stinging nettle and pit vipers providing excellent cover from German and SS army units. I can only imagine that my parents breathed a huge breath of relief at landing so far away from the hurt of the prison camps and the nervous tension of an uneasy normalcy in occupied Paris. La Chezotte was to provide real comfort to the new couple, both that year and in years to come, especially for my father. He was then 28. Sylvia was 29.

Chapter 23

Wartime Honeymoon

However remote the tiny village of Ahun, the new couple's actual residence nearby would have been hard to miss. La Chezotte, where they set up house, was a 15th Century chateau that was the German-Ribon family's country estate. The castle, while built during the Renaissance, loomed as fully medieval, with two round towers, crenellated battlements and a dank *oubliette* beneath the wine cellar (that is, a dark, very deep subterranean dungeon, literally translated as "a place to be forgotten"). The chateau stood three stories above a working moat that served as the sewage system, and was traversed by a hand-made stone bridge. The main fireplace, which inhaled large oak logs and big fagots of kindling, was so big one could stand inside it. The property also included a variety of outbuildings. Besides servants' quarters, a farmhouse and barn, it had its own chapel, a laundry for drying and pressing clothes, a huge, donkey-drawn stone apple press, and a garage. There was no washhouse, though. Laundry was boiled in a big tub outside the farmhouse and the help used a well-worn stone angling into the property's trout stream, rather than a washboard, to scrub out dirt and grime. An apple orchard, a large vegetable and flower garden, and a pine-tree farm, criss-crossed by a fast-flowing trout stream, also chockfull of crayfish, were part of the estate. A man-made stone grotto on the hillside beneath the orchard housed a statue of the Virgin Mary. Fat, bottom-feeding carp cruised the moat. Thus, although German troops were largely garrisoned in Guêret, the departmental capital about 11 miles away, or Limoges, 50 miles away, it was inevitable that La Chezotte became something of a magnet for occasional, roving Wehrmacht army patrols.

"The scariest time was when I came in one evening and the dinner table was lined with German machine pistols," my father recalled years later. "The patrol wanted to see my papers—and the only thing I had was a fishing license from the village of Ahun." My father went upstairs, supposedly to find the papers, while

Sylvia and her mother plied the patrol with apéritifs: local wine, hard cider and a raw, fiery applejack made locally from the fruit of the estate's own orchard. Amazingly, the patrol never came upstairs to find Francis or look at the papers. The escaped prisoner of war and his new bride also benefited from the goodwill of farmers and villagers from Ahun and other nearby hamlets, many of whom, like the Gatins couple and a growing network of men and women joining the local Resistance movement, made no secret of their disdain for occupying forces. As Eglé said in her memoir, "They led a most comfortable life, securing provisions on bicycles from the nearby farms, where, after a while, they were cherished." But Francis had other close calls.

"Everything was going well until the day partisans killed two German soldiers," Eglé continued. "So, there was a huge stir to find the guilty parties. One day, a patrol came to La Chezotte and asked where Francis was. They were told he was a freed former prisoner of war. The platoon leader asked for his papers. And he didn't have any, for good reason. The platoon leader then said, 'OK, get them all loaded up.' He was put onto a truck. Francis kept on saying he was a freed prisoner. He was asked the name of his last prison camp. He gave it to them and told them that he'd worked as a busboy in a neighboring village.

"By extraordinary happenstance, one of the German soldiers knew the spot perfectly well, since that's where he often went to drink. So, Francis was told to get off the truck. Which was fortuitous, as all those gathered up in this sweep were shot to death in Montluçon. Sylvia always said that this miracle was due to Saint Anne, to whom she'd begun praying upon entering our family." (I'm not really sure why my mother adopted St. Anne as her special saint, but if Catholic doctrine is correct, Anne, mother of the Virgin Mary, reputedly was a special protector of housewives and women in labor, as well as the patron saint of Brittany, which would have had special applicability in Sylvia's case. Anne was a saint with many varied interests, according to Catholic myth, and also granted special protection to sculptors, goldsmiths, broom and glove manufacturers, washer women, rag merchants, navigators and miners.)

Similarly, sometime later, my father was able to talk a German patrol out of arresting a youngster from a nearby farm, again because he was able to let the platoon leader know that he'd been held as prisoner in the German's home area. Another time, Francis was visiting his cousin and close family friend, Paul de Villelume, at a nearby property in Aixe-sur-Vienne, *L'Osmonerie*, below Limoges. "The Gestapo showed up one day and said, 'We're here to arrest the marquis [Villelume],'" Grandmother Eglé said. "The manservant kept talking to the Gestapo while his wife quickly went to warn Paul and Francis, who skedaddled out a back window, jumped on their bicycles and dashed toward Limoges on back lanes."

At other times, Francis did what he had to do to keep himself below German radar, sleeping in nearby barns or in a smallish worker's hut at the far end of the vegetable garden at La Chezotte. With the help of Baptiste, my Grandmother Elvira's loyal butler, he buried all their shotguns and rifles in the garden beds so as to not have any on the premises if a German patrol searched the chateau.

There was a constant search for victuals for Baptiste to cook up, including one memorable day, when they got Larivière, the local butcher in Ahun, to secretly help dress a large pig. Fresh meat, even in the country, often was scarce. Another time, they secured enough eggs, flour, sugar, butter and milk to make a heavy pound cake, thereafter nicknamed the "Choke-a-Christian" cake by the family.

Eglé found that Francis and Sylvia made enough friends in their rural retreat to serve them in good stead, as was confirmed one day when she came down from Paris to visit the young couple. She was astounded at the tenor of the times in and around La Chezotte. "One day, as I was coming back home on foot from having attended mass, I was stopped by a gang of bizarrely dressed people who asked where I was going. When I told them "I was Free French, too, and I'm going to La Chezotte, one of them took the rest aside and said, 'She's OK. Let her pass. She's one of us. She's with La Chezotte—she thinks like us.'" Even years after the war was over, a large wooden double cross of Lorraine, the official symbol of the Free French Forces of the Interior (and also the heraldic symbol for Joan of Arc) could be found affixed to the walls of the chateau's gatehouse.

Despite the ever-present, threatening undercurrent of the German occupation, the young couple appeared to enjoy times of pure domestic tranquility. Photo albums kept by both Sylvia and Eglé depict a life of rural simplicity at La Chezotte, with my mother herding a gaggle of geese on the farm, cows in the field behind her; riding a donkey-drawn cart; eating a picnic outside the chateau; and throughout, pictures of the new groom often with a small, wry smile, looking very much like he'd just caught and swallowed the canary.

Always, however, in the background of their lives, the violence and brutality of war loomed. It was inescapable, even in this remote, rural backwater, even after Allied forces had started pushing inland from their D-Day landing sites in Normandy. In mid-summer 1944, a German security detail dubbed the Jesser Brigade, operating some 60 miles from Ahun in Clermont-Ferrand, swept into La Creuse. Its mission and specialty was the elimination of Resistance units. On July 21, just outside Ahun, the brigade stopped four Italian laborers who apparently were trying to make their way back to Italy from the engineering and construction works of the Todt Organization, which was then building an "Atlantic Wall," along France's coast. The Todt Organization, named after the Nazi engineer, Fritz Todt, was a key engineering subsidiary of Nazi war efforts, building autobahns, armament factories, the Siegfried line, air raid shelters, and launching facilities for German V1 and V2 rockets, in addition to the huge "Atlantic Wall," the long line of concrete bunkers and fortifications constructed to guard against Allied invasion from the sea.

The Jesser Brigade soldiers interrogated the Italians at a roadblock outside Ahun, searched them and stripped them of their cash. Deeming them terrorists, they led the hapless Italians to an isolated side road leading away from La Chezotte, the pathway to the hamlet of La Couture, made them dig their own graves and, without trial or hearing, shot them dead around 6:30 p.m.

The next day, my father helped local farmers exhume the bodies, and take them to the cemetery in Ahun for proper burial. The smell of the dead bodies was so pungent that Francis never again could wear the jacket he wore that day. But the story did not end there. A local doctor, Jean-Baptiste Michard, 28 years old, several days later was shot dead by a German officer in the courtyard of the local elementary school in Ahun after he reproached the Germans for the Italians' slaughter. Later that summer, on August 4, Giraud Albert, an assistant to Ahun's mayor, was arrested, allegedly for having provided a false identity card to a Jew and for organizing a Bastille Day celebration on July 14. He was locked up in Aubusson and shot to death on August 11, along with 41 other hostages. All told, about 40 men gave their lives for the Resistance in and around Ahun alone. More than 450 others were killed for the same cause in this remote department of la Creuse.

Years later, Francis helped raise funds to set up a small memorial stele along the rough trail where the four Italians were killed. Ten years after this murder, this trail (*Le Sentier de la Couture*), was so overgrown by briars and bushes that it was hard to negotiate. As children, my brothers and sisters and I saw it as a dark place, to be avoided on blackberry-picking outings. One of my sisters, Eglé, believed the path was haunted and said it gave her the willies. Indeed, it remained haunted for our family through the mid-1950s, when memories of war were still raw and very much on the surface around Ahun. By the turn of the 21st Century, however, the trail had been bush hogged and widened and smoothed and obviously was being used by motorized farm equipment and four-wheeled vehicles. I saw the memorial stele standing upright against a rocky outcrop that looks very much like the foundation of an old Roman structure (Roman ruins dot the countryside of la Creuse). The monument overlooks a rolling plain of farm fields and forest. To me, the site appeared remarkably peaceful, in huge contrast to the emotions the site evoked when we were children. Maybe time does heal youthful fears, I thought.

It is unclear if Francis ever joined any of the various Resistance groups that gathered in the *maquis* of la Creuse. According to my sister Eglé, a truck swept by La Chezotte one day, looking for volunteers, but he was out and did not join any of the various crews of Resistance fighters in the department. However, correspondence with Sylvia some two years later suggests they had shared a tender good-bye in the small garden hut "when I was leaving for the *maquis*." He also noted in a draft resumé after the war that he had "worked with the Underground" during the years 1944-45. Whether he joined the *maquis* or not, it is certain that he knew the *maquisards*, many of whom in this section of the Creuse were Italian, and many of whom were avowed Communists—because dating from that time, he learned to sing the Internationale, the Communist hymn, in Italian! (Just as many French workers were transshipped to Germany as laborers, so many Italians were dispatched to supplement depleted labor pools in France during the war.)

Francis' children also believe that he tried at one point to join Free French Forces of the Interior in Algeria, but did not get further than Toulouse, where he was provided phony French army demobilization papers. As his son Martin recalled it, Francis was told he wasn't needed: The end of the German occupation was already in sight.

Finally, the tide of the Allied forces began to turn, and in all of France. One day, my mother and father recalled, they were walking on the farm path behind the nearby farmhouse owned by the Marcel Victor family. They looked up to see hundreds of Allied planes overhead. It was D-Day in Normandy, June 6, 1944, the beginning of the end for the Nazis. This eventually was followed by the liberation of Paris, a world-shaking event closely followed by Eglé from her post in the French capital.

Chapter 24

"Kicking the Anthill"

The Allies landed on the beaches of Normandy on June 6, but it took American and French units until August 19, 1944, to reach the French capital and then another six days of sometimes harsh street-to-street skirmishing involving both French and American forces, as well as French civilian irregulars, to drive out the German army for good. Grandmother Eglé was witness to it all. She saw fighting, shooting and dying on Avenue Kléber and rue Dumont d'Urville, only a few blocks from the large apartment on Place des Etats-Unis that she, her brother Charlic and her mother, Jeanne de Madec Fischer, called home. As a Red Cross official, she was given a helmet to get around the streets when the shooting broke out.

"They were fighting on avenue Kléber, with firing from the rooftops. It was very, very dangerous," she said years later. "We were crazy with excitement. It was extraordinary. We went to *l'Etoile*. We saw the German flag taken down and the French flag put back up. That was something—it was a great, great time.

"I saw the Germans arrive on the 14th of June [1940,] but I saw them leave too," she remembered. "They said, 'We're going on vacation,' and I said, 'I hope you have a good vacation.' And they never came back."

Grandmother continued in the same vein in her memoir. "It was very emotional because the Place des Etats-Unis was still in the German sector of the Hotel Majestic. All the church bells were ringing, but we were somewhat still prisoners, so to speak. [The nearby Hotel Majestic had been taken over as German military headquarters in Paris.] We clambered to the top of the roof and it was really very poignant to see the German flag come down and the French standard go up in its place," she said. "We ran like mad toward the avenue Kléber at the risk of being hit, as partisans and Germans were shooting all over the place."

A very similar thrill of liberation coursed through the little village of Ahun,

Eglé said. She heard that "the people of La Creuse learned of the good news and began dancing in the village square of Ahun. They rang the church bell so hard that it cracked." She also remembered little ironies, as when her parish priest at Chaillot, apparently having learned of the D-Day landings, asked the congregants, including numerous German soldiers, "to sing the *Te Deum* and a Hallelujah—which was a bit strange, but we did it. We had a lot of very Catholic Germans who regularly attended services there, and these men sang the *Te Deum* with us—which signaled their defeat," Eglé said.

Her emotional memories of liberation were tempered by knowledge that Paris was not a bed of roses during the occupation. Some people were starving and my siblings and I remember being told a decade later that many infants and young children growing up in that era had never seen a white-bread *baguette* (as we munched through as many croissants and *baguettes*, all lathered with as much butter from Normandy as we could gorge). Times definitely were tough in Paris by mid-1944. Gas and electricity and foodstuffs were in short supply. The subway, the *Métro*, wasn't running on a regular schedule. Public officials, police and postmen often were on strike. Eglé was still working for the Red Cross, running the care package program for French prisoners of war from the 16th arrondissement. She and her brother and mother would still have an occasional, more-or-less spontaneous tea for friends and neighbors. Sometimes, they would secure a bit of luxury—chocolate or little *patisseries*—from black market teahouses. But getting enough "food was difficult," she said, in what I thought was a most understated fashion, given the reality of a war quickly unraveling for the occupiers. "Food was rationed. The food was very scarce. Your grandmother [Sylvia's mother, Elvira] would send food from the country. And Philippe [Manset] would bring eggs from Argeville."

Eglé, then 51, transcribed her day-to-day experiences of 1943-44 in letters to her son and new daughter-in-law at La Chezotte, a dozen of which were saved by Sylvia. They read like a diary, recording daily events from the mundane to the earth shattering, from having neighbors come by for tea, to more serious reports of looting and last minute arrests and killings. Take her letter of August 19, 1944, the day American forces reached the gates of Paris, and its sequel two days later:

My dear Mitou,

The postal service is on strike, but I am still going to try to tell you everything I have heard or seen in recent days and I'll send my letter as soon as it is possible. My last letter to Sylvia of 16 August, must be resting somewhere in a mailbox.

Since Thursday, Paris gives the impression of an anthill that has been kicked over and all the ants are saving themselves as best they can. Various [German] units are leaving in order, but others are fleeing in great disorder. Many individuals are taking off in stolen cars, or even German military vehicles whose tag numbers have been erased. Bikes also are being used.

A lot of them have left, but there are many still here and I even think that certain combat units have returned.

As I wrote to Sylvia, we've had some SS troops for better than 30 hours in la place [des Etats-Unis] with caissons of ammunition. It was unbelievable. Thursday, they started taking away all the reserve supplies they had in the garages: St. Didier, Chaillot, Lauriston and in all the arrondissements of Paris. The stores were packed: Underwear, shoes, food, telephones, soap, etc. What supplies they could not take, they started to distribute to the people and then after a while, they closed the garages. During the night and into the next day, French people popped the door locks and pillaged. People whom one would have considered well behaved took away bicycles and all sorts of goods. It's awful. The Germans, disgusted, ended up firing on the crowds. Everything calmed down. Yesterday, Friday, their departure seemed to go well. We went up to Sacré-Coeur [church], Charlic and I, and since there was no Métro running, we did the round trip on foot and everybody seemed happy and calm as the departures accelerated. What I forgot to tell you is that the looting was possible because, since Wednesday, the police are on strike, as are the railroads, the post offices, the Banque de France,

(Continued...)

etc. The self-styled police do not want to go back into service until the Americans are here.

The police stations are closed. It's said there's a civilian workforce inside; but you don't see anyone. Moreover, everything is strange. At the same time as the Germans, or German women wearing grey uniforms, were selling or giving away bicycles, others only 500 meters away were requisitioning them. [The women in grey refer to the German auxiliary forces, whose grey uniforms resulted in their being dubbed "les Souris Grises," the grey mice.]

This morning, the army of the Resistance had to get into action—placing, it seems, French flags on certain public buildings. As for me, I saw some at the police station [of the 16th arrondissement]. It's said that skirmishing is breaking out between Germans and French near the ministry buildings, at the Concorde, on the bridges. At last report, we were told that at the mayor's office in Neuilly, it's real serious between the Army of the Interior and the SS. I know nothing of it. Here, there's nothing going on up until now. You hear canon fire and machine guns. It's curious. I wonder if this shooting isn't a bit premature and that it would have been more intelligent to await the Yanks' arrival before putting up the flags. The main thing, as I see it, is to get rid of the others [that is, the Germans.]

For the past eight days, we've had American plenipotentiary officials at the Hotel de Ville, trying to get Paris considered as an 'open city.' Thursday night, we had hoped it was done, but everything seems broken down this morning.

Without a radio, we don't know anything for sure, but it's said many new units are at the gates of Paris? Let's wait and see. It's probably idiotic to write you—my letter probably won't get forwarded, but I'll keep writing and we'll see later. I imagine that with new arrivals, we'll be cut off. I think that it won't be long before we see you again—at least I hope that is the case. I hope that my last cigarettes [sent on] the 14th finally will get to you. I went out this morning and

(Continued...)

I got the feeling things were turning for the worse. I sent everybody home at 11:30 a.m. [This refers to Grandmother's care-package workforce.] Some of the girls live so far away.

This afternoon, I did not go out. Neither did Charlie. You're at the mercy of gangs that have drunk too much and are firing their machine guns or revolvers like mad. It's said at the mayor's office that a lot of passersby were wounded, and others at Neuilly or at the Hotel de Ville, where there was skirmishing. The SS had halftracks and trucks. I just don't see the worth of this fighting today, which only delays the departure.

Monday, 21.

We're beginning to understand. At Neuilly, it was really the Resistance that wanted to recapture the mayor's office, but they only had a half-hour's worth of ammunition. So, it wasn't very smart to begin with. In Paris, they are not stirring and it's the Communists who are firing on the Germans, and have taken over the Hotel de Ville and occupy, to a certain extent, various mayor's offices, ours for one example. They look unbelievably fierce, are very young and have taken over the first floor. The mayor and our friends are on the second floor, with very few employees. It's pretty hard to get around certain arrondissements, so the employees stayed home.

The situation is very confused. What is certain is that various Communists are running matters at the Hotel de Ville. Taittinger ... president of the municipal council and [others] have been arrested by them. Our brave leaders, [meaning Vichy government representatives] as you must know, folded back to Nancy or Germany. It's said that an entire train-full of 'collabos' left the station. Saturday and Sunday, fighting broke out all over Paris, but especially in the 17th and 7th [arrondissements]. Unfortunately, there were a lot of victims. Yesterday, there was a truce—but it was announced everywhere that it was over, that there was an accord between the Hotel de Ville and the Germans. Notes

(Continued...)

were sent to the mayors' offices and loudspeakers announced it, but there were liars on one side and the other and the truce did not hold. Everything started back up today.

Up until now, our neighborhood is mostly calm. Tonight, one hears a lot of artillery fire. If only it could be the Americans approaching. The presence of their army is really needed here. The spectacle of Paris is really not very pretty. I love you and je t'embrasse.

By the 25th of August, a day full of shooting and house-to-house and roof-top-to-rooftop hunts for German snipers, Parisians were ready to move from a mop-up operation to open jubilation at finally being free of the heavy yoke of the Occupation.

Eglé related that she could hear heavy firing across the Seine River and in the vicinity of l'Etoile and the Trocadéro. But in her neighborhood, the Germans were simply surrendering to civilians, the Resistance. "The [civilians] were wonderful, but, unfortunately, several were killed or wounded."

Other Germans, though, fought a rear-guard action, sniping from roof-tops and from the Arc de Triomphe at anything that moved. "I'm told it was pretty bad," Eglé continued in a letter of August 25. "Here, it was an incredible manhunt, on the roofs and on la Place des Etats-Unis, totally conducted by the Resistance on the hunt for Germans and, what's more serious, for *miliciens*." The mention of the miliciens refers to France's homegrown jackbooted brown shirts, the French Militia, created by Vichy as a counterforce to the *maquisards*. The miliciens included ultra-collaborationists, toughs and some smattering of "respectable bourgeoisie and even the disaffected aristocracy," according to one author. Grandmother reported that miliciens had joined in the death-throes of the German forces in Paris, hiding out with SS units and "firing on innocent Frenchmen.

"The Parisians have been splendid and it's beautiful and I am wild with joy to feel the Krauts gone," Eglé continued. The next day, the Free French forces marched down the Champs d'Elysées, with General Charles de Gaulle on foot, surrounded by a few officers. "The enthusiasm of the crowd was indescribable," Eglé wrote. "It was nothing like the majestic parades, even the little ones of the war of 1914-18. But it was like a spontaneous demonstration, a bit disorderly, but exhibiting the giddiness of a populace grateful to have been freed." The American troops, Eglé continued, were massed around l'Etoile that day, but did not take part in the parade. "It was as if they wanted the French to have the honor of retaking Paris and to show themselves."

The arrival of the American GIs, in fact, stirred Eglé in coming days and seemed to awaken memories of America and Atlanta that long had been dormant. She had not lived full time in the States since 1923. Now, her Americans were in the French capital, powerful liberators.

"I am so proud of America," she wrote her son on the 24th of August. "Despite the bad times, I have a gentle recollection of your dad—there was so much good in him—and today he is so deeply in my heart and thoughts." (As best any of Eglé's grandchildren can tell, this brief footnote represents the only expression of love or tenderness that Eglé ever recorded for her American husband. I do not remember her ever mentioning him, not even once.)

Two days later, she ran across an American Army unit on the avenue d'Iéna, and shook hands with one of the Yanks. "He was speaking softly and I asked him where he was from and he said from Atlanta, Georgia! A bit of a cracker, but he knew the Georgian Terrace. Admit it, it's strange. The world is really very small."

In another letter, this one to Sylvia, dated four days after that, Eglé expressed awe at the American troops. "This American army is something formidable. It's a world of materiel on the march—and what marvelous equipment! I'm over-joyed to see them in Paris ..." About a week later, the Americans got their own parade, starting at the Bois de Boulogne, going down the Champs d'Elysées, and all across Paris. "It's amazing the number of troops that were marching and the quality of their equipment," Eglé said. "It's beautiful! The people were really touched and couldn't stop saying, 'Thank you, thank you,' which they pronounced '*chank you.*' Since then, we're seeing Americans everywhere in Paris. Some are just passing through, others are staying. Paris has taken on the mood of festivity and gaiety. Those 'nice' women who used to go out with the Krauts are now showing the same tenderness to the Yanks—but it's all done with a lot more happiness." A day later, Eglé reported that she and Charlic were having tea at home with an American military physician and his chauffeur and another G.I., a very civilized interlude in the midst of war.

By the 10th of September, in another letter to her son, Eglé reported one could have imagined being back in one of the black neighborhoods of Atlanta, next to Oakland cemetery or at the old train station. "There's a veritable army of trucks lined up along the sidewalks of the Place des Etats-Unis, driven by black soldiers," Eglé wrote. "They run, they play, sing, call to each other, speak to the kids, swap out their cigarettes and soap, etc. It's enchanting."

In honor of the liberation, Eglé and Charlie put up flags on all their apartment windows: "French, British and in the big living room window, an immense American flag that we got on loan, big as a ship's colors. It's sensational! I really wish you could see all this."

Eglé's liberation letters also frequently expressed an immense sense of gratitude that her only son had managed to get out of Germany, as she did in a letter of September 3, 1944, five years to the day after war had been declared and Francis was getting ready for his call-up to Coulommiers. "Who could have predicted the events that unfurled since then? Not only do I see the Krauts out of my Paris, but add to that the infinite joy at my knowing you got out. I've got to admit that if you were still 'over there,' I'd be going a bit crazy. I am truly grateful to God to have brought you back from over there and put you in the arms of my Sylvia."

Letters from this period do not dwell on it in great detail, but here and there, interspersed with mention of day-to-day events, Eglé made allusion to the last-minute throes of the German occupation, the arrests of acquaintances she knew in Paris. Many of them were being shipped to the notorious internment camp at Drancy, too often nothing more than an intermediate stop on the road to the gas chambers at Auschwitz. After the Liberation, she wrote of the equally swift decision of the French authorities to arrest and dispatch known collaborators and German sympathizers—"*bochophiles*," she called them in one letter—to the same internment prisons. Scores were to be settled, and settled in a hurry.

A couple known to the family was arrested for being "too close to the Krauts," she wrote on September 10. The same treatment was allotted to one of the Vichy officials who let the last death train pass through Paris. Another acquaintance, president of a mining concern, had counseled his shareholders to sell out at a huge profit, rather than let the company be taken over by the Germans. The result was that the Germans secured majority control of the firm. This man's wife thought he was going to be slapped in prison for about six weeks, Eglé reported. "Drancy and the prisons are full to capacity—one doesn't know where to put the internees," she said.

By mid-September, though, the capital began to get back to some semblance of normalcy. There was enough food and gas, and electric service was being restored. One of Francis' friends decided to visit them at La Chezotte, by bicycle. Eglé used the opportunity to bundle up all the letters she'd written during the liberation and send them down to her son and daughter-in-law. She herself was busy helping set up a welfare liaison office between the American forces and needy Parisians.

The Americans were wary, Eglé reported, of possibly being put in contact with people who might have collaborated with the Germans. "We've promised to provide guarantee for every contact," Grandmother wrote on September 13.

Similarly, the Free French forces of the Interior (FFI), General de Gaulle's troops, were wary of taking on men who'd stayed in France, among them Eglé's and Francis' good friend, Paul de Villelume. "In Paris, it's said that Paul was not taken back by the de Gaulle army because they felt this brave colonel got there too late," Eglé reported in a letter of August 30. Grandmother also provided some greater explanation in her memoir, suggesting there was bad blood between de Gaulle and de Villelume dating back decades. "After a while, Paul decided to go to Algeria to find General de Gaulle. He crossed over the mountains. But on arriving at Algiers, he was very badly received by de Gaulle. He'd loathed him for a long time because Paul successfully escaped from a prisoner-of-war camp [in World War I] while de Gaulle, a prisoner in the same camp, had failed."

Francis's childhood friend, Philippe Manset, had better luck, allying himself with an American infantry recon unit stopping outside the Manset home in Argeville-sur-Boigneville, in the country south of Paris. Philippe recalled it for the family decades later. He was playing tennis that day when villagers ran to him, exclaiming, "The Americans are here!" Because Philippe spoke English, he helped the unit fix its bearings and was taken on as an interpreter-scout for the next few months, as the unit moved east and north toward Germany. For the most part, that involved Philippe's finding the head of the local Resistance unit as the American recon forces went from village to village across France, claiming each for the Allies.

Francis and Sylvia then decided to return to Paris—on bicycles again—as the railroad system "had been totally destroyed by partisans," Eglé said in her memoir—and made a new home at Sylvia's mother's house at 4, rue Dumont d'Urville. (The railroad station nearest to La Chezotte, at Busseau-sur-Creuse, was located adjacent to a viaduct over the Creuse River more than 1,000 feet long and 188 feet tall. Partisans blew it up twice in 1944, on April 30 and June 14.)

Francis too tried to find a home in the U.S. military and was knocking on the doors of the U.S. Embassy in Paris by December 19, 1944, initially to get registered as a U.S. citizen after "protracted foreign residence," as State Department files described the application. "My reason for now applying as an American citizen is for the purpose of obtaining a valid American document in order to join the American Army," Francis stated in the affidavit appended to the application. Indeed, later correspondence showed that Francis got as far as receiving three different American Selective Service cards beginning in late 1944, the last of which classified him as eligible for service (A-2), following a physical. But he was eventually turned down; he'd become too old to serve, the files suggest.

The application also explained a bit more of what Francis had been doing as V-E Day approached. "Since D-Day, I have been working with the French Forces of the Interior. I did not take an oath of allegiance to France in connection with this work. During the time of the havoc, in connection with my work with the FFI, I was put on the Free Committee Council for the arrangement of the distribution of food for the French people in my district. This council consisted of people of different nationalities and who are members of the FFI. As there was no legal government in France, several of us accepted this temporary position, which position we will hold until Election Day."

But the application went nowhere fast. First, the embassy forwarded the paperwork to American Army intelligence, but not before January 17, 1945. The G-2 intelligence people then reported on March 21 that they had "no derogatory information" on Francis. Hitler committed suicide April 30. A week later, Victory in Europe! On August 29, 1945, the war in Europe essentially all over, the U.S. Army let Francis know by letter that "only those applicants between the ages of 18 and 25 years are now being accepted for enlistment. It is regretted, therefore, that your application can no longer be considered. The offer of your services is appreciated."

By mid-March of 1946, Francis was back in the United States, accompanied by Sylvia, but he was not there for fun. Grandmother Eglé put it this way: "Francis had woken up one day with a terrible flu. A night nurse hired by his mother-in-law said, 'You've got to do a lab test. I'm afraid it's TB.' And, in fact, that's what it was."

Francis and Sylvia, by then pregnant with their first child, decided to go to New York to consult with pulmonary disease specialists. Said Grandmother Eglé: "As I drove them to Orly, I wondered if I'd ever see him again—he looked so sick."

Chapter 25

Tubercular in Love

Francis and Sylvia faced a decidedly uncertain future when they took off from Orly airport for London and thence to La Guardia in New York, deplaning that March 18, 1946. At the time, there was no guaranteed cure for the dread disease afflicting my father, the same malady that had helped lay low his own father and that had resulted in the early deaths of so many fellow soldiers in German prisoner-of-war camps. He quickly was admitted to Doctors' Hospital for treatment, while my mother repaired to the Ritz-Carlton Hotel at 46th and Madison Avenue. In early April, physicians collapsed one of Francis' lungs under a procedure called a thorocoplasty, a common treatment then in vogue for tuberculosis. "At the time, they didn't treat TB patients with drugs," Eglé noted in her memoir. "The doctor said only one thing would save him—which would be to get to the mountains."

With the help of Francis' aunt, Mary Jackson, then living in Manhattan, the couple was able to move Francis from the hospital in New York City to the remote town of Saranac Lake, in the middle of the Adirondack Mountains. This was the location of the well-regarded Trudeau Sanitorium, which had been treating TB patients with its "outdoor cure" since its establishment in 1884. This regimen was remarkably similar to what the family believes my grandfather had undergone when he spent time in Asheville, N.C. in the mid-1920s: Isolation (so as to not infect family and others who came in contact with the patient), long hours of rest in cold, mountain air and, occasionally, surgery.

My father, for example, slept on an outdoor porch of the house the family purchased in Saranac. He "wore a mask and always kept himself at a certain distance," Grandmother recalled. "But sometimes it was so cold that we decided to let him sleep in the bedroom, with the windows open." As Francis and Sylvia subsequently remembered, he also received periodic "pneumo-thorax" treatments

Dancing on a Volcano

from the Trudeau Sanitorium, in which his collapsed lung was pumped up with air every two weeks. The lung collapse operation left a scar that took a long time to heal, my father noted in letters to his bride from this period.

By September 1946, Francis was set for an extended stay in the frigid reaches of upstate New York. A combined cook-and-nurse's aide was hired. Eglé came from France to help take care of her son, as Sylvia, then more than eight months pregnant with her first child, stayed in Manhattan to give birth. Her mother, Elvira, joined her there, as did her sister, Beatrice Manset.

Beginning in mid-September and continuing pretty much daily for the next three months, Francis wrote Sylvia a total of 79 consecutively numbered letters, which the new mother-to-be saved for posterity. Of her own letters, only one was saved. The love letters—that is the only real way to describe them—are full of Francis' longing for his bride, and chafing at the physical separation the two had to endure. To put it simply, it was obvious from Daddy's letters that my parents thoroughly gloried in their bodies as they celebrated their love for one another.

"It's very pretty and cold today. But the house is really sad without you. Yesterday, your bedroom still smelled of you; today, it's a sad room as anonymous and dead as an hotel room," he said in Letter No. 2, of September 12, 1946. "I think of nothing more but to repeat: I love you. I love you. I love you. I love you …God bless you," he said in Letter No. 3, dated September 13, 1946.

The collection of letters is replete with my father's reaching and longing for his Sylvia, in such detail that it might make the unwary blush. The letters are replete, too, with the mundane: How their two dogs, Brownie and Ruffles, were doing; how he had hired yard help to clean the garage and cut out some dead tree branches; how he ensured Sylvia had enough spending money, (usually, a check for about $1,000 each month, a handsome allowance in those days). There also was talk about pending visits by friends and family from France, which by the time the Saranac period had ended, included Uncle Charlie, Samuel Arrellano; Beatrice and her husband Philippe; Mary Jackson and her brother, Ben Gatins and his bride, Dorothy. But Francis, facing possible death from a terrible disease, kept his main focus on Sylvia, and on the baby that was soon due.

September 19, 1946 (letter No. 9).

I reread your letters and my morale gets better. I think especially of our past, and the days are more pleasant. We have

180

(Continued...)

so many good memories in common. You were speaking to me, the other day, of that first kiss when I was on my knees in front of you on the carpet of the small living room. (Mother is just back from the mailbox — nothing from you). But do you think of that day when you said, "No," and let yourself be kissed in the Citroen parked on Avenue d'Iéna, far from other street lights? I thought of it during those three years of separation that followed that sad good-bye. And do you remember, at Argeville when we first engaged, how we stopped every hundred feet to kiss each other? Your mouth is so fine and I miss it so much. Then, I think of La Chezotte, where we were so free and easy and alone. I see it all.

Letter No. 12, undated.

I'm always thinking of you — you're the only one I have fun with. I love your spirit, the way you see things, your laugh, the blues you get in the fall. I have so many warm memories of you that we could spend years remembering them. But especially, you are always new to me. I often wonder what you're really like, what you think. So often, you surprised me. You looked so determined killing your pig, driving your big Packard, leaving in difficult circumstances for an unknown country. What I love in you is that you are so young, always ready for fun, even with little things. I'm really looking forward to seeing you as a mother. Because your dominant strengths are your freedom and your kindness. That's what makes you so desirable: Your native ease for making love. You gave me your mouth one day, so simply, so kindly and with such a good, open heart. The same way, one night, you gave me the best gift in the world, your entire body, all the sweetness of your skin, all your perfume and your virginity. I sometimes wonder if you know how much I appreciate that gift...

> *September 29, 1946 (letter No. 19).*
>
> *I've read the paper and especially all the news from France. It's odd how far away and uninteresting it all seems. I feel no sense of attachment or patriotism. France's fate seems so small, small compared to our fate and the arrival of the baby. As for patriotism, I don't give a damn. Would only that we could return to La Chezotte from time to time. The only flag that I venerate, for which I would give my life, is the hot, perfumed blouse you just took off. To defend a country that isn't even mine, and whose inhabitants I find despicable—all that got me is a three-year separation from you.*

The young couple also remained in contact with telephone calls almost every evening, with Sylvia occasionally breaking down in tears at the separation. But it is clear too, that Francis, debilitated from the disease, and often dulled by tranquilizers—he couldn't walk very far, much less do yard work—poured most of his energy into the letters. Years later, the Gatins children got the feeling that this correspondence between our parents gave him the heart to live and definitely helped him survive the tuberculosis, just as his mother, with her letters and care packages, had helped him immeasurably through the prisoner years. The Saranac correspondence is liberally laced with page after page of tender words and anticipation of an eventual reunion.

> *September 30, 1946 (letter No. 20).*
>
> *For me, this separation and disease, however sad they might be, serve a useful purpose. First, we'll have the joy of starting all over again. The biggest enemy is the routine. Your body must be as sensually exciting as the red bullfighter's cape is to the bull.*
>
> *Whatever our jobs, whatever family concerns, whatever the sad times, we must every year manage to take a honeymoon trip where we will take care of each other to help our love progress. What do you say?*

Ten days later, at noon, my father wrote my mother to tell her how proud he was "of your baby." That letter also makes plain that it was a difficult birth, Sylvia having endured 33 hours in the delivery room before bringing me, their firstborn son, into the world. (Mother gave me the name Joseph Francis Miguel Gatins, adding the extra middle name in honor of her brother, Miguel.) A follow-up letter, dated that same evening of October 10, is full of questions. Had little Joe been given his tuberculosis immunization vaccine, the BCG [Bacillus Calmette-Guerin]? Where would the christening be held? Could it be held in Saranac? Would Philippe Manset, the baby's godfather, be willing to attend? Telegrams had been sent to everyone in Europe about the new baby. Family and friends in Atlanta got phone calls. Francis and Eglé had celebrated the event with a toast of cognac. (My father also made plain in one of his subsequent letters, dated October 18, that he was not particularly pleased that Sylvia had tacked on a second middle name to my birth certificate. "Pity to have given him the name Miguel! I wonder if it wouldn't be better to correct this error. If you agree, I'll take care of it." But the change was never made.)

He also noted the need to support his growing family, the same day I was born. "We're going to have to make some money to bring up this child. So, I've seriously started writing my memoirs, in an attempt to get them published and to make a bit of money. My baby, I will never be able to thank you for this gift. I love you. [Letter No. 30, October 10, 1946.]

My mother herself penned a wonderful letter that same day, one of the few saved by my father. He kept it in an end table drawer in their bedroom and the children often read it as they were growing up. Unfortunately, it disappeared at the time of his death decades later. It was funny, tender and bawdy all at once and makes me regret that I was never able to read any of my mother's letters to our father, especially those from the war years.

My father's letters from the Saranac period suggest that Sylvia had remained in the hospital for at least a week, to recuperate from the difficult birth. In keeping with the medical tenor of the times, she did not breast-feed me (which the couple obviously thought was just fine: Both of them wanted her breasts back to normal size). Judging from the letters, Sylvia was exhausted, maybe a little bit depressed with post-partum blues and Francis was counseling bed rest for her. Grandmother Eglé had gone to New York to visit, as had Mrs. Fraser, the cook at Saranac, taking with them a nanny from Saranac hired to help with the new baby.

Francis realized he was going to have to share Sylvia's time and attention with their son, as in letter No. 49.

> *I'm so anxious to resume a normal life with you and the baby. When are you going to be done with this confinement? You no longer tell me if you're still hurting. I'm a bit sad this evening, and it would be so good to roll myself up on you in your arms. To mold myself to your body and to go to sleep protected by your body, because there are some days when I do not feel like a husband, but like a brother to little Joe, and, like him, I love feeling so protected by you.*

Francis also reported receiving periodic house calls from Dr. Pierre Trudeau of the sanitorium, who could offer only a guarded prognosis for recovery. In fact, despite the progress seen in his lung cavities, there was still a good chance he'd test positive for TB, my father said. Still, his weight had crept back up to 155 pounds—15 pounds more than when he landed at La Guardia seven months previously. By letter No. 55, Francis' TB tests had come back negative. In another letter, he reported that their beagle, Raffles, had won third place in a dog trial in Saranac. In letter No. 62, he quoted verse from Baudelaire and Verlaine, in anticipation of their reunion, planned for some few days hence.

> *Letter No. 62, undated.*
>
> *You know how much I need you, my baby. But as huge as that desire might be, there's my tenderness, my admiration, my friendship and my love for you. All this seems indivisible. You're my boon companion, but I respect you. You're my wife, but you make me laugh. I pinch and pummel you, but I'm a little bit afraid of you. You're little Joe's mother, but the most sensual of mistresses. You are my Sylvia and my letters never let you know enough why I love you and how much I love you.*

The much-anticipated reunion was then put off for another eight days—Sylvia was still exhausted, the letters suggest—but eventually they did have a week together in Saranac before Sylvia returned to Manhattan. Francis kept on counting the days until they could be back together again for good.

Eventually, mother and newborn left Manhattan and made their home in Saranac, too, finally joining Francis and Grandmother Eglé. They got through the winter of 1946-47, but the snows were sometimes so deep that they could not open the front door of the house. The two women often wore slacks rather than dresses to negotiate the drifts, family photo albums from this period show. Grandmother Eglé also recalled that she and Sylvia attended mass every Sunday at a nearby Franciscan monastery. "Their chants were so beautiful that we preferred the monastery to our own parish church which, nevertheless, was nice."

Little by little, the patient was able to get up, walk a few steps and even take meals with his family. By springtime, Francis was able to go out fishing, which delighted him, my grandmother said. By the fall of 1947, with Sylvia finding herself pregnant a second time, Francis was given permission to travel south for the winter. Atlanta was their destination, and the Georgian Terrace Hotel, intimately tied to Gatins family fortunes, was to be their winter home for the next three seasons.

Chapter 26

Not White Trash

Once in Atlanta, the Gatins family—Francis, Sylvia, Eglé, baby Joe (that is, me) and my nanny, Nana Clark—made our home at the Georgian Terrace Hotel on fabled Peachtree Street. Family history repeated itself. This was the same hotel that was Eglé's first home in Atlanta, when she had followed her new husband there some 33 years previously, and to which they had returned with their young son Francis in 1916.

The Terrace, located at the corner of Peachtree Street and Ponce de Leon Avenue, had experienced something of an economic renaissance during World War II, as both visitors and some Atlantans found it advantageous to live there. These long-term residents included lawyers, businessmen and well-off widows who had moved there because they could not find domestic help during the war. The hotel had entered into Atlanta's collective unconscious as one of the best hotels in town after my great-grandfather Joseph F. Gatins Sr., the first-generation American in this branch of the Gatins clan, had built it in 1910-11. Its imposing, 10-story brick façade was punctuated by a set of circular tower apartments. An expansive, west-facing porch was lined with rocking chairs from which a "rocking-chair brigade" watched the passing scene on Peachtree and across the way at the Moorish-looking Fox Theatre, erected in 1929. Years later, the porch also served as playground and tricycle track for the likes of me, as it did for my father before me.

The New York Metropolitan Opera stayed there when it was in town, because Gatins Sr.'s brother-in-law, John Murphy and his wife Julia, were instrumental in bringing the Met to Atlanta. And it seemed all of Hollywood had stayed at the Terrace for the premiere of *Gone With the Wind* in mid-December, 1939. Through economic thick and thin, the hotel benefited from a stellar publicity machine. More than 5,000 residents were said to have walked through its doors for the hotel's grand opening on October 2, 1911, praising it, according to a contemporary press statement "for the general appearance of an up-to-date Fifth Avenue hotel... This hotel marks a distinct step forward in southern hoteldom and is truly, as we expressed in our advertisements, 'a Parisian hotel on a noted boulevard in a metropolitan city.'"

The well-known Atlanta chroniclers, the late Franklin M. Garrett and Harold H. Martin, gave the hotel prominent mention more than a dozen times in *Atlanta and Environs: A Chronicle of Its People and Events*. Enrico Caruso, the renowned opera tenor, wrote a glowing letter of appreciation after the Met's visit in 1913. Warren Harding and Calvin Coolidge made it their headquarters during visits in 1921. And in 1947, it served as home to another generation—technically, the fourth to call Atlanta home—of the ever-expanding Gatins family.

The hotel also was a wellspring of my father's finances in that his one-third share of the room and banquet and restaurant proceeds dutifully had been saved during the war years in Europe. His grandfather, who built the hotel, had placed it in trust for his three children and their descendants in 1912, making clear that he did not believe his direct progeny were qualified to run it as a business—and obviously believing them better suited to spending money than making it.

By the time Francis assumed his share of the Georgian Terrace, after his father's death in 1927 and his grandfather's death in 1936, the main trustee for the hotel was an Atlanta lawyer, Welborn Cody. He'd had the distinct pleasure of informing Francis after his last escape and the liberation of France, that some $57,200 was being held on his behalf, a real fortune for the former army corporal! This share of hotel profits for the World War II veteran "far exceeds what we originally anticipated," Cody wrote my father in a letter of August 7, 1945. Unfortunately, this money had been placed in various bank accounts that had been frozen during the war. So, Francis spent a good bit of time and stationery writing to Cody from Saranac, and even before, from France, to make sure he could access this cash, and get the money invested in interest-bearing accounts or securities.

"Now that the war is over, would it not be wise to start the identification of these accounts and try to have them freed, as all formalities seem so long nowadays," Francis wrote Cody from Paris on October 25, 1945. "Otherwise, arriving in Atlanta, I will have to live there as white trash." In a business letter to Cody on September 14, 1946, he added a personal note: "I have no intention of staying in Saranac. In a year, I hope, I will be well enough to leave this place for good. I have spent enough cold winters in Germany and Poland that, as soon as possible, I will never spend a winter north of the Potomac."

He relied on Cody for specialized, personal legal advice as well, asking the Atlanta lawyer on one occasion, for example, to get U.S. Customs to release a case of French armagnac that Philippe Manset had sent him from France. He also usually checked with Cody on real estate and automobile purchases. Eventually, with his bank accounts duly un-frozen, Francis and family were ready to live large at the Terrace, where the manager had reserved a string of suites for the Gatins party, rooms 824 through 828. Not like white trash at all. I have very little memory of this period and the next few years except that I remember thinking that we were living very, very high above the street below and that Nana Clark often pulled me back from the open windows overlooking Peachtree. I remember she would read me the "funnies" from the newspaper—I thought Dick Tracy was so cool, with his radio watch. The comical antics of Terry and the Pirates, Snuffy Smith and Beetle Bailey also got my attention. When I was a "good boy," someone sometimes took me across the street to the Rexall drugstore adjacent to the Fox and treated me to a special fountain drink, a small, iced Coca-Cola in a triangular fountain cup, liberally laced with cherry syrup.

About this time, too, the State Department moved to regularize my father's status as a U.S. citizen, finally closing a long, bureaucratic chapter in his efforts to choose one country or another as his own. In a clear reflection of the tenor of the times, he also took his duties as a citizen seriously enough to contact the Atlanta office of the Federal Bureau of Investigation on December 29, 1947, to report the sighting of a former prisoner of war that he thought might be "used by the Russians as an espionage agent in the United States." That man, whose name still remains excised from the public record by the FBI, was described as a native of one of the Baltic States who had lived off and on in America but who had been captured by German forces during the early years of the Second World War. The man had returned to his native country—whether Estonia, Lithuania or Latvia, the memo is not sure—"to join the Russian Army because he believed in the Russian system."

"He told Gatins that he had lived in the United States off and on for a number of years but felt no love for this country and classed it as [a] 'Drugstore Civilization,'" the one-page memo concluded.

I don't recall my father ever talking about this episode or his feelings about Communists and purported Russian spies, but I find it interesting, and somewhat odd, that he would turn in the name of former prisoner with such tenuous connection to any specific wrongdoing, particularly given the hate he often voiced for prison rats and informers (*mouchards*, in French), whom he had crossed paths with during his own prisoner days. The "Red Scare" brought to white-hot pitch during America's McCarthy period was just in its infancy, but there was apparently enough thinking in America about the oncoming Cold War that Francis, a newly minted American citizen, harked to the recently completed war he had experienced.

Eglé had sharp memories of this period at the Terrace, especially of a round of parties thrown for Francis and Sylvia, and then, on February 15, 1948, the premature birth of my first brother, Charles. "Strange as it may seem, a mouse ate through one of the wires leading to the transformer and the hotel where we were staying was plunged into darkness. We went down the eight flights on foot, after which Sylvia was struck by birth pains and transported to St. Joseph Hospital, where Charles was born," Eglé said.

The entire family went to Saranac Lake for the summer. Eglé, like her son, had developed a keen sense of belonging in the United States, and fondly remembered the road trip back to Atlanta in October of 1948. Philippe Manset had joined Eglé, Francis, Sylvia and the children and drove them through the Adirondacks and the Shenandoah Valley of Virginia, "full of red maples," and on to Atlanta, she recalled. All I remember of this time was pushing a toy lawn mower behind my dad's real push mower in Saranac. Family photo albums also show him teaching me to shoot a homemade bow-and-arrow. As for my brother, Charles, what a pain! I don't know if it was sibling rivalry or what, but I do recall he pushed me into a lake at one point, which was not a lot of fun, as I did not yet know how to swim.

But storm clouds were brewing over the young family, now three children strong with the birth of Sophie on July 7, 1949 in Saranac. My parents were having a tug-of-war over where to settle down, the U.S. or France. Sylvia, in a bureaucratic battle thoroughly reminiscent of her husband's long skirmish with the State Department over his passport and citizenship issues, was facing a stiff fight of her own with the U.S. Immigration and Naturalization Service, which had serious doubts about a Colombian citizen extending a tourist visa in the U.S. "For reasons that I don't really recall very well, Sylvia said she wanted to go back to Paris to raise the children," Eglé said. "Francis, he preferred the United States. She left and set up shop at her mother's house. Francis was not very happy."

What an understatement! Married less than seven years, my father and mother essentially created separate households on two different continents.

Chapter 27

Intercontinental Interlude

The young Gatins family, soon to grow from three children to six with the birth of twins Martin and Eglé, and then Miguel, spent the next three years batting between Atlanta and Saranac Lake and Paris, trying to figure out where to make a permanent home. Francis preferred the freedom of America. Sylvia preferred France, or Colombia, especially since the U.S. Immigration and Naturalization Service actively had been trying to deport her since 1948. My mother, had overstayed a temporary tourist visa originally secured to accompany her husband to New York for treatment of tuberculosis. The INS deportation effort, involving voluminous documentation, formal hearings and findings, filings of some 16 different birth and marriage certificates and the like, faced repeated delays as the file was shipped back and forth from Atlanta to upper New York State. It was all collected in an inch-thick compendium no less bureaucratic than the file documenting Francis' earlier fight to establish his U.S. citizenship.

There were also hints that the foundation of my parents' union had developed a few cracks, as Francis and Sylvia moved into their sixth and seventh years of marriage. Essentially, the couple established a bi-continental living arrangement.

As Grandmother Eglé said in her memoirs, "They decided to buy an apartment and found a very pretty one on Boulevard Suchet [in Paris]. Francis preferred the States. He went there frequently and when he came back to France, he went to La Chezotte, which he really loved." It is obvious to me and all my brothers and sisters that our father had a true and abiding sense of place for the charming chateau located in the backcountry of La Creuse. He'd walked every little pathway in those parts, knew the headwaters of every little trout stream, which he fished with local guides, and remembered it fondly as the site of an extended and safe honeymoon. (I, too, have memories of this special place. One of my small enduring recollections of this period involved being driven by Daddy to La Chezotte in the middle of a harsh winter. The water in the moat was frozen solid, but he built a huge fire in the main fireplace and pushed a sofa close up to the coals to keep me warm that night.)

Francis was very frustrated by bureaucratic snafus affecting his family, as he made plain to the INS inspectors who interviewed the couple and in letters to lawyer Welborn Cody. "I am quite worried," he wrote Cody on June 18, 1949. "Sylvia is again having some troubles with the Immigration Office. You will see at once the consequences. Sylvia still has a warrant of arrest and deportation hanging over her head. Those people do not seem to worry about breaking up a family," he continued. "I don't understand why the wife of an American citizen cannot live quietly with her husband and children."

Both Francis and Sylvia said the same thing under oath during the deportation hearings, after INS agents suggested bluntly that the couple was rich enough to withstand separation (both, the file noted, were living off the proceeds of trust funds). "It isn't a matter of economic detriment, it is the moral side of the picture, that of separating a family," my father retorted. "I do not want to have my family separated. I want to have my children brought up as United States citizens and they need their mother's care. Surely, there must some way this can be straightened out."

But it could not. The eventual outcome of the INS procedures was that Sylvia was forced to "voluntarily" go back to France and from there re-apply for permanent resident alien status, which is what she did in the fall of 1949. The file suggests the INS had looked askance at the fact that Sylvia had attended an International Red Cross conference in Paris right after war's end, as a representative of the Colombian government.

According to Francis, these were not happy times in Paris. "The change has been too big for the children," Francis wrote Cody in November of that year, 1949. "Sophie had a bad case of anemia and Joe cannot get rid of a cold. And in terms of morale, it was tough for them to be among people they do not know and who do not speak English."

My own memory of this period is that my brother Charles and I forgot English, quickly learned French, and generally learned to behave like well-behaved, upper crust French kids. One did not hit girls in playground fights, "even with a flower." One did not drink *café au lait* out of bowls like every peasant in France," that's just too common." Older women were greeted with a light kiss on the hand.

And if my father was gone half the time, it didn't register on me. I do recall that he was pretty religious about remembering my birthdays, even if he was in the States, and on one occasion, shipped me a cowboy outfit, with a real cowboy cap pistol. The carton arrived half-opened, half-broken, but the pistol was a great toy to have on our daily walks to the Allée des Fortifications and the Bois de Boulogne, which were just across the street from our apartment. These grassy play areas were still dotted with German pillboxes, leftover from the Occupation, which Charles and I used as hiding places and play "forts." Talk of war was never far from the surface, even for the children, and I remember asking our new French nanny, Manelle [Marie-Louise Sonet] "What is it, the atomic bomb?"

Francis, meanwhile, was having a hard time finding gainful employment on either side of the Atlantic, despite the best efforts of a legion of business associates from Atlanta and New York to find him a future as a company man. He was 34 years old, a veteran of the big war, but he'd never had a paying civilian job in his life. Was the post-war economic boom passing him by? Francis hinted as much in chatty letters from Paris to a good drinking buddy in Atlanta, Jack Spalding, and to lawyer Cody.

"We have been awfully busy doing nothing much. Just trying not to be overrun by the children," he said in a letter to Spalding dated October 17, 1950. "Sylvia, trusting the price of coffee to go up forever, has bought us a nice seven-room apartment..." (Sylvia had brought her own funds to the marriage, most of them invested in holdings in Colombia, whose value by 1955 was the equivalent of almost $6 million in today's dollars.)

Efforts to land a job in Europe with the Atlanta-based Coca-Cola Company had come to naught. The Coke man who interviewed him was "a very nice man, but he did not like me. I am not so anxious to work for our big Company as I do not feel so sure that war is not arriving one of these days, and then I really would hate to have the kids stuck in Europe," Francis continued. "I hope that you will be glad to know I did not get the job, as I am, as it will give me a chance to go back to Atlanta. Sylvia was very much disappointed. I know that you will enjoy thinking that your old friend Francis is a worse bum than yourself. You do not stick too much to a job, I cannot even get one. So, let us hope that we will be soon be at the bar of the P.D.C. [Piedmont Driving Club] just talking about all those fools, so good and so dumb, that we see around us."

Similar job applications to the Ford Motor Co. and General Motors in New York also came to naught, amid my father's self-doubts about his ability to secure a real job. Those doubts had surfaced as early as five years previous, in a September 1945, letter to another acquaintance in Atlanta. "I hope I will find a job in spite of the fact that I am getting pretty old, and that since I left college, I never had a chance to settle down to business."

But Francis was still flush with the remainder of his grandfather's trust fund and monthly draws from the Georgian Terrace Hotel, and while ostensibly look-ing for gainful employment in the States, he could—and did—sample the fast life of Café Society in New York, with show girls, nightclubs and restaurants. This brought him into contact with the denizens of Manhattan's *demi-monde*, some of whom he collected into a tight little coterie of late-night companions. Very little of this would be known to the children today, except for his being linked, if only peripherally, to a scandal involving a New York show girl and an amiable rogue and ladies' man who became one of his close friends in Manhattan, Mario Enzo Gabellini.

The headline in the *New York Journal American* of May 13, 1950 was hard to miss: "Finds Actress Dying In His Midtown Apt." According to police reports cited in that article and other articles in the New York press, a 25-year-old show-girl and divorcée had taken poison (a nicotine-based insecticide) in an "apparent suicide" in Gabellini's apartment—and subsequently died at Bellevue Hospital. The papers concentrated on Gabellini, as this incident represented the second violent death linked to him in New York in less than 10 years. In the first such instance, Gabellini was the last man to have seen heiress Patricia Lonergan alive before she was bludgeoned to death by her estranged husband, one of the most lurid murders to occur in New York during October 1943.

Daddy, as my sister Eglé recalls it, is believed to have been the last person to see the showgirl alive that night. (Gabellini was able to prove he had been out of town.) But the papers made no mention of this possible Gatins connection, and a slim paperback volume that alluded to this fact remains lost in my sister's bookcases.

Although the Gatins children did hear suggestions decades later that Francis might have been having an affair in New York during the period, Sylvia took her strict Catholic upbringing seriously and divorce was taboo for the faithful in those days. Nor apparently was a formal separation seriously considered as had occurred with Grandmother Eglé and her own mother, Jeanne Madec de Villelume-Sombreuil Fischer. In any case, Sylvia and Francis were still making babies, apparently with the help of divine intervention. Before I was born, Sylvia, who'd been told she would have a difficult time bearing children, had contacted an order of nuns in France who, if given a dozen eggs, would pray for the moth-er's fecundity. After the sixth child, their friends suggested, "Enough with the prayers!"

The twins, Martin and Eglé, were born prematurely on July 27, 1950, at the American hospital in Neuilly, an upscale Paris suburb. For reasons not clear today, Sylvia and Francis and the three older children then went to La Chezotte, while

Grandmother Eglé, who was at the hospital the night of the twins' birth, stayed with them and "an elegant nurse."

"The nurses went every day to get mother's milk from a lactation center," Eglé recalled. "Then the twins grew big enough to be sent to La Chezotte." But they were still tiny, especially Eglé. The older children clearly remember the twins could both fit inside an apple basket and were carried around that way. (As for the lactation center, then as now, French women who were not breast-feeding were encouraged to donate their mother's milk to official "lactariums" in Paris and across the country for donation to infants who could use it and whose own mothers, for whatever reason, were not breast-feeding.)

Despite Francis' early concerns about dislocating his first three children away from the life they knew in the States, Charles and Sophie and I readily assimilated ourselves into French culture. We spoke only French and essentially forgot English. We had a wonderful time, especially since in the summers we were given the run of La Chezotte under the watchful eye of our French nanny, Manelle. The twins, once born, were placed in the care of a second nanny, nicknamed Manou.

Manelle assumed most of Sylvia's maternal duties. She washed us in a big tub, dressed us, played with us, took long walks with us, either in the countryside of la Creuse or in the Bois de Boulogne and tucked us into bed at night. Only after that would Mother come up for a ceremonial goodnight kiss and, in deference to her Catholic faith and superstition, inscribe a sign of the cross on our foreheads with her thumb. Every afternoon in the country, there would be a ceremonial washing of the hands before afternoon tea, which, in our case, involved buttered peasant bread, sugared orangeade or *cassis-water*—and occasionally that great tool for disciplining children, scrapings of dark chocolate layered on top of the bread and butter. Baptiste, the long-serving and loyal butler for Grandmother Elvira, took me and Charles fishing with cane poles, teaching us the right way to bait worms on the hook. The moat around La Chezotte was populated by schools of carp, while the nearby trout stream was full of small, freshwater baitfish that were caught by placing a bit of stale bread in a wine bottle whose bottom had been knocked out. The fry could get in, but never seemed to find the way out. The family usually would stay in Paris through July 14, Independence Day in France, to watch the military parades down the Champ d'Elysées, but the rest of the summer usually was spent at the chateau. And it was back to Paris in the fall of 1951, with Sylvia pregnant again with her last child. My father was in New York. When birth was imminent late that year, Francis tried to rush to Paris. Unfortunately, there was a terrible fog and all the Paris airports were socked in, as were most of the others in Europe. Francis landed at Shannon in Ireland, and then found a flight to Brussels. Meanwhile, "Sylvia was running back and forth from airport to airport, waiting for her husband. But finally, she had to go to the hospital and her chauffeur got lost," Eglé recalled. "The child was aborning as she finally arrived at the hospital. She was undressed in the birthing room and Miguel, a splendid boy, was born." That was December 17, 1951.

Shortly thereafter, with Francis becoming more and more adamant, the couple "came to conclude that life would be easier in the United States," said Eglé. There were other motivations than convenience, it seems. My father suggested to friends like Philippe Manset that there were business reasons for making a permanent home in the States. Income taxes, for example. Indeed, the business correspondence with Welborn Cody, the lawyer in Atlanta, suggests this motivation weighed heavily on Francis' efforts to secure U.S. citizenship for himself. There would have been a tax surcharge if he'd been deemed a resident alien living in America, which had occurred when his U.S. tax return was first filed in 1937. "He was promptly notified of this action and he in turn promptly notified us that he was an American citizen and not an alien, and directed that his tax be handled on that basis," Cody wrote an IRS official as early as 1944. Francis' citizenship fight with the State Department had led him to formally renounce any claim or right to French citizenship, particularly since it seems the French tax authorities were after him, too. This formal renunciation, initiated in mid-1948, finally was sealed and delivered on page 9,221 of the *Journal Officiel de la République de France*, on September 11, 1949.

Francis had filed a similar formal declaration with the U.S. Department of State on January 15, 1946, even before going to New York for tuberculosis consultations. The form was termed an "Application to resume citizenship in the United States by a person while a citizen of the United States lost his citizenship in order to perform military service during the Second World War in the army of a country at war with a country with which the United States is or was at war." The form required an oath of "renunciation and allegiance," as follows: "I hereby declare on oath that I absolutely and entirely renounce and abjure all allegiance and fidelity to any foreign prince, potentate, state or sovereignty of who or which I have heretofore been a subject or citizen; that I will support and defend the Constitution and laws of the United States of America against all enemies, foreign and domestic; that I will bear true faith and allegiance to the same; and that I take this obligation freely without any mental reservation or purpose of evasion: So help me God. In acknowledgement whereof, I have hereunto affixed my signature."

It is also very likely that Francis did not have much respect for the politics and postwar actions of his former French compatriots, as he signaled in his correspondence with Sylvia. It would not have escaped his attention, for example, that his interlocutor in the punishment camp of Rawa-Ruska, Georges Scapini, the Vichy government's minister for prisoner of war issues, had seen his indictment cleared sometime after 1949. According to my sister Eglé, Francis thought it had been his duty to try to escape from prisoner of war camps, and that he looked askance at fellow French soldiers who had seemed willing to accept incarceration so long as they received packages from home. My brother Miguel said it this way: "I was under the impression that Daddy wanted out of France as a result of the humiliation it experienced as well as that of himself and 1.5 million other soldiers, which he blamed on the spineless political dynamic that existed at the time. In a few words, I think he just lost faith in the country and its leaders and never forgave them for the debacle." My brother Martin thought the move "had a lot to do with the fact that Daddy liked the U.S. and the fun life in New York and Atlanta and thought that there were more job opportunities in the U.S.A." My sister Eglé also recalled the rationale for the move as more nuanced, and forced on Sylvia by Francis, who apparently feared a Communist political take-over in France. She believes it was hard on Sylvia to finally agree to give up family, childhood friends and, ultimately, an entire way of life.

In any case, the need to permanently settle somewhere came to a head. As one granddaughter, Anne Stewart Mason, heard, Francis eventually gave Sylvia just 24 hours to make up her mind. "We're leaving Paris for good. We can live in New York, Atlanta or go to Colombia. Which is it?" Sylvia picked Atlanta.

They quickly moved to sell the apartment on Boulevard Suchet and purchased a home on Rivers Road in Buckhead, a highly landscaped and comfortable Atlanta neighborhood shaded by immense tall pines and hardwoods. Sylvia went first to pave the way. Sometime in 1952, Francis took a ship back to the States with the first five children and a lot of luggage and belongings. On the boat, the three oldest children began relearning the English they had forgotten. I recall discovering, for example, that French-fried potatoes were the same thing as the *pommes frites* we had been eating for the past three years, but I recall nothing more of the trip to Atlanta. The last child, my brother Miguel, remained with Grandmother Eglé for nine months before also being brought to the U.S., largely so his immigration and travel papers could be put in perfect order.

The family stayed first at the Georgian Terrace, then moved to its new home, a two-story, yellow-brick house with a green ceramic tile roof, shaded by huge oaks and sweet gum trees, with an expansive garden and yard. The lush green lawns were framed by vigorous plantings of large azaleas, daffodils and scented jonquils that created a pink, yellow and orange fringe in the spring. The back of the property had once been set up as a grass tennis court, which the boys promptly turned into a combined practice baseball and football field. A long narrow extension of land at the back of the property was a jungle, overgrown with forsythia, poison ivy, honeysuckle and some very old, tall pine trees. A big wooden crate arrived with furniture and furnishings from France and the Gatins family settled in to what would become home base for the next three decades. The crate was eventually painted a battleship grey and served as a combined play fort and baseball backstop for the children for years thereafter. The new home in Atlanta reflected my mother's taste in interior decorating, with Louis XV chairs and sofa (most uncomfortable), and a large array of bibelots and trinkets and knick-knacks layering each end table, including a collection of gold vest-pocket timepieces handed down over the years. She knew the pedigree of every piece, down to where and when it had been acquired or given as a wedding present. The French magazine, *Réalités*, came by one day to do a photo shoot of the living room. But we all spent most of our time either in the kitchen or its small breakfast nook or in the airy and sunny "red room," which was the most comfortably furnished room in the house.

Soon after we settled in, our French nanny, Manelle, rejoined the family in Atlanta, ensuring a continuing French connection, French upbringing (and very French discipline) for us six children. When the entire family knelt together to say evening prayers, we said them in French. We prayed in Latin at church, but our missals were all in French. While the children were inescapably thrust into American life at school, the family in many ways maintained old world, French ways at home, and settled into something of a dual life.

Back to Paris: Francis and Sylvia and the three oldest children hurriedly sailed back to France from New York in 1949, with the U.S. Immigration Service hot on Sylvia's heels for overstaying a tourist visa. (Below), the couple relaxing in Atlanta.

At peace: Francis was perhaps nowhere more at peace than at the beach, in the Swiss Alps or cruising on mountain lakes. Sylvia, shown here next to a historic Roman mile marker, thrived at La Chezotte in the 1950s,

ke-and-hay brigade: The Gatins children were happy to help with raking hay at La Chezotte in he 1950s and also had the run of the property on bikes and tricycles. The farm managers, André and Alice Deluchat and a young helper (with beret) took care of the haying operation, while their nanny Marie-Louise Sonet kept a watchful eye over the bicycle runs.

American kids at play: The Gatins gang was more informal in Atlanta. Joe (at top) watched over Martin (holding hat) and Charles, while Eglé, (at bottom left), Sophie and Miguel scanned their favorite Tintin comic.

Children made to be seen: And not heard. That unofficial guideline was often enforced on the Gatins children in Paris.

All grown up:
Sophie (with scarf),
turned into a lady,
while her sister
Eglé (left) pursued art
studies. The boys got
all dressed up for
Sophie's wedding,
(from left) Joe,
Charles, Miguel and
Martin.

The grandmothers: Elvira de German-Ribon (right) could not have been more different in temperament from Eglé Gatins (left).

Grandes Dames of Atlanta: Eglé (right), renewed a strong friendship with her niece, Katherine Murphy Riley, upon returning to Atlanta.

Chapter 28

Culture Shock

In many ways, the Gatins family's permanent return to Atlanta proved to be a culture shock for both the family and for their new American friends and neighbors.

To begin with, none of the children spoke English in 1952. The oldest three had forgotten it, the youngest three had never spoken it. Sylvia spoke English with a somewhat British accent, and chain-smoked her Marlboro cigarettes in a long cigarette holder, while Francis had a high-pitched, very distinctive French accent that did not sound at all like the sonorous Southern accents of Atlanta. And he never totally mastered the English language, for example using the term, "It is," when he really meant "that's it." For Sylvia in particular, who had only visited Atlanta previously, this was a strange new world.

In Paris, there was the underground *Métro* for transportation; in Atlanta, electric streetcars going up and down Peachtree Street. At night, the headlights from passing cars shone through my open bedroom windows or near-transparent blinds. In Paris, the dark at night was complete, as everyone retreated behind metal shutters. In America, the children had the funny papers, Dick Tracy and Snuffy Smith, and later, the very irreverent *Mad* magazine. In Paris, there was *Tintin's Hebdomadaire*, which Grandmother Eglé religiously shipped to her grandchildren. Most of the Gatins' neighbors had televisions, which were just coming on the market. Their children talked of watching Superman and "soap operas" and seeing Elvis grind his hips for the first time on the Steve Allen show. My family did not get a TV until 1963-64. Instead of listening to the radio in the evenings, my parents read aloud to the children, from French fables to Jules Verne's adventure books—the same books that Francis had had as a child in France. The family subscribed to *Life* magazine, but also received *Paris-Match* and *Réalités*. The Gatins kids looked and dressed differently from American children. In elementary school, the boys all wore shorts with long knee socks (flannel shorts in winter, khaki cotton in summer) and high-top leather shoes from France, usually fitted with prosthetic lifts to discourage flat feet. American kids wore T-shirts and jeans and rubberized, high-top Keds.

The food was strikingly different, too. There were no French bakers, hence no crusty *baguettes*, no delicious *croissants* or *pains au chocolat* hot out of the oven. As a substitute, the children were permitted to sandwich a block of semi-sweet baker's chocolate between pieces of Merita white bread, so soft it tasted like putty. American kids ate chocolate ice cream for dessert. Sylvia whipped up meringues and chocolate *éclairs*. In France, we ate macaroni with butter and Parmesan. In America, spaghetti was lathered with Ketchup. Sylvia made sauce *Béarnaise* to put on steaks; in America, there was Heinz 57 Sauce. In France, we drank orange-ade or carbonated mineral waters. In America, there was Coca-Cola and a host of sugary soft drinks—Nehi Grape, Nehi Orange, ginger ale, Dr. Pepper, root beer and the like, the Cokes especially favored in Coca-Cola's headquarters town. Fresh milk and heavy cream in heavy glass jugs was delivered daily before dawn by the R.L. Mathis Dairy. In France, children hardly ever drank milk. Classmates at Christ the King School ate tuna fish salad sandwiches on Fridays (in pre-Vatican II days, Fridays were a meatless day for Catholics); we brought sardine and onion sandwiches to school in our lunch boxes, to the bewilderment of both teachers and pupils, many of whom weren't familiar with sardines. Hot dogs liberally covered with mustard, relish, onions, slaw and Ketchup, also proved a tasty novelty. In Paris, neighborhood grocers prevailed. On Peachtree Street, Sylvia found Kroger's and the Garden Hills Grocery and so many frozen vegetables that we hardly ever ate fresh greens again. Jello and canned fruit became staples. Instead of hot roasted chestnuts bought from Paris street vendors in newspaper cornets, we stopped at the drive-by watermelon-and-fruit stand at the intersection of Peachtree Street and Peachtree Battle Avenue. And there was hot popcorn at the movies in Atlanta!

It was also a new world for my parents, who were accustomed to a veritable army of servants in Paris, two nannies, cooks, Spanish maids and a chauffeur. In Atlanta, they made do with one nanny, Manelle; one cook (after a series of disastrous hirings, settling on the talented and loyal Bernice Dallas), and a big, hungry one-day-per-week yardman named Harvey. Harvey was a gentle giant of a man who worked very hard that one day, but insisted on getting breakfast out of the deal. Bernice would fry up some bacon and two or three eggs, on which he layered a heavy dusting of black pepper, a condiment we had rarely seen in France.

Still, assimilation did occur, somewhat faster for me and Charles and Sophie, who'd been born in the U.S., than for the youngest three. By dint of daily repetition, I recall learning to say the Pledge of Allegiance and the Hail Mary every day at Christ the King School by rote memory and sound—not having the faintest idea what all the words meant. Instead of ending the Hail Mary with, "the fruit of thy womb, Jesus," for example, I heard and mouthed the words, "the broom, Jesus." Similarly, I remember learning to sing *America, the Beautiful,* just as I had picked up *Frère Jacques* and *Sur le Pont d'Avignon* in France. I survived Sister Saint Louis in the first grade and won a spelling bee in my second-grade class. Little by little, we children learned to how to behave in this new country. Men and little boys kissed ladies' hands when introduced in Paris, but not in America. Instead of *La Marseillaise* we sang the Star-Spangled Banner (and Dixie). We were introduced (by one of the kitchen help prior to Bernice) to what it was to "play the spoons" with wooden clappers whittled down just for that purpose.

We also found another part of the extended Gatins clan in Atlanta, Joe and Ina Gatins, and their two sons, Joe and Michael, the latter about the same age as Martin and my sister Eglé, descendants of the original John Gatins who immigrated to Georgia with my great-great-grandfather Joseph, the railroad clerk.

Charles and I stopped dreaming in French, and with the help of little crystal radios attached to a metal night-light, learned idiomatic English while tuned in to Atlanta Crackers baseball games, Georgia Tech football games and the Grand Ole Opry, whose AM broadcasts from Nashville were powerful enough to reach Atlanta. Cousin Minnie Pearl, with her trademark greeting, "How-deeeeeee," was our favorite. Rather than Citroën sedans and 2CV economy cars, we learned to recognize the sweeping lines of Plymouths and Buicks, Chevrolets, Fords, the ill-fated Edsels and every version of the modified hot rods that teenagers used to cruise up and down Peachtree Street. Since my parents decided not to buy one for more than a decade after moving to Atlanta, we were fascinated by the neighbors' television sets: On one side, the Brooks family and their son Scott let us watch the soaps and Howdy Doody after school. On the other, Jesse and Cencia Shelton kept their TV in a combined office and Florida room, where we were dispatched on Sundays to watch *Meet the Press.*

The children essentially had the run of the lower half of the Rivers Road neighborhood, between Muscogee Avenue and Habersham Road, so long as they heeded the dinner bell, which usually rang around 6:15 p.m. Up until then, after school, I roamed through backyards and across the street along an unnamed stream that eventually made its way to Peachtree Creek, chief of a little band of funny-looking French kids. When it rained hard, the stream would overflow and inundate the street. When it was dry, we "played Tarzan" with a huge, old grapevine that permitted us to vault over the creek. The family's two dogs also marked their territory. These hound dogs possessed a native cunning for survival. They would sun themselves in the middle of the road every afternoon, waiting for the arrival of the Northside High School bus, which stopped in front of the Gatins house every day to deposit a neighbor's children. When the bus started back up, Silly and Chibcha would race it to the end of the street, snarling and nipping at the front wheels of the bus.

I learned to "trick or treat" at Halloween and, from the second grade onward, how to craft red paper hearts on Valentine's Day, pagan holidays that did not then exist in France. Charles and I were transferred to the private, Presbyterian-affiliated Westminster Schools by third grade, (at which time I convinced my mother to let me wear long pants and high-top Keds like the other boys), but Atlanta's Catholic diocese apparently convinced Francis and Sylvia to keep the other four children in Catholic schools. Westminster was the successor school to Washington Seminary, which Daddy had briefly attended at the turn of the century.

Although we had no particular background for it, Charles and I took to sports with gusto: Football, basketball, baseball (fullback and lineman, guard and first baseman, respectively), and later, when I got to high school and college, tennis, soccer, lacrosse and even the bone-crunching game of rugby. Football was a special passion in Atlanta. When the Georgia Tech Yellow Jackets played football at home, the end of the game was signaled by a long, loud steam whistle that could be heard all the way up to Buckhead, some several miles away from the stadium. The games were all preceded by the singing of the national anthem, which always brought the crowd to its feet in a mighty roar. Georgia Tech also had a rousing fight song about drinking one's whiskey clear and dispatching the rival Bulldogs at the University of Georgia in Athens straight to hell, a song the Gatins boys thought was pretty cool.

Like our one-armed grandfather and his brother, Uncle Ben, both of whom had turned into magnificent and able sportsmen (on horseback), Charles and I turned out to be fleet of foot and fearless on the gridiron, with many memories of particularly satisfying, small victories. Early on, we played single-wing football, a quick and bruising no-nonsense formation that required artful faking by the quarterback, but straight-ahead charging by the fullback. Most times, I played fullback, and I still remember how satisfying it was to run over the opponent, which I did one day on the Westminster playground at recess. A teacher seemed horrified and gave me an earful of discipline. I thought it was the right thing to do, plus sports were the ticket to acceptance by fellow students. I don't think Daddy ever understood the intricacies of American football, but he was there for me, ferrying me to schoolboy football matches on Saturdays, especially once I got to the sixth and seventh grades and our classes were part of the "Gray-Y" league. I have a particularly strong memory of a hard-fought, sloppy game against R.L. Hope Elementary School, played out in a steady rain. Daddy watched it all from the sidelines, hatless. The rain, which eventually came down in a torrent, rolled down his face and extinguished the cigarette he'd been smoking. Of course, my memory centered primarily on my intercepting the R.L. Hope quarterback's lateral pass, which I ran in for a touchdown. I was also the punter during that game and managed to loft the football over the opponents' heads at each kick, having practiced punting every afternoon in the back yard.

To this day, I am amazed at how brightly some very small sports memories still burn in my mind, and how easy it was to gloss over the wrenched knees, twisted thumbs, busted collarbone, stitches over the left eye and the loss of two front teeth given to this cause. I made the all-state football team as a guard and linebacker in a prep league in high school, but I better recall a one-handed catch that broke a touch football tie in the backyard of a fraternity at the University of North Carolina. And a special goal notched against the University of Virginia rugby team—played that day before the coeds of Sweetbriar College. I was hoping to be just as good in baseball and remember trying out in the 7th grade for a local Little League team in Buckhead. But Sylvia, to my enduring irritation, pulled me very loudly from that public tryout to make me attend tea at some old lady's house. To this day, I can stir up resentment over her interference that day.

While Manelle drummed the intricacies of French history into our brains at home and despite Mommy's old-world ways, we learned at school what it meant to be an American and got steeped in the history of this new world. By fifth and sixth grade, I remember biking to the Ida Williams public library branch in Buckhead and taking out and reading and re-reading Hardy Boys mysteries as well as slim biographies, all bound in orange covers, of noted American historical figures. I learned about Paul Revere and his midnight ride; George Washington and his cherry tree; Ben Franklin and his kite; Lewis and Clark and their trek to the Pacific; of the frontier exploits of Daniel Boone and Davy Crockett and their raccoon-skin caps; Kit Carson and Geronimo and The Alamo. For me, these stories eventually overwhelmed much of the French history that Manelle tried to teach us, about Vercingétorix, Charlemagne, Louis XIV, and Napoléon Bonaparte. (But I never forgot Ravaillac, the assassin who knifed France's King Henri IV to death, and who in turn was put to his death in front of a wild crowd in Paris. Ravaillac was savagely tortured and eventually drawn and quartered by

211

four horses—an unforgettable, bloody scene richly depicted in one of the French history books we used at home.)

Becoming American did not occur as quickly for my three youngest brothers and sisters. "I for one felt French until I was in my twenties," my sister Eglé reported in an e-mail exchange with family members. "I always felt it was incidental that we lived in Atlanta. France was our spiritual home. Everything was French—the language, the books, the countless children's magazines, the food, the dress, the thinking ..." Her twin brother Martin experienced much the same thing. "I didn't start feeling American until I went to Tennessee [to attend college] in 1968."

At the same time, as the oldest of this band of six, I recall that we children stuck together against all comers and other neighborhood children. We *were* different and knew it. I remember feeling mostly French and somewhat Colombian at home, American at school, but not having any particular difficulty straddling this huge cultural divide. This dichotomy was reinforced because the family spent some several summers abroad during the 1950s, usually at La Chezotte, and once, during the summer of 1958, in Colombia, where Sylvia's brother Miguel and his family lived.

Coming home from those trips, we did our best to extend memory of our stays abroad by sneaking as much French food past U.S. Customs as our small travel bags could hold. Visualize six children in a row, all in matching outfits, each carrying identical raincoats over their arms and a Pan American Airways travel bag over their shoulders. The raincoat pockets were stuffed with *saucissons secs* and French chocolate, the bags with French bread and smelly French cheeses, croissants and, sometimes, the fiery applejack made at La Chezotte, all carefully wrapped in sweaters by Manelle. No customs agent ever got wise or inspected our hand luggage. Thus did the Gatins family keep one foot firmly planted in the Old World and the other in the New, never exploring the vast United States any further west than Gatlinburg, Tennessee.

What exploration was done by the family was most often done in France. In Paris, Mommy would take all the children to visit a seemingly endless parade of churches and museums, like the Louvre to see the Mona Lisa, and the Musée Rodin to see the sculptures. Grandmother Eglé often took us to Vincennes Park or, by Métro and by bus, to Les Invalides to visit the military museum and all its artifacts and, more importantly, the cenotaph erected there to the memory of Mademoiselle de Sombreuil, the forebear who vainly had tried to save her father from the guillotine. She also amused the children by patiently playing short silent films from the Charlie Chaplin, Buster Keaton and Harold Lloyd era on a small, hand-cranked Pathé Bébé projector, which dated to Daddy's childhood. We loved the enormously unlucky Keystone Cops!

One time, there was a visit to the top of the Eiffel Tower, but most of the time, we were never taken to sites that might have been a bit more fun, like the Paris catacombs or its spectacular sewer system; that would have been "too common." We heard that term a lot. Don't pick your nose—so common. At breakfast, don't slurp your *café au lait* from a bowl like 99 percent of the French—"too common."

The summers at La Chezotte were simply idyllic, serving as a restorative respite for Daddy especially, and as a gateway to a fascinating, rural experience for the children. No one there seemed overly preoccupied with what was "too common." Elvira, our Colombian grandmother, spoiled her grandchildren, buying us all bicycles and tricycles for the summer, and letting us help with the milking and the haying. Having bicycles to ride was special, as we did not have bikes in Atlanta, only little scooters. Daddy won an English bike in a church raffle when I was in second grade, but it was too big and we had to wait a few years before we were able to ride it. At La Chezotte, the children also hitched an old donkey named Charlotte to a cart and got around that way. Charlotte had been rescued from a nearby coalmine operation and liked to bray loudly—a very bizarre sound when I heard it the first time.

André and Alice Deluchat, the brother and sister who ran the farm for Grandmother Elvira, crafted special, children's-sized wooden hay rakes for us and let us lead the cow-drawn cart that was used to carry the hay. The two cows, Butterball and Whitey, were docile, obedient in the extreme to two words—"hu" to go, "ooooh" to stop—and the guidance of a long stick with a nail sticking out the end. Haying was a long process, as the hay was scythed by hand. André and a helper would resharpen their scythes with a whetstone after each row. When it came time to take a break, they dipped a water glass in a nearby spring bubbling out of the hillside. Then the hay had to be turned over twice, again by hand using handmade, long-handled hay rakes, to dry before being collected with pitchforks, placed into the long wooden cart and stored in a large barn. The process took up most of the month of August. Sometimes, the children and Manelle also helped with the haying at the farm of a neighbor, Marcel Victor, whose extensive family also worked a small-grain operation that produced wheat, rye and oats. Toward the end of summer, the Victors' grain was harvested and threshed in a huge, steam-powered threshing machine pulled in by a team of horses, which occasioned a long workday for all adult neighbors for miles around. The machine huffed, puffed and clanked, its large flywheel spinning, to spit out pure grain from a small chute into burlap sacks. Neighboring peasant men, fortified by liberal doses of local red wine and snacks of peasant bread and cheese, hoisted the heavy sacks onto their backs and moved them into the Victors' granary, on the third floor of the farmhouse. I got a small, child-sized sack to help. That was an exciting time, especially since children got a taste of the wine, too. Back in Atlanta, we got a Coca-Cola on ice if we behaved, but in France, particularly in *la France profonde* that was the ever-so-rural Creuse department at the time, nobody thought anything much about offering everyone, little children included, thimble-sized drams of local liqueur (*la goutte*, literally "the drop"), usually homemade applejack or cherry-infused liqueur. It was custom to greet visitors that way.

The workday was broken for the adults at La Chezotte by a return to the farmhouse around 4 p.m. for red wine and huge slabs of bread and cheese and *saucisson sec* carved out and eaten with pocketknives. We got to sample the meat, bread and cheese—I'd gotten my first small pocketknife about this time—while André and his helper eased their wooden sabots off their feet. Back at the chateau, Grandmother Elvira presided over daily tea on the terrace or under a tent set up just across the moat. It was quiet and peaceful there, often the only sound the buzzing of bees and wasps lighting into a bee-bait contraption full of rose-colored sugar water and fiery spirits.

We children had the run of the entire property. We helped feed the flock of chickens in the barnyard, and learned to tuck a chicken's head under its wing to disorient it before it got its head chopped off, and then how to pluck its feathers. We learned how to liberate fresh cow's milk from the cream in a hand-cranked separator. We fed the rabbits in the rabbit hutch. On one memorable afternoon, I remember going with André to hunt for rabbit with a big hunting dog, which netted a large hare, quickly hung outside the farmhouse. André bled the animal with a deft knife punch to the eyes, dribbling the fresh blood into a plate of raw onions (quickly eaten later that day), and then peeled the fur off the animal like a pajama. The guts were quickly distributed to the farmer's hunting dogs.

On Saturdays and Sundays, after a big lunch complete with hard cider made from the local apples, Francis would spend the afternoon working the complicated crossword puzzle in the *Paris-Match* magazine, often with the help of Marie-Louise (Marise) Tavernier, a family friend who often spent summers at La Chezotte. Marie-Louise was a Red Cross nurse who had tried to help the hapless Jewish victims of the *Vel d'Hiv* pogrom in Paris during the war. Another family friend was something of a sensitive, and could locate a person's exact location on Michelin maps with the help of a gold chain and pendant, which fascinated the children. One of Grandmother Elvira's friends from Colombia, Maria-Teresa

Saravia, another regular at La Chezotte, spent hours painting watercolor still-lifes of the many bouquets pulled out of the flower garden. My mother stayed busy hand-knitting sweaters for all the children, and sometimes enlisted our aid in turning skeins into more useful balls of wool.

When we got bumps and scrapes and bruises, Manelle turned to a medieval pharmacopoeia of remedies: Tincture of arnica for bumps and bruises; pure alcohol for cuts; Balm of the Pyrenees (a cocoa-butter base), and an Inotyol salve, for burns; charcoal dust for stomach-aches; a steam inhalation for colds, and a mustard plaster for chest congestion. For truly serious fever, she'd resort to using cupping glasses. This entailed burning a bit of alcohol in a glass, turning it upside down on the afflicted's back, which created a vacuum that "pulled the fever and infection" from the skin. Usually, a half-dozen glasses were placed on our backs. Manelle served as mother to all six children in many respects, nurturing us as my mother did not seem comfortable doing, and did not believe she was expected to do, according to her understanding of what was proper. Mothers were made to run the household—as *maitresses de maison*—but not necessarily get involved in the sometimes grubby, difficult business of raising kids. Manelle used a native intellectual curiosity to spark general learning in the children. In Atlanta, she drilled us unmercifully in French grammar so we could write in both French and English. In France, Manelle stocked up on all the patent medicines and collected dried linden tree flowers to be used in infusions in Atlanta. Lavender, thyme and other herbs were harvested and dried, and placed in sachets to keep bugs away from the linen.

Once a week at La Chezotte, everyone would pile into a car (I remember a pre-war-vintage Citroën) and go to the large outdoor market at Guéret, capital of the Creuse department. Grandmother's chauffeur made daily treks to the nearest village, Ahun, for fresh bread and croissants. On Sundays, there was church in the village of Ahun, where the parish priest would permit the Gatins boys to pull the bell rope to summon parishioners to mass. The priest would come out to La Chezotte and its private chapel for special occasions, such as the first communions for Charles, Sophie, Martin and Eglé, with mass celebrated in the chateau's private chapel. (I made my first communion in Atlanta, Miguel in Colombia).

Everyone took long afternoon walks, picking wild blackberries along the many small pathways edged with centuries-old rock walls, the same country byways Sylvia and Francis had traversed when they hid out during the last months of the war. Or, we took to nearby fields and with Manelle watching nearby, did endless cartwheels and games of leapfrog. Or Baptiste, Elvira's loyal butler, would take the boys fishing. Charles always had the most luck. Baptiste, whether digging for worms in the manure pile, or collecting wood for the fireplace, also had a knack for awakening the venomous pit vipers that inhabited the Creuse. He'd quickly dispatch them with a hatchet or hoe.

Talk of war often dominated the conversation. Francis would tell and retell the stories about German patrols coming to La Chezotte, and how he and Baptiste had buried the family's shotguns in the garden, and how they were so rusted after the war that they never could be used again. How Francis had helped dig up the four murdered Italian laborers and later helped set up their memorial marker. How he hid out from time to time in small gardener's hut at the far end of the vegetable garden. During the summer of 1957, Sylvia and Francis took special pains to thank all the local *Creusois* who had helped them during the war. They threw an energetic drinking and singing party at La Chezotte on July 14 (French independence day). I remember how proud I was to have been asked to sing at the party. Dozens of farmers and villagers from miles around came to the chateau to be fêted, and to toast their friends, Francis and Sylvia. Some came in old cars or jammed onto a tractor, but most either walked or biked to the party.

That same summer, the couple took me, Charles and Sophie on a quick trip to Switzerland, to see the village of Gruyères, where Francis had first started to fall in love with Sylvia in 1939, and Pontrésina, the Alpine resort town where Francis had spent so much of his youth mountain climbing. For five days, Francis, wearing hobnailed boots, hiked us up and down nearby mountain paths. At times, when we were above the snow line, he would break into bawdy French Army marching songs, which (my wife says) are the only songs I can sing on key.

All this happened under the watchful eye of Grandmother Elvira, whom we grandchildren remember as *Abuelita* German-Ribon, nicknamed Pata. She was a colorful character, quick to dispense treats to her grandchildren. She chain-smoked Craven A cigarettes, played flamenco guitar for us, and taught us card games like solitaire or Canasta, which she played for high stakes once a week with other Colombian expatriate women in Paris. When she lost, she would issue a terse "*ai, caramba.*" She was comfortable showing emotion. Often when saying good-bye to us, her tears would flow. Pata never saw a *patisserie* that did not require a stop and purchase of croissants, brioches and innumerable *pains au chocolat*. She put out a lavish table daily, spiced with odd dishes that the children got nowhere else—rice with fried eggs and plantains on the side, for example, or frothy hot chocolate with a piece of *Gruyère* cheese melted into the cup. Pata was definitely an international bon vivant, whose self-flagellation as a young teen was well behind her and who, thank God, did not try to pass that practice on to her grandchildren!

Eglé, nicknamed Mé by the children, was more reserved than Pata and something of a saint, when it came to self-denial. Servants saw her that way, and Manelle reported that Grandmother Eglé made a particular point of taking on physical pain, holding her legs away from the floor when kneeling at the prayer stools at Chaillot parish in Paris, which I remember as being the most uncomfortable kneelers ever devised. With Grandmother Eglé, there were hardly ever any tears. As my sister Eglé recalled her, our Grandmother Eglé was "a bit hard, opinionated and severe," while Pata was "warm and loving, but difficult."

In sharp contrast, the family spent the next summer (1958) on Sylvia's territory, the expansive high-altitude savannah outside Bogotá, Colombia, where her brother Miguel and his family lived. It proved an intriguing, eye-opening visit to a very different culture and gave us a much better feel for our German-Ribon grandmother, so different in so many ways from Grandmother Eglé. That summer, the family was still living large, so flush that my parents bought a Ford station wagon in Atlanta and had it shipped to Bogotá to get around Colombia. My siblings and I remember the trip to Colombia as something of a special interlude. We had to get special immunization shots, more than when going to France. We stayed with Uncle Miguel, Aunt Laura and their two sons on a large country property outside Bogotá, a large-walled *finca* with exquisitely manicured lawns, flower gardens, a man-made lake, tennis court, horses for riding, and a veritable army of servants. Sometimes the horses were saddled, sometimes we rode them bareback, using an old rope as makeshift halter. To this day, the six children have indelible memories of that summer: Visits to neighboring *fincas* and their polo ponies and bulls being tested for the bullfighting rings, the grinding poverty of the urban poor and often-barefoot peasantry, a side trip to the Colombian coast city of Cartagena where half-naked little boys dove for coins thrown off the sides of a boat. New tropical fruit, like guava, which was made into a special jelly. Visits to huge waterfalls and hot springs.

Another side trip took us over the mountains surrounding the savannah plateau where Bogotá is located and down into semi-tropical coffee country, where we visited a plantation founded by one Carlos Rodriguez, arranged like a French village, complete with theater and blue-and-white Parisian street signs. Of course, we had to make a special stop to visit the village church in this *tierra caliente*. There was only one sign of life inside, a big poisonous snake coiled on the stone flooring, sunning itself in a ray of sunlight. A worker was called, machete at the ready. He cut it to pieces, striking sparks on the stones as he put the snake to death.

This was the last vacation the entire Gatins family took together.

Chapter 29

Tabasco in Buckhead

Atlanta in 1952 still had the feel of small town, with a population of about 430,000, a far cry from the 5.3 million people living in its metropolitan area today. Most of its people were either black or white. Atlanta's multicultural Hispanic and Asian population booms were still decades away. Buckhead, a tree-covered neighborhood where the Gatins family made its permanent home, had just been annexed into the city. It was then essentially a small crossroads commercial area at the intersection of Peachtree, Roswell and Paces Ferry roads, with a barbershop, a menswear shop, a sports shop, hardware and stationery stores, the Wender & Roberts drugstore and the Buckhead Cinema. Lenox Square did not yet exist and Phipps Plaza (now another expansive covered shopping mall) was still a smallish enclave of black residents known as Johnson Town. In contrast to today's sub-urban sprawl, the Atlanta environs were still mostly played out farmland dotted with low pine forest hardscrabbling out of the area's deep red clay soils.

The world that the Gatins family moved within also was small geographically, bracketed by home, Christ the King Cathedral (the Catholic church less than four blocks away), the Piedmont Driving Club, the Georgian Terrace Hotel in mid-town and, a bit farther downtown, the Davison's and Rich's department stores and the small office Francis and his small import company, Allied Trading Company, Inc., shared with several other business people. Municipal trolleys powered by overhead electric wires connected Buckhead to downtown via Peachtree Street. Decatur and Dekalb County were another country, Roswell and Marietta, rural outposts.

The couple stood out within that world, given their foreignness, their accents, their obvious and sometimes ostentatious wealth and, in Francis' case, a reputa-tion for the unexpected. One of those times when Mother was in Paris with the children, Francis attended a dance at the Piedmont Driving Club, in the company of a family friend, Joan Zillessen, then unmarried and called Joan Smith. "He got to waving a switchblade around the P.D.C. bar that night," Zillessen recalled, which would have been most unusual in the button-downed world of that private club. Jack Spalding, another old family friend, and the eventual editor of *The Atlanta Journal*, remembered him this way after his death. "Your dad was like a drop of Tabasco on the Atlanta scene."

Sylvia stood out, too, according to contemporaries. She did her hair differently than other women in Atlanta. She was blunt and had an earthy side that was a real novelty in the equally buttoned-down woman's world of Atlanta in the early 1950s. Gina Kennedy, a social friend, recalled Sylvia teaching various Atlanta women how to make French croissants. Rolling out the pastry dough, Sylvia alluded to the shape of the croissant and that she looked forward to "taking care of Francis tonight." The ladies of Atlanta were shocked—but also delighted to hear someone speak freely about sex, Gina recalled. Sylvia also delighted in needling American historical sensibilities, once engaging in a vigorous argument with friends about whether President George Washington had smoked pot, to the puzzlement of two young men in the room that day. (Whether the first president smoked the weed is unclear, but he did grow hemp on his Virginia plantation outside Washington.) Sylvia often would be asked if she intended to become a naturalized American citizen. Never! "First, the United States would have to give Panama and the canal back to Colombia," she would say.

The permanent move to Atlanta represented the first time, except for their honeymoon period at La Chezotte, that both Francis and Sylvia had truly lived apart and really away from their mothers. They charted their own social course. They entertained and were entertained, following the unofficial motto, "Let's not be boring." About once a year or so, they invited the membership of the Alliance Francaise to the house on for a well-attended lecture and cocktail party. Every year, they held an expansive party at the Georgian Terrace Hotel in connection with the annual visit of the Metropolitan Opera, a party that started well before the opening act and usually enticed many opera-goers back to the hotel at intermission. For such occasions, Sylvia, fingernails lacquered, hair coiffed, and wrists heavily perfumed, wore Dior dresses acquired the last time they were in France. Francis looked resplendent in a maroon smoking jacket and patent leather black pumps, gold cufflinks on his tuxedo shirt, his gold cigarette case tucked inside the jacket.

They used finger bowls for special dinner parties—a rarity in Atlanta—and Sylvia spent hours manufacturing delectable gourmet sauces from recipes she'd learned at the Cordon Bleu school in Paris. These parties sometimes turned boisterous, with loud peals of laughter and a bit of rebel wildness in the air. Quintessentially Southern men with quintessentially Southern names like Finlay and Strother, Phinizy and Welborn, and Sims and Willis downed their drinks, which were given an extra measure of liquor; the silver jigger was actually my baby orange juice cup, which held an extra ounce of liquid more than most jiggers. Some of the crowd entertained the children with parlor tricks, one man in particular, who could make an entire deck of cards disappear from his large right hand—and then "remove" his thumb as well.

Sometimes, our parents' dinners and gatherings would take on a bizarre air. My father would entertain the guests as Sylvia called them from the red room to the dinner table, leaping from a small three-legged milkmaid's stool into a heel-clicking salute, right arm outstretched: "Heil Hitler, Sylvia!" usually followed by an incongruous cackle of laughter. A commemorative SS ceremonial dagger kept on the windowsill behind the couch in the red room often was a conversation piece. Unnerving and strange as this might seem to the outsider, this was just passed off as Francis being Francis—never boring.

In retrospect, my father was probably turning the corner into serious alcoholism around this time. Just like his own father, Sylvia, and later the boys, he developed a strong taste for Scotch whisky, in particular the King William IV brand. Anyone who believes that alcoholic allergies are not a genetically driven family malady does not comprehend the disease of alcoholism. Like his father before him, Francis eventually succumbed to the deadly spiral of acute alcoholism. Only, no one called it that at home. He's just drunk, Mother would say, mixing disdain, exasperation, sadness and excuse in the same breath. No one ever breathed the term alcoholic at the home, nor was there ever any mention of my grandfather, who had been shipped off to "disintoxification houses." No talk of shipping Daddy to a rehab joint. Getting drunk, as the children saw it in the 1950s and 1960s, was just one of those things, a part of day-to-day life. As children and grandchildren of alcoholics, they were simply bewildered by the drunkenness and really had no idea until many decades later how it was affecting them emotionally, psychically and spiritually.

During the day, Daddy went downtown, where he and other small business people shared an office in the Candler Building. Those who knew him then recall that the office, sparsely furnished except for stacks of yellow legal pads and a large crystal bowl full of impeccably sharpened yellow pencils, served as the jumping-off point to long, multiple-martini lunches, usually at Herren's Restaurant nearby. On the way home, there was usually time for a quick refresher at the Georgian Terrace Hotel, or at the bar of the Piedmont Driving Club, where he sometimes spent hours observing the high-stakes gin rummy games that took place there daily. For some, this essentially was a cocktail-driven society, where three-martini lunches and scotch-on-the-rocks at 5 p.m. were part of daily adult routine.

Francis, the great-grandson of a likely Yankee sympathizer—no one is quite sure if he knew of this fact—also spent countless hours studying the Civil War, obviously taken with the Lost Cause. He took the children on frequent visits to the Cyclorama (a large painting depicting the battle for Atlanta in 1864) and Kennesaw Mountain battlefields, where Confederate forces had put up a last, brave stand before Atlanta fell to Sherman's forces. He bought records of Civil War ballads, playing Dixie and the Yellow Rose of Texas *ad nauseam* on the record player. He took the entire family to see *Gone With the Wind* when it came to town for re-release in 1956 and 1961. (The crush on re-opening night at the old Loew's Grand Theater in 1961 was horrific. People were pushing and shoving madly to get in line to get tickets.) At weddings, Francis, with the help of his old drinking buddy from the days of the Club 122 in Paris, Sims Bray, would declaim a dog-gerel "Good Old Rebel Song," to the tune of the Georgia Institute of Technology fight song, "Ramblin' Wreck from Georgia Tech," hoping to shock any Yankees in the wedding party. The boys in the family took to this rebel business with gusto.

It cannot be overestimated how memory of the Lost Cause suffused Georgia and Atlanta in the 1950s. Gov. Herman Talmadge has just been succeeded by an equally adamant segregationist, Marvin Griffin. Confederate flags flew every-where after the state flag was changed in 1956 to include the stars and bars, as a protest to the U.S. Supreme Court's desegregation ruling, Brown v. Board of Education. The little Studebaker sedans still driving around Atlanta traded in their "I Like Ike" bumper stickers for vanity license plates depicting a scruffy, mustachioed soldier in grey. The tagline: "Fergit, Hell!" Sometimes, sinister-look-ing redneck ruffians rode around town with Ku Klux Klan posters affixed to the sides of their big sedans, sidearms on their dashboards, after another cross burn-ing on the top of Stone Mountain.

Sylvia, meanwhile, busied herself with church, school, running the household and, with the extraordinary help of Manelle and Bernice, the care and feeding of the children, and instilling in them proper notions of French behavior. "Children are meant to be seen and not heard," she'd say. "One must be as well-behaved as an engraved image" (*sage comme une image*). Following a European model, the children were drilled in the discipline of being orderly in public, of putting on a brave public face. The boys had to shine six pairs of shoes daily, theirs and their sisters'. The girls had to iron their wool skirts, pinning each pleat and steaming it into order. At Christmas, Manelle drilled the children into putting on a nativity pageant in French, costumed in homemade versions of Middle Eastern garb. But there was huge reward at Christmastime for those of the children who believed in Santa Claus. The living room a week ahead of time was sealed off with a big sheet for *Père Noël's* arrival, and only unveiled after breakfast on the 25th of December—I remember I could hardly wait. It was magical to see the tree with all its ornaments and the multitude of gifts. We would say a prayer *en famille* and then sing a few Christmas carols around the tree, also in French, before diving into the gifts.

Discipline was left mostly to Manelle who, especially in Charles' case, sometimes found it necessary to apply a solid slap of the *martinet*, a leather whip used to discipline children in France. This was part of a home and church culture that also had rigid religious duties, more of it drummed into us by Mother than by Father. Heaven was a very nice place. Hell was a living, breathing and fiery damnation, with purgatory not much better, however temporary one's stay there might be. The family said its nightly prayers on its knees. If there was a new Catholic church, we'd visit to say a prayer, or light a candle at the altar. The Catholic faith of my childhood still trafficked in something called indulgences, a tally wherein one could secure favors as far as getting into heaven was concerned (or shortening one's stay in purgatory). If one spent a franc or a dime to buy a candle, that was one indulgence. Three Hail Marys and three Our Fathers, that was another indulgence. Visiting a new church added to our total, too, each indulgence putting us a step closer to eternal bliss. While this practice was severely abused in the early years of the Catholic church and led, in part, to the Protestant Reformation, we took every opportunity, it seemed, to visit and light candles at every Catholic church we ever saw, whether in America or in France, and to invoke the names of patron saints at every opportunity. One summer, Mother led a family pilgrimage to Lourdes. We all secured many more indulgences for every rosary we said during that visit (and came back with several thermos-fuls of holy Lourdes water). What I recall most about Lourdes is that some of the faithful crawled up to the Lourdes grotto on their knees; that had to hurt like hell, I thought.

In keeping with a practice of Roman Catholicism that was as much superstition as religion, Sylvia made sure a crucifix hung over every one of our beds. Angels were important, too. Each of the children had his or her own personal protective angel to call upon when beset by childhood fears or turmoil. Of course, we all wore scapulars under our shirts, as a private sign of Catholic devotion and Godly protection. We went to High Mass every Sunday, said at that time in Latin. Women wore mantillas or kerchiefs to cover their heads. Sometimes, on holy days, the priests would spread the pungent smell of resinous incense from the censers that they would swing around the altars, leading some women to faint from the heat and the piquant odor of the burning spices.

Francis, while faithful enough in the Catholic practice of going to mass on Sundays, had a much more skeptical, intellectual and worldly view of the church than Sylvia. He was prone to talk about its sham aspects, as well as the writers, theologians and thinkers who wrote about it. He knew, for example, who Pope Joan had been, and could recite chapter and verse of the corruption of the Borgian pope, Alexander VI. The veritable panoply of saints revered in France was part of the reason he was most often called Francis, rather than Joe or Joseph. His grandmother, the formidable Jeanne de Madec Fischer, had insisted on calling him Francis because Joseph, to her mind, was one of the patron saints of cuckolds. French Catholics paid homage to an army of patron saints, carefully chosen from among the more than 10,000 individuals sanctified by the Vatican. By contrast, Sylvia was possessed of a more emotional faith, replete with ceremony, devotions, superstition, and many, many rosaries dedicated to the Virgin Mary. Jesus also lived in our midst in the form of a large polychrome bust of a very pained-looking Christ, sallow in color except for the blood dripping out of his chest wound and the crown of thorns on his head, which greeted visitors in the entrance hall. The "constipated Christ," Daddy wryly called it.

Having Manelle at home permitted Sylvia and Francis to take extended weekend trips, often with other couples. Sometimes, Charles and I went with them. There were fishing trips to Florida and Opelika, Alabama; weekend mountain getaways to Highlands, North Carolina, and Tate, Georgia; boating trips to Watts Bar Lake in Tennessee; weekend escapes to the hydro-power lakes in Rabun County, Georgia; and later, after the Chattahoochee River was dammed, to Lake Lanier. There were quick Appalachian treks to the Indian reservation at Cherokee and weekend excursions to Gatlinburg, Tennessee, and the Great Smoky Mountains National Park. Besides La Chezotte and Switzerland, I don't think I ever saw my father quite so much at peace as when he was hiking a mountain trail, walking the beach or guiding the tiller of small outboards on the lakes of north Georgia and east Tennessee.

Somewhat restless, Francis also permitted himself occasional, men-only duck and pheasant hunting trips to south Georgia, or quick escapes to the Kentucky hunt country or the summer resort towns of Lake Michigan. It helped that one of his companions, a builder and general contractor named Frank O'Neil, flew his own private plane on these bachelor-like escapes. One time, my father and O'Neil flew all the way to Michigan to pick up my brother Charles, who had been vacationing with a good friend, George Branch, whose family often spent their summers there. Daddy served as navigator on this trip—by looking down below and following Interstate 75. But neither he nor Sylvia ever trekked west of the Mississippi to see the rest of the vast United States, which, when I think about it, seems to mean they had only an East Coast curiosity.

When Daddy was away, Sylvia sometimes took all the children to the Terrace for lunch, to show the flag, as it were. We would have to get dressed up, which was a pain for the children, but we learned new things during these outings, like the hotel restaurant only used thousand island dressing on its salads. At home, a tart vinaigrette was all we knew. The lamb chops at the hotel came all dressed up with frilly paper booties to keep the fat from dripping all over one's fingers.

Francis' business, which began with the importation of ladies gloves from Belgium and later, of gold-leafed picture frames from Italy, finally settled into a more regular routine when he became the southeast representative for a German hardware manufacturer. That work took him on the road from Miami to Washington, calling on small hardware retailers and textile plants across deep Dixie and the spine of Southern Appalachia, to sell them pick mattocks, axe handles, sledgehammers and the like. He knew somebody in every small town, especially the textile mill towns that still dotted the South then, and where to find a drink in Bible-Belt locales that were still legally dry. The roads then were mostly two-laned blacktop (this was well before the Interstate highway era) and before all cars had air conditioning. To stay awake in mid-summer, Daddy said he would stop at a country restaurant every few hours for a glass of iced tea. Then, back on the road, also staying alert by tuning in to country and rock-and-roll radio stations that dotted the AM dial at the time (FM radio was still something of novelty). Daddy marveled at the goofiness of some of the songs he heard, especially the likes of *Itsy-Bitsy, Teenie-Weenie Yellow Polka Dot Bikini*, which came out in 1960. A year later, when I turned 15 and got my first driver's permit, I would accompany him on the back roads of the Deep South, where we often passed convict work gangs, usually toiling along road rights-of-way. They weren't locked to ball and chain anymore in Georgia, but were still attired in striped prison clothes. Daddy always would throw the prisoner gangs one of his packs of cigarettes, knowing from his prisoner-of-war years how tobacco served as currency behind barbed-wire fences. I saw him do this several times and did it myself through the 1970s.

One of the German company's representatives, a bald man with a big head, joined Francis on one of his business trips across the South. The trip ended in Miami, which provoked a strange flashback from the former Rawa-Ruska prisoner. "We were at the hotel trying to get a drink, but it was six-deep with Jews," he recalled years later, around a steak barbecue at home. "So, we started talking in very loud voices about the camps in Poland and what it was like unloading the cattle cars. We got our drinks in a hurry." At odd times, like the middle of Sunday dinner, Daddy would relate wartime and prisoner-of-war stories, for entertainment or shock value, or to take the measure of the men present, or perhaps in a misguided attempt to exorcise painful chapters from his scarred life. While he never taught the rampant anti-Semitism of his youth to his children, it sometimes seemed to bubble up, as in the Miami bar story. It was as if he was more resentful of Jews for having been taken as one of them, and tortured for that reason, than at his Nazi torturers. Today, I wonder if he had a case of the "Stockholm syndrome," in which prisoners and hostages show loyalty, rather than hate, to the captors who abused them. In contrast to the sentiments he voiced in letters to Sylvia during the "phony war," Daddy never spoke ill of the German soldiers afterward, often declaiming that they had always treated him perfectly correctly. "They were just doing their job," he'd say. Contrast that to what he wrote Sylvia in 1940: "Don't consider this war like a crusade. I'm in this not for an idea, a principle or a sentiment, but simply to kill as many Germans as possible, including women and children, so that our children, at least, can live in peace. Without hate or passion, I want the destruction of Germany."

If he'd somehow excused the Germans, Jews were another matter. Don't wear your caps and hats inside the house, Daddy would say. "The only people who wear hats inside are Jews." Francis liked to assume a pro-Palestinian stand when it came to political affairs of the Middle East, and he often penned letters to the editor of the local newspapers that voiced this position. While he did very little to explain his resentment, or the anti-Semitic training of his youth, the blunt harshness of his attitudes toward Jews was often unmistakable.

More often than not, though, the conversation around the dinner table and during Daddy's outings with his children turned to more general affairs of war, which were never far from his mind and, therefore, from the minds of his children. While he forever carried (and never really managed to exorcise) the burden of his prisoner-of-war traumas, it also was plain that he had never been more alive than during the war, having to hone instincts for survival to an unusual degree.

Sometimes, out of nowhere, the children would hear him say, "There is no one tougher than a God-damned U.S. Marine," a statement often used to elicit comment and thereby take the measure of other men and contemporaries, and to quickly find out what they had done during the war. It was clear from this kind of talk he did not appreciate wimps, who, as he put it, "had never slept with a man or a woman."

So, whether crisscrossing country lanes for blackberries in France or listening to the chatter around the dinner table, the children paid close attention to the war talk and the lessons of life that they provided. They inhaled all the tales about escaping from the Germans and learned multiple, if unusual, lessons from those conversations. These lessons often emanated from Daddy on weekend hikes along the Chattahoochee River, or Sope Creek or up to the top of the only mountains within easy striking distance of Atlanta, Stone Mountain and Kennesaw Mountain. At the time, the riverine areas were still fairly remote from Atlanta's population centers, jungled places cross-hatched by muddy jeep trails cutting through old tree stands and dense underbrush, and we children often had them to ourselves. Stone Mountain, best known for its huge carving of Confederate icons Jefferson Davis, Robert E. Lee and Stonewall Jackson, also was the site of the rebirth of the hyper-racist Ku Klux Klan in 1915. It routinely was used for KKK ceremonies and cross burnings during my childhood and early teens. At Kennesaw, Daddy usually would lead the children to "Little Kennesaw," a smaller outcrop that was still dotted with the remains of Confederate defense trenches from 1864, which he used to teach us all the fine art of *défilade* and *enfilade* military ambush tactics. By then, all the children knew Daddy's marching songs, used to keep us going uphill and down. But woe to those who did not want to keep up the pace. Francis would break into a mocking French ditty about weaklings "crying like a fountain" in an effort, it seemed, to "toughen up" his brood.

Sometimes, these expeditions included a fun stop at The Varsity, a drive-in restaurant renowned for its chili hot dogs and french-fried onion rings, or ice-skating at the old Lakewood Fairgrounds. One Saturday, Daddy packed all the children up in the station wagon and took us to Atlanta fire station No. 27 on Northside Drive for a memorable outing. I never found if he'd won a bet from, cut a deal with, or simply implored Jesse Draper, one of Atlanta's aldermen, to let the firefighters give the Gatins children a private ride on one of the city's fire trucks. It was a grand day, roaring down Mt. Paran Road, pulling the rope that activated the truck's fire siren, all the way to the house of one of Daddy's fishing buddies. The occupants rushed outside, thinking their house was on fire!

Sometimes, these outings were mainly for the boys only, to teach them how to shoot, for example. One memorable afternoon, the Gatins boys and a passel of other young men were brought by their fathers to a Kennedy family cabin on a bluff overlooking the Chattahoochee to get an unforgettable lesson in shooting from Bobby Lamar "Lucky" McDaniel, an expert marksman from South Georgia whose "instinct shooting" techniques were legend. He had us lighting matches on the ground with BB guns and hitting clay pigeons with .22 rifles before the day was out.

And always, there was talk of war and its many lessons. Among them:

- Trust no one and never forgive informants. Francis said a fellow prisoner had turned him in during an early escape attempt from a work detail. Decades later, he still sent the snitch one letter per year, with the same message every year: "You little shit, if I ever see you again, I'll cut your balls off."

- Attempt escape alone. "You're under nervous tension [with a fellow escapee]," he told a newspaper interviewer in 1951. "You spend all the time fighting, you feel like the other is making more noise, he is eating more, and you argue about which direction to take."

- Choose your priests carefully. A Catholic priest turned him in during his second escape attempt, after refusing him asylum in a church sanctuary. For the rest of his life, Francis was careful in choosing which priests to be friends with. He was especially fond of a Dominican in Paris, who had shared time with him in the prison camps, even though this cleric had repeatedly denied him permission to drink the wine reserved for mass. In Georgia, he found solace with members of the Monastery of the Holy Spirit, a Trappist monastery in Conyers, which he visited periodically for silent weekend retreats. I accompanied him on one of the Holy Spirit retreats as a boy of eight or nine. I have no real idea why I was there among the monks who practiced permanent silence. It might have been part of my mother's overall vision to dedicate one of her sons to the priesthood. My guess today is that Daddy was still trying to exorcise the dark evil, shame and guilt he'd experienced during the stay in the Rawa-Ruska prisoner-of-war punishment camp and perhaps make spiritual amends for having taken part, however unwillingly, in the diabolical history of the Holocaust.

- Develop and trust your sense of smell. "Daddy used to tell us he always could smell when someone was dying, or when they were to be executed the next day. They smelled like dust." Other smells were gruesomely unmistakable, like the dead Soviet woman shot and left to rot outside the barbed wire of one camp. "They called her Chanel No. 5."

- Learn to navigate at night. The North Star on clear nights could serve as a reference point; and a rising moon, up until it became a half-moon, could be used to point southward. Draw an imaginary straight line from the top of the moon through its lower tip down to the earth—that way points south, he often told his children.

- Avoid walking on dry leaves. They make noise, which prison guards can use to find escaped prisoners. Francis hardly ever failed to remind his children of that fact when they took walks in the woods around Atlanta.

- Stay warm. To survive harsh winters in prison camps without blanket or overcoat, cuddle up like spoons with fellow prisoners and blow your hot breath onto your neighbor's back. Daddy spontaneously demonstrated this maneuver on a young woman for a somewhat nonplussed band of dinner guests in Atlanta well after the war. When your shoes and boots wear out, wrap your feet in newspaper or blankets.

- When escaping, don't walk when you can take the train. In his first escape, Francis simply walked off a work detail. Subsequently, he found it better to take the train.

These teachings and other topics of discussion also were imparted at meals at a long, highly lacquered mahogany dining table. (Given my mother's superstitions, she never permitted 13 at the table at the same time, lest one be a Judas-like betrayer. In such cases, Mother would set up a separate card table to arrive at a proper number of people for dinner.) Everyone served themselves buffet style and took part in what often turned into a cacophony, loud give-and-take on the events of the day: Racial integration, the latest priest assigned to Christ the King parish. Everyone learned to be quick about getting a word into the conversation. Eglé, after returning to Atlanta to be with the family, always ate her meal hurriedly without saying very much, as if she could not wait for the meals to be over, witness as she was to the rampant and active alcoholism all around her. The conversations swirling around the table were often in both French and English—and woe to the poor visitor who could not follow both languages.

When discipline needed to be meted out, regardless of which child was guilty of a behavioral infraction, Daddy usually meted it out to all the children, often herding them into line with liberal (but fairly gentle) swats of his belt and barking orders he'd often heard in Germany: "Los, los" (faster, faster), "Schnell, schnell" (on the double), or "Balek, balek" (out of the way, in Arabic). He also would call out the words, "Fissa, fissa," probably meaning "Quick, quick" in Arabic.

Inevitably, the children at one time or another asked their father if he had killed anyone during the war. He'd usually brush away the question, saying that he did not know if he'd ever hit anyone when he fired back in his first and only skirmish with German forces before being captured in 1940. He repeatedly stressed that he never held anything against the German soldiers who had been his guards and his enemies. The fact that Francis owed his job to a German concern whose principals included some of those very soldiers was simply one of those odd life connections that added to the aura of foreignness that enveloped the Gatins family in Atlanta.

By the late 1950s, the German hardware enterprise evolved into a partnership with an Atlanta businessman, with offices on 14th Street, under the name Cargo Sales Co. It was a few blocks away from the Piedmont Driving Club and its bar and, just as important, a small, efficient automobile body shop at the intersection of 14th and Peachtree streets that could ding out and repaint body damage to one's car the same day it was brought in.

As the children grew, Francis traded in a wood-panel Ford station wagon for a roomier, 1958 blue Ford station wagon with a powerful V-8 motor, which he used on his road trips and family trips to the beach those years they did not go abroad for the summer. Daddy taught all the children (and several of their teenage friends) to drive a stick shift on this station wagon, taking over the ample parking lots and entrance lanes to the private Westminster Schools property as a driving course.

A garage apartment behind the house was let for rent, serving as temporary shelter for a varied set of interesting people, including young unmarried couples looking for privacy, an internationally renowned concert pianist, a Cuban refugee family, and two young college graduates whose bourbon-fueled bachelor parties in the little guest house often lasted until morning—we children would watch them jitterbug and boogie until all hours—and one of whose girlfriends drew a large charcoal nude in an erotic pose on the wall of the bedroom. To cure hangovers, the college roommates played recordings of William Faulkner reading some of his most famous books.

One day, a friend from Francis' time in New York, Mario Gabellini, dropped in unexpectedly, to Sylvia's undisguised displeasure; he was a reminder of Daddy's days on the prowl in Manhattan. It was a memorable visit, though. Daddy was in the driveway, the children running around him on their scooters, helping me build a new doghouse for Silly and Chibcha, the family's two hound dogs that had been fished out of the Chattahoochee River as puppies. Mario drove up in a tan-colored, tiny Renault Dauphine. He was out of gas and out of cash, asking for help in French, and looking for a place to stay before moving on to an appointment in Salt Lake City, where his first wife lived.

Help yourself, my father said. Mario pulled a long rubber hose from his trunk and siphoned several gallons of gas from the family station wagon into his car. To say thank you, he decided to cook an authentic pizza for the family. Into the kitchen he went, ordering Sylvia to find flour, eggs, salt and yeast for the crust; tomato paste, garlic, herbs, cheese and anchovies for the topping. He turned into a pizza dervish before the family's dazzled eyes, finally serving a memorable pizza pie to us and joining the panoply of memorable characters that Sylvia and Francis collected around them.

Very occasional visitors from France came to spend the night. Grandmother Elvira would spend several months at a time. Hopie Simpson and her sister, Dorothy, sometimes visited from New York. So did Uncle Ben. Aunt Mary hung out at the Terrace, becoming more of a recluse after her last divorce.

Mother was a whirlwind, keeping the house organized and well supplied, and the children properly clothed. Every other week or so, she would drive to the state farmers' market in southside Atlanta and pick up cases of fresh oranges from Florida, or cases of apples and peaches in season, and bananas, which were quickly gobbled up as after-school snacks by the children. In winter, all six kids stayed warm in sweaters knitted by Sylvia. At first, she knitted these by hand; later, she mass-produced them on a Swiss-made automatic knitting machine. Sylvia's kitchen was a home within the home. On its two stoves, the children watched her whipping up desserts and cakes, and got to taste the sugary batters; there on Saturday nights, they sometimes got to mass producing *crèpes Suzettes*, flipping them from their pans with ease before rolling them and stuffing them with raspberry jam, or deep-frying sugary *beignets*; and there, for several summers, all the children helped Sylvia make gallons of peach preserves. Perhaps in honor of Grandmother Elvira, who made them frothy hot chocolate at La Chezotte, Sunday nights were hot chocolate nights for the children, along with plenty of hot buns and butter. Every Christmas Day lunch, Mommy would whip up a buttery *bûche de Noel* and Daddy would pour flaming rum over a plum pudding. Sunday lunches, to Francis' delight, often included *pot-au-feu*, boiled beef brisket and vegetables, which reminded him of the simple food at La Chezotte. Sugar, however, was the essential and key ingredient of the Gatins children's diet, so much so that we were offered cubes of refined sugar dipped in black coffee if we'd behaved at the Sunday dinner table.

Yet, in spite of the French-ness of home and Sylvia's best efforts, some of us began behaving like typical American kids. Completely unlike his own upbringing, Francis drilled the children in the value of hard work, getting jobs and doing well in their studies. I bagged groceries at the Garden Hills Grocery store for several Christmas seasons, later working the holidays with my brothers for Irving Gresham, owner of a downtown florist shop and one of Father's favorite lunchtime companions.

Sylvia tried to instill a love of classical music and opera in the three older children, taking them to the occasional Atlanta symphony concert. In my case, there was also dancing instruction in the 7th grade. Truth to tell, we were more attuned to the melodies coming out of our crystal radios and car radios, rock-and-roll from Elvis and Jerry Lee Lewis, rhythm-and-blues from the likes of James Brown and The Famous Flames or Dr. Feelgood and the Interns. The transition from the class-conscious polish of Europe to the more democratic brashness of America was subtle, but unmistakable. And after the many changes Francis and Sylvia had already lived through in the 1940s and 1950s, a whole new set of problems was revealed in the dawn of the 1960s, another period of great social change. These proved to be their free spending ways and the family's growing dependence on gin, vodka, Scotch whisky, six-packs of beer and cheap Gallo table wine.

Chapter 30

New Reality of the 1960s

For the Gatins children, the 1960s largely are remembered as an accumulation of small, often-disturbing family episodes that incrementally led us to realize that things no longer were the same on Rivers Road, or in Paris. Small things, at first. Having been sent away to prep school in 1959, I remember coming home at Christmas and for summer vacations to find my father subject to huge coughing fits. Daddy had switched to smoking Kool cigarettes, but the menthol had no effect. He often seemed to have withdrawn into himself, reading quietly or seemingly daydreaming on a comfortable armchair in the red room, an enclosed porch that served as a sitting room. It was hard to break through his shell of isolation during this period. I had been looking forward to coming home to Atlanta from school in far-away Rhode Island, touched with a bit of homesickness. It was a rude awakening to realize that everything was not perfect at home.

Everyone in the family grew accustomed to a very loud, strange and awful rasping sound coming from our parents' bedroom at night, haunting us through the walls and doors: Francis grinding his teeth. Daddy obviously was suffering from posttraumatic stress disorder, as it is termed today, and recognized by the medical community as an official mental disorder. It was called "soldier's heart" during the American Civil War; "shell shock" after World War I; "battle fatigue" and "combat neurosis" after World War II. According to one researcher, "more than 50 years after wartime internment, survivors of Nazi concentration camps continue to demonstrate post-traumatic symptomology as well as neurological concomitants, especially in the domain of verbal memory." Survivors, this researcher found, were prone to sleep disturbances as well as problems with nervousness, irritability, memory impairment, emotional instability and anxiety, all problems experienced later in life to one degree or another by my father. Daddy had been prophetic in previewing this internal confusion and uncertainty when he noted in his first letter to Sylvia as a prisoner (on July 15, 1940) that "I will never get over all of this." I don't think he ever found a way to fully exorcise, or talk himself out of, this turmoil. My sister Sophie, who found a second career as a licensed professional counselor, believes Daddy was trying to numb himself emotionally, in his case, by manifesting feelings of detachment, estrangement from others, alcoholism, irritability or outbursts of anger. Another recent study noted that posttraumatic stress disorder "shatters sufferers, sense of trust, intimacy, self-esteem and safety, often altering their behavior and making it difficult for them to reconnect with their families and old friends or to hold jobs." Some 88 percent of men and 79 percent of women with this disorder have "additional mental health issues, including substance abuse, mood disorders, anxiety disorders and unhealthy behaviors," according to that paper's author.

For my brother Miguel, the new reality sank in at family prayers one night, when it became obvious that Daddy was too drunk to kneel upright, and had to hold onto a chair. I never saw this, but later in the 1960s Francis would sometimes be found in the back yard, passed out on an old grass tennis court that once had served as a sandlot baseball diamond for me and my brother Charles and later as a dog run. Miguel would bring him back into the house and put him to bed, but it seemed to him Francis was reliving old escapades, catching sleep in the open outdoors, as he had had to do during any number of prison escapes.

Martin recalls that family money problems began around 1963, when Charles (who was hiding underneath a table in the living room) overheard Francis and Sylvia discussing the fact that they were "out of money." Charles had already contributed voluntarily to family cutbacks, transferring to a parochial high school in Atlanta from the more expensive prep school that he and I attended in Rhode Island. I got a scholarship, went on to graduate and was accepted into college, only to find during that summer of 1964 that a securities fund Mother and I thought was being saved for college costs had been sold off by Daddy years before. That was my financial kick in the gut, a real wake-up.

Up to that time, Francis and Sylvia had sought to insulate the children from their new financial realities, or only to hint at them indirectly. I remember taking a road trip up the east coast with Daddy in the early 1960s, partly to visit college campuses, but also so that he could confer with money managers in New York to try to increase yield on certain investments. That trip also provided an excuse to drop in on Mario Gabellini, who seemed to know everyone in every small Italian restaurant on New York's East Side, and who said hello in the most international of manners. "Ciao, ciao," he would say, with a slight wave of his right hand. I'd never heard that before.

In Paris, meanwhile, Grandmother Eglé was experiencing another family reversal of fortune, largely due to her brother's spending habits. What had been a substantial Fischer fortune had been frittered away to the point that Uncle Charlic was pawning some of the silver and household furnishings. His only real income was derived from ownership of a small printing press, and the small monthly allotment received from the French government for having won his own Chevalier de la Legion d'Honneur award after serving in both world wars. To make do after their mother died in 1957, brother and sister abandoned the expansive apartment on the Place des Etats-Unis and moved to a smaller, less costly place on rue Raynouard, but still in the tony, hyper-class conscious 16th arrondissement.

Grandmother put the move in the best light possible in her memoirs, explaining that the rent had become more and more expensive. "We were able to exchange it for a smaller apartment. It had a wonderful view, overlooking the Invalides, le Val de Grace," she said. "It was strange, but I had the impression I would not stay long in this place." In fact, events quickly came to a head. The loyal help told our grandmother that the silver and other objects were disappearing from the apartment. She confronted her brother, who got very huffy and told her finances were "none of a woman's business." She in turn got very angry with him. Charlic then had a stroke, fell into a coma, and never recovered. In Grandmother's written version of these events, much more expurgated, Charlic fell ill shortly after the move to the new apartment, and was hospitalized. Eglé sat at his bedside praying, and trekked every day to Sacré Coeur cathedral to pray for him. Physicians diagnosed him as having cirrhosis of the liver, she said, although he'd never been known as a heavy drinker. He lingered, unconscious, for about a month and died May 27, 1963. My father rushed to the funeral service at Chaillot and told his mother: "Now, it's over. You're going to come live with us in Atlanta. We have a little guest house behind ours that will be perfect for you."

First, though, he had to help untangle what was left of Charlic's and the Fischer estate. There was not much. Indeed, Grandmother Eglé and my father found a pile of debts and, according to the long letters Francis wrote to Mother that summer, evidence that Charlic had quietly been dipping into an employee benefit fund for a group of Paris actors, which he'd served as treasurer. He'd also managed to abscond with the quarterly checks Francis and Sylvia had been sending to France for Manelle's social security contributions to the French government and taken out substantial loans against the printing company's profits. My father's letters from that summer, which detailed the mess Charlic had left, were not saved, but mother read them out loud to the children at the dinner table. I remember them as if it were yesterday.

My father and grandmother reimbursed the social security and actors' funds, repaid the printing company loans, and assured the cost of her flight to the states and the shipment of some furniture, by auctioning off Charlie's *cabinet*, a valuable collection of books and monographs on the French Revolution. Her engagement ring also was sold to pay everything off, in a truly final break with her late husband. "We organized a sale that made a lot of money," Eglé recalled. "I was thus able to assure the move and my trip to the United States." She also sold off some additional furniture to the couple that had taken over the old apartment on Place des Etats-Unis. Finally, she resigned presidency of the Red Cross chapter for the 16th arrondissement, a post she had held since 1948.

Grandmother landed in Atlanta December 1, 1963, almost 50 years after the final separation from her husband. She was fondly remembered in the Georgia capital by her many women friends, even after all those years, and quickly renewed acquaintance with her cousin, Katherine Murphy Riley, (Katherine, then married to her third husband, had become one Atlanta's most financially secure and generous philanthropists, operating from the expansive mansion property on West Paces Ferry Road, Villa Juanita, which had been the scene of so many wild parties in her youth.) Later, after the death of her third husband, Jim Riley, she and other Atlanta women like her were called "Coca-Cola widows," living handsomely off the proceeds of Coke stock acquired early in that company's business cycle. Grandmother also reconnected with "my marvelous friend, Edna Thornton" and other old friends and made many new ones. "It was a series of dinners and cocktails," she recalled. "Everyone was so nice to me."

Indeed, Katherine and Edna were very generous, establishing small trust funds whose income helped tide over the essentially penniless Eglé in Atlanta. After close to 35 years of wearing the black garb of a widow, she purchased new shoes and neatly tailored grey suits, often worn with jaunty silk scarves. She got her hair done weekly. The Atlanta newspapers found her again, writing up yet another article about the Gatins family as a welcome-home present, this one by Yolande Gwin, the society columnist successor to the papers' Sally Forth, who had written about Grandmother in the 1930s.

ATLANTA CLAIMS MRS. GATINS

When the news swirled around that Eglé Gatins was coming back to Atlanta—to live, no less—her legion of friends were delighted and pleased.

After an absence of many years, she still was a favorite among a socially elite group here. Because of her very distinctive qualities, her ties of friendship here were not broken during her stay in her native Paris, but were actually strengthened.

"I have worked long and hard for other people and for the poor. Now, I want to rest and relax and enjoy my life with my grandchildren," she said.

The article described Grandmother's 23 years of work with the Red Cross in Paris, as well as her energetic efforts to get her son back from the prisoner camps in Germany. She described Atlanta as "home," while still retaining her French citizenship. The photograph accompanying the article, published in the spring of 1964, had all six of her grandchildren, dressed in Sunday best, surrounding their grandmother.

She moved into the old garage apartment behind the main house on Rivers Road (I'm the one who repainted it and blocked out the charcoal nude from the dining room), and turned it into the Atlanta version of the salon she'd inhabited in Paris, with many of the heaviest furniture pieces still intact. But there was hint of the incongruous, too. Two of her lamps were made of brass artillery shells from World War I. Still, it was a warm haven of gentility and quiet grace compared to the whirlwind habitually swirling in the big house. Most evenings, Daddy would spend some time at her little house, talking of current events and the gossip of the day, before escorting her to the main house for whatever dinner Sylvia had prepared. In winter, she kept the thermostat on "high," blasting heat throughout her new salon as if to forever banish memory of cold winters in Saranac and in Paris during the war.

Grandmother was as generous with her grandchildren as she could be. She scraped together enough cash to help my brother Charles purchase a used car, an old, pink-colored, four-door Rambler sedan with an amazing push-button gearshift off to the left of the steering column. It was very roomy, with an equally amazing feature that let the front seat fold backwards to make a huge bed inside the vehicle. Charles and his high-school buddies would take this bed-on-wheels to the drive-in movies after cruising to the liquor stores on Cheshire Bridge Road to get one of the hangers-on outside the stores to buy him and the under-aged group a case of beer. I had little need for such subterfuge, finding that most liquor and package stores in Atlanta at the time were happy to sell booze to any young man wearing long pants and tall enough to peer over the counter. For good measure, I had a doctored driver's permit showing I was older than 18 years old, the legal age for drinking at the time. The State of Georgia permits of the era were filled in by pencil, easily and quickly erased and reconfigured to the right age.

After such escapades, the Rambler sometimes ended up way out of town the following morning, pushed to the limit by Gatins boys so liquored up they did not recall how they got there in a blackout. "One morning, I ended up in Chattanooga [about 120 miles away]," Charles said, which set a record none of the other boys ever were able to match.

By late 1964, the family was foundering in comparatively difficult financial straits. My father's partnership business, Cargo Sales, had failed, although on paper he maintained presidency of the firm. He then batted from dead-end job to dead-end job: Selling polyethylene plastic film; selling shoes in the basement of Rich's, one of Atlanta's premier department stores; peddling pots and pans door-to-door in Atlanta's black neighborhoods; counting ducts in a heating and air conditioning company; selling men's clothes, first at Parks-Chambers, then for Brooks Brothers. What small salary he was bringing in often never made it home, getting wasted away in a bar attached to a second-rate motel along the interstate highway bisecting downtown Atlanta. It all made me feel both sad and mad at the waste. The situation came to painful light that summer, when Sylvia and the children intervened to find out where the money was going and to try, under the direction of Charles, who had a knack for finance already at age 16, to develop a realistic family budget. Francis did not appreciate being confronted with the many checks made out to the motel bar. His blood-curdling, primal screams of anger and resentment at this confrontation were unforgettable and scared the wits out of Grandmother, who said she feared she might experience another suicide in the family. I drove away from the house that night at breakneck speed to get away from the madness, stopping only at the Chattahoochee River about eight miles away, by which time I had finished the half-empty six-pack I'd grabbed from the refrigerator on the way out. I was looking to quiet the clanking in my brain. I was already well on the way to knowing that alcohol could numb as well as intoxicate. My parents had permitted and encouraged me to drink at home, beginning about age 15, in a vain attempt to help me learn "how to hold my liquor like a gentleman." Sylvia by then was imbibing Scotch whiskey quite as much as Francis. It quickly became clear that I, too, loved the stuff—like grandfather, like father, like son, three generations in a row—and that it worked instantaneously on my psyche, so much so that it was obviously more than a social lubricant. I could navigate, both cars and social gatherings, in a blackout. I could pass out in the middle of a party.

The family, meanwhile, turned inward. My parents had already cut back on spending. No more repainting of the house or hiring yard men. No more dinner parties and cocktails. In fact, their social life was nil for several years, and Sylvia, like her husband, also began to succumb to the family disease. The faithful Manelle had been sent back to France, adding to a sense of dislocation that the younger Gatins children, then in their early teens, were already feeling. Bernice, the loyal cook, was let go. Charles and I, with our father's help, found summer jobs. I worked in construction, physically working harder than I ever had before, first helping labor crews renovate the Rialto Theater downtown. The next summer, I worked on a new Rich's department store in the Avondale suburb and the summer after that, on the new Veterans Administration Hospital in Atlanta as well as a railroad car repair shop. Charles found summer employment in an insurance company office. During the school year, he worked long hours after classes pumping gas at a nearby service station, in part to repay the small bank loans he was taking out at the time. (These were co-signed by Daddy's good friend, Deezy Scott O'Neill, a former reporter and public relations executive who dated to the days of the shared offices in the Candler Building. His own credit was not good enough.) Miguel got his own after-school job as a butcher's helper at a nearby A & P. I remember being struck about this time by the fact that no one in the family was taking photos of family gatherings anymore or maintaining photo albums, which seemed really strange to me. I went out and got a small Kodak camera and started a new album.

About the only time the family splurged anymore was on New Year's Eve, when bottles of champagne, foie gras and sometimes, small expensive tins of caviar miraculously made a brief appearance. Everyone got festive, especially when Daddy entertained these soirées with hilarious readings of Rabelais' bawdy poems.

In an effort to maintain sanity around the dinner table, the family decided to ban gin, controlling a situation that was very much already out of control. Martinis or gin-and-tonics, everyone decided, made people combative and mean, but vodka and Scotch were OK, as were half-gallons of Gallo wine on the dinner table.

Sylvia, who had never held a job in her life, found one with Edith Hills Co., an interior-decorating firm of very solid repute in Atlanta. It was not why she had studied Beaux-Arts back in Paris, but her schooling served her in good stead when it came to recommending certain furniture styles to paying customers. In a soul-wrenching effort to put food on the table and stay abreast of household bills, she also decided to secretly sell off some of the Colombian emerald jewelry that had been passed on to her by her mother. The children well remember that, with the help of Edith Hills, she took the cache to New York and sold it to a trader in the diamond district. There was so much cash that it was placed in a carrying case and Sylvia was provided an armed escort to her hotel. Mother made plain in a tearful phone conversation with me that she was devastated by the decision to sell the jewelry, but proud at the same time to have taken this drastic step to ensure the family's survival. That money, subsequently socked away in a bank box, along with the job at Edith Hills and regular extra help from Grandmother Elvira, tided the family over for the next few years.

Mother also found solace and an anchor in her Catholic faith, and especially with the Jesuit priests who had been assigned to work in Atlanta, both as parish priests and at a Catholic retreat center, Ignatius House. She made tabernacle covers and altar cloths for these priests and invited them all to Sunday lunches, from the archbishop on down. In this same period, Mother worked with a counterpart, Elena deGive—another South American woman who had married an old Atlanta family man—as a volunteer in the civil rights movement and the new War on Poverty. The two taught poor black women how to cook the surplus foodstuffs distributed for free. Elena was married to Henry deGive, descendant of early Belgian immigrants who had brought culture and class to Atlanta with the building of deGive's Theater, property that later became the Loew's Grand, best known for hosting the premiere of *Gone With the Wind.*

The Gatins children recall this period primarily as one of bewilderment. Our special and different world—so cozy, so rich, so comfortable—had turned topsy-turvy. Where had all the money gone, anyway? Much blithely had been spent on family vacation trips abroad, but there was never a full explanation or understanding of where it all went. Many years later, I wondered if Daddy had been playing, and losing, big money on those gin rummy games at the Piedmont Driving Club, rather than simply observing from the sidelines.

Less than five years before the financial crisis of 1963-64, the family had been sitting pretty with Francis' one-third share of The Georgian Terrace Hotel, and a portfolio of blue chip securities conservatively estimated around $36,400 in value. The hotel, however, was about to enter a period of decline, victim of changing driving habits and the advent of motel economies—and a deteriorating neighborhood. That was the year the family spent the entire summer in Colombia. The family, in fact, "audited" the South American country that summer, with a view of possibly moving there permanently. But Francis opined that he did not like Bogotá or its society— "All the men do is get drunk and do long lunches." So, we came back to Atlanta.

Even as crisis swirled around us in Atlanta, Grandmother Elvira's generosity was used to send some of the children back to France for occasional summers at La Chezotte, or to Bogotá and a tiny but very well appointed private island off the Colombian coast. (Charles, who spent one summer there, was sent home early from Colombia after he started pushing and motivating island residents and servants to ask for higher pay from Uncle Miguel!) The Gatins brood was fortunate enough to thus extend an already international education and point of view. All six children were bilingual and several, trilingual. Elvira's gifts and generosity became increasingly important to day-to-day life. Sophie and I, for example, were dispatched to spend the summer of 1966 in France, which I recall as an attempt to give us a last taste for a way of life that was soon to end, and to introduce Sophie to Parisian society.

I particularly remember realizing how thoroughly Americanized I had become. One of Mother's childhood friends had us to a formal lunch, using the occasion, at Mother's behest I believe, to remind us two that we were descendants of and still much part of "one of the greatest families of France." That rang hollow for me, striking me as just so much chauvinism, a remnant of faded French glory.

Rather, that summer brought back memories of how the ideas of American democracy crept into my consciousness as a child, from reading and re-reading all the biographies of American historical figures, which seemed to overwhelm all the French history that Manelle had also tried to drum into my brain. Like my father in the army, my sense of democracy grew from working one summer on an all-black construction labor crew, led by a very smart labor foreman named Paul, and another as a carpenter's helper for rough-hewn, all-white mountaineers from north Georgia. Georgia crackers, the historians call them, people like "J.C.," who'd lost his right thumb and two other fingers to a saw accident, or the carpenter foreman, nicknamed "Heavy," who looked after me when I was still a very green construction helper. These men lived as brightly in my mind as a French corsair named Madec or the royalist Villelume-Sombreuil family.

My parents and sister Eglé spent the summer of 1967 at La Chezotte, which proved to be restorative for my father especially. When he got there, he literally seemed gray. La Chezotte, which he had first visited in August of 1939, was really therapeutic for him, young Eglé recalled. "He was in terrible shape. But Mother slowly nursed him back to life with good food, no stress, less drink and the fact that he adored La Chezotte. After two months, he was a changed man."

Grandmother Elvira, fondly remembered by her grandchildren as a fun-loving bon vivant and gourmet, died one year later, and settlement of her estate eased the family's financial situation. Uncle Ben also died that year (of a heart event), facilitating the dissolution of the trust that had handcuffed Francis to the Terrace hotel and its trustees for so many decades.

The United States was in turmoil that year of 1968, having suffered through the virtual abdication of its president, Lyndon B. Johnson, over his handling of the Vietnam War, and two more political assassinations, those of Dr. Martin Luther King, Jr., the Atlanta-based civil rights leader, and Sen. Robert F. Kennedy, the slain president's brother. For me, just graduated from the University of North Carolina, the chaos was much worse than after the first Kennedy assassination in 1963. Keeping alive the national unease were continuing civil rights and anti-Vietnam War demonstrations, marches and violent, urban strife, the often drug-and-alcohol-fueled revolt of a younger generation and a deteriorating political situation, shockingly illustrated at the Democratic National Convention in Chicago. Daddy and I watched that convention on television together. We saw Chicago Mayor Richard Daley's verbal explosion on the floor of the convention and his police mob clubbing demonstrators in the streets outside the hall. By the 1960s, Francis had become a Kennedy-era Democratic supporter and often volunteered as a campaign worker for political candidates, notably the anti-segregationist congressman from Atlanta, Charles Weltner. Less than three months after the Chicago convention, my brother Charles and I enlisted in the army, following our father's footsteps rather than the protests all around us. By May of 1969, Grandmother Eglé was doing what she had so much experience doing: Sending care packages to a loved one on the front lines—in this case, to me. I had been dispatched to Vietnam, where I spent the next 11 months. She sent me weekly copies of *Le Monde*, food packages, and saved every one of my letters from Southeast Asia. She was to undertake much the same care giving for her other grandchildren and a whole new slew of great-grandchildren over the next two and a half decades.

Chapter 31

Tempest Fugit

Dark days and family turmoil eased somewhat by the 1970s, as the six children, the fifth generation of Gatinses trying its hand at settling down in America, began to sink their own roots deeper into the soil of the United States.

Grandmother Eglé saw all of her grandchildren go on to college and eventually get jobs and get married and start making their own way. Francis and Sylvia became grandparents. The children all worked hard and, having grown up with such good teachers in this department, they knew how to play hard. Like their parents, they, too, could "dazzle the bourgeoisie" when necessary, at their own huge parties on Rivers Road. By the late 1970s, their Christmas night party was legend, attracting friends, hangers-on (and sometimes total strangers) from out of town, and even, sometimes, the notice of the Atlanta police who had received complaints from neighbors about the noise. Those unable to drive home from these parties were steered to the library, where an old bed with a brown cover served many as refuge for the night. Daddy loved the hubbub and the attention of the local constabulary. It brought out the contrarian in his nature, the same twist that made him wear orange on St. Patrick's Day instead of green in much the same way that he liked to tweak the Nixon Republicans who were his friends.

The children did their thing. I got into journalism in Washington and Richmond, after my own stint in the military. Charles blossomed in the real estate business in Atlanta after his military service, and became a collector of expensive automobiles. Sophie found a calling first as a chef, then as a stay-at-home mom and later as a licensed professional counselor in Atlanta. Martin proved a most energetic entrepreneur, first in Atlanta, then eventually in New York. His twin sister, Eglé, became an artist and painter and moved to Columbus, Ohio. Following a divorce, Miguel, a sometime businessman, ended up making a second home and family in Mexico.

I had come back from Vietnam physically unscathed but with my own version of post-traumatic stress. Spiritually, I survived base camp duty about two hours drive outside Saigon with a subscription to the Sunday edition of the *New York Times*, daily letters from family and friends and regular delivery of care packages. Assigned to stateside duty in Washington, I found it a really wonderful place to erase wartime memories with drink, celebration and more-or-less serial monogamy. Washington had some great bars. I remember how lovely it was to see the planes landing at night at Washington National Airport from an apartment perch high up on the hills of the Adams-Morgan neighborhood—it reminded me of the bright flares that parachuted down around the base camps when shooting erupted in Vietnam. Hearing the national anthem at that time stirred strange, sometimes tearful emotion. I was proud to have served my country, but what price had I paid? One night at the Adams-Morgan apartment, I woke up screaming from a black, wartime nightmare, soothed only when a police helicopter flew over the neighborhood with its sodium vapor floodlights, so reminiscent of the base camp at Quan Loi, a fortified French rubber plantation. It was only many years later that I realized that I had lost all remaining innocence in Vietnam. Like many veterans, it took me years to get over the family dysfunction, increased smoking and drinking and reduced "life satisfaction and happiness" that "a substantial minority" experienced even decades afterward. Vietnam was not a prison for me but a moral quagmire. I kept all these feelings well-wrapped, though, unless circumstances exploded around me—like when Sylvia one night asked why I had not received as many good conduct medals from the Army as my brother Charles (who served his overseas tour in the relative comfort of Germany). I don't remember what I said, but the comment so angered me that I stalked out the kitchen and slammed the back door so hard that one of its glass panes shattered. It also had unsettled me that my bedroom at home had been totally redecorated while I was gone, my desk moved and new curtains put over the windows as if they were not expecting me to make it back. Somehow, though, I became the last Gatins to serve in the military and no one else in the family, to date, has found himself or herself in a far-off war overseas. For a family whose ancestors' experience included the Crusades and many conflicts from India and Africa to Latin America and the United States, from Europe to Southeast Asia, this appeared a very real break with an often-violent past.

Meanwhile, my parents saw their financial circumstances ease with the distribution of various estates and the sale of the Georgian Terrace and various family holdings. The bill collectors stopped making phone calls at the same time as Sunday dinner. They took trips abroad again. The changes allowed my parents, at

Sylvia's insistence, to make it possible for the two girls to make their debut with the Atlanta Debutante Club. In Sophie's case, that led directly to engagement and marriage upon graduation from college. My sister Eglé had little interest in this social scene and basically skipped most of the deb season. She was in France studying art that summer.

The family's intercontinental restlessness eventually seemed to slow down and everyone appeared to make their peace with Atlanta as home base, but neither the children nor my parents totally severed international ties. Some of the children became more American than others, while some kept at least one foot firmly planted abroad. Charles and I, having served our country in the military, were firmly rooted to the U.S., but Charles used his linguistic talents to sell commercial real estate across the South to legions of European investors. Sophie ended up in Atlanta, but her eldest daughter Nathalie married a Frenchman. Martin hopscotched five continents in pursuit of international business deals in a variety of industries, as did Miguel. Eglé, an accomplished artist, moved to Ohio after marrying a college sweetheart there, but, like Sophie, was very religious in maintaining ties to relatives and old family friends in France and Switzerland.

By the 1980s, Sylvia and Francis had become grandparents many times over, while Eglé, great-grandmother of the growing brood, was one of the *grandes dames* of Atlanta. When the family gathered for holidays, weddings, or christenings, she would marvel at how large the extended family had become. "All this," she would say, "from just one child!"

With the financial help of her friends and an annuity from her brother Charlie's printing company in Paris, she had the financial freedom to pass out occasional allowances to her grandchildren (and liberally finance her youngest grandson Miguel's activity on the teen dating scene). She adhered to a set weekly schedule that included daily walks to mass at Christ the King Cathedral, about four long blocks away; purchase of a six-pack of Coca-Cola to give to the garbage men who weekly came up to dispose of the household trash; and employment of two black servants to polish the family silver one day per week. She drank a ceremonial, annual martini on New Year's Day, often followed by a hike up Kennesaw Mountain, a practice she adhered to well into her eighties. She received and responded to countless letters from friends in France, often staying up late at night to pen the letters in something of a correspondence ritual, complete with stylized letter openers and occasional use of sealing wax. She still maintained an account at Morgan Bank in Paris. The tellers there easily recognized her distinctive, triangular handwriting (very difficult to read, like cuneiform) and cashed her checks for visiting family members with little question. Eglé was sought after by family friends and others to tell of her many memories of an Atlanta and a Paris that was long past, essentially establishing her own intellectual salon. John C. Calhoun, an architectural designer who had come into the Gatins fold during the Edith Hills days, often came over to hear about the characters and Salon Society intellectuals she knew in Paris during the Lost Generation era, and to tell her of Atlanta society while she'd been in Paris. (Calhoun's description of "Atlanta pinks" was priceless—haughty debutante belles so taken with themselves they were virtually unapproachable.) Al and Pat Lawton, fellow parishioners at Christ the King, and their three children, faithfully dropped in from time to time. Two well-known Atlanta philanthropists, the late Mary Branch Close and Anne Cox Chambers, came by for tea one afternoon when I happened to be present, to take in Eglé's wisdom and tell tall tales of bygone eras in the Georgia capital. Mrs. Close and Mrs. Chambers at the time were a pair, making it a habit of going to benefits together, to check out who was doing what with whom and what the women were wearing at these parties. As the tea wound down, Mrs. Close spoke of her keen appreciation for Grandmother Eglé and for my father, who had been a steady friend to her children after her own husband died. She also appreciated his contrarian bent. "Sometimes, those who break the rules are the most interesting," she said. (For me, who had never lived in Atlanta at the same time as she, Grandmother Eglé was always a steely cipher, very loving but remote. Other family members, friends of an intellectual bent, and the grandchildren who lived for a time in the same house, grew to know her as I never did.)

Francis and Sylvia also maintained their knack for deflating Atlanta convention and did not lose their capacity to shock in their waning years. At a large Sunday dinner held to welcome their son's Martin's fiancé's family, the Clarks, into their circle Daddy exclaimed, "Well, Mr. Clark, your daughters will never go hungry. They are all so pretty, they can always be hookers." Mother, not to be outdone in the outrageous department that day, had recently undergone a mastectomy due to breast cancer. She complained out loud that the falsie she was wearing was "damned itchy, you know," and promptly drew it out from under her sweater and flopped it on the dining room table.

Several years later, she managed to dumbfound a grandchild, my son Demian, by liberally feeding rich Belgian chocolate to her two dachshunds, Helmut and Silly, complaining of its expense and never offering him the smallest bite. When parties got too loud and too rambunctious, even for her, Sylvia would raise her voice to tell everyone to go home, or throw ashtrays down the stairs to get everyone's attention. "Go home, young man, go home," she once told Demian, too befuddled to realize that he was a member of the family.

Sylvia and Francis also had their routines. They maintained old friendships with Skip and Joan Zillessen (Skip spent hours weekly gossiping with Sylvia over the telephone while Francis had a weekly lunch date with Joan). They renewed friendships with Katie and Joe Hutchison, the building contractor who'd given me my first summer job and with whom the family often had partied on week-ends on Watts Bar Lake and Lake Lanier. They kept up with Beau and Irving Gresham, who'd put the Gatins boys on the florist shop payroll at Christmas, and Deezy O'Neill, who dated to the old shared offices in the Candler Building in the 1950s. (Her husband Frank, who piloted to Michigan with my father as an informal, seat-of-the-pants navigator, died a premature death from cancer). They cocktailed with Finlay McRae and his longtime companion, Ann Meadors. Francis still worked from time to time as a salesman in the men's clothing depart-ment of Brooks Brothers downtown. He was called to criminal grand jury duty and did it so well that he was called again and again and joined an informal "grand jurors association." He maintained contact with the Trappist monks in Conyers, but did not seem to have a need for silent retreats anymore. Rather, he bought bonsai trees from the monastery and lovingly cared for them at home, lining them up on a long, south- and west-facing refectory table and giving them an outdoor soaking once per week. He also had the time to plant and nurture a large rose garden. On Sundays, he drove the two daschunds to a nearby city park to give them a weekly run.

Daddy around this time took me aside one day in Atlanta and spoke to me about my own drinking. "I'm not one to talk," he said, "but you really have to watch your drinking." That was the closest we ever came to talking about the dis-ease that had so affected everyone in the Gatins clan.

Sylvia volunteered to teach English to the Spanish-speaking inmates at the Federal Penitentiary in Atlanta until she was dismissed for mailing inmate let-ters that bypassed the prison censorship system. The episode came to light when two FBI agents came knocking at the door one Sunday morning, much to the children's consternation. They were just there to ask Sylvia and Francis about their volunteer activities and not, to the children's relief, for a pot bust or to ask about the hookah that had a semi-permanent home in the red room. During that period, Francis and Sylvia also put up a French woman in the guest bedroom for about a week, the girl friend of Joseph Lucarotti, a French inmate at the Atlanta pen. Lucarotti's claim to criminal fame was that he engineered the inception of the famous "French Connection" heroin trade between France and New York from his penitentiary cell! Before she was cashiered from volunteer service at the peni-tentiary, Sylvia and Francis befriended another drug-dealing, French-speaking expatriate at the prison, Maurice Rosal Bron, formerly Guatemala's ambassador to the Netherlands, who'd been arrested by federal agents in New York in 1960, carrying more than 200 pounds of pure heroin. Rosal, just before his release, prevailed on my father to provide him with a new suit from Brooks Brothers, so he could walk out of prison with a touch of class.

Francis, more than Sylvia, had a somewhat uncanny knack for collecting casual acquaintances and strangers, bringing them home for a visit or a meal, often to the surprise of the children. My parents also maintained a distant connection with another denizen of the *demi-monde*, Mario Gabellini, who had remarried for the last time, lived for a time in Atlanta, headed back to New York, and then eventually retired to Nice, on the French Riviera. He stayed in contact by letter and by showing Gatins children around Provence when they went to France.

My father died in 1983, of complications arising from blood cancer. He'd beaten TB after the war, and eventually given up smoking, but his luck ran out when it came to leukemia, and it ran out very quickly. His liver was so shot, the family was told, that it was basically impossible to initiate the strenuous drug therapies often prescribed in these instances. He and Sylvia had just celebrated their 40th wedding anniversary on December 8 of that year with a black-tie dinner at my brother Martin's home. They knew something was wrong when his hands were shaking so hard that he was unable to remove his cufflinks after the dinner. His subsequent weeklong stay in a hospital's private room and adjacent suite (with icebox and icemaker) turned into a "pre-wake" of monumental proportions. The liquor flowed day and night. Although he said he'd lost the taste for alcohol in the hospital, his last, prophetic words to his four sons were: "Drink all you can," which we were all doing already. Old friends came to say good-bye, including James G. Kenan, the Atlanta history expert who often had trekked with my dad to Civil War sites, and Mary Branch Close.

My father died in my arms on the bright, very cold morning of December 18, coughing up and choking on his own blood. I was the one who had spent that last night with him. The family went on a weeklong wake, more Irish than French. Lots of whisky. Said Grandmother: "There is nothing harder than losing your son." True to Daddy's final suggestion, I drank even more after his death than before to try to erase his loss. Beer before breakfast, wine at night before passing out on the couch. I felt like I was falling into a very dark and deep hole.

In 1985, Aunt Katherine Riley died, leaving significant legacies to the extended Gatins clan, which eased everyone's financial circumstances. The old house on Rivers Road was sold. With decades of accumulated smoke, whiskey, perfume, wine, and delectable cooking in the kitchen, the old house had a homey scent that newcomers were quick to detect. I believe the aroma added up to a hint of rot as well, aided by the mold and mildew of Atlanta's hot and humid summers. Until the late 1960s, the only ventilation had come from two large attic fans, as air conditioning was not yet in general vogue when the house was built in the late 1920s. The Gatins family indeed had imprinted the house with its aura. Its current occupants sometimes hear a weird thumping on the second floor, which that family attributes to "the ghost of Mr. Gatins."

Mother and Grandmother moved to more modern, smaller townhome on Peachtree Street. Mother died a little more than two years later, January 9, 1987, from a stroke brought on by a dose of tranquillizers. The pills had been prescribed to help her stop her own uncontrollable drinking. "I'm dying, you know," she told her children. "What a bore!" But her death and its aftermath were much calmer than our father's, as all four of her boys by then had somewhat miraculously stopped drinking. How this happened is pretty much beyond belief, but I think we were all at that point beginning to fear for our own lives, not wanting to crumble and die like Daddy. We did not have need for a weeklong wake after Mommy's death. Instead, we gloried in how rich her life experience had really been. Contemporaries remembered her as having been just as intriguing as her husband: "We didn't know how boring we were until we met your parents," one friend said.

The passing of Francis and Sylvia also left Eglé fully in control of her financial destiny for the first time in her life, at age 94. With her grandchildren's assistance, she bought a separate condominium on East Wesley Road, conveniently located next door to Christ the King Cathedral.

"I remember her crying when I showed her the East Wesley condominium," her grandson Martin recalled. "And when I asked her why, she said it was the first place that had ever belonged to her where she was not living at the mercy of others!"

On New Year's Day in 1989, she suffered a crippling stroke at her granddaughter Sophie's dinner table after downing her one, annual martini. She lingered for over a year, comfortably enough with nurses at her side, but pretty much nonresponsive to speech, before expiring at the age of 97, on January 28, 1990.

It was the end of an era. One generation of family lava cooled. Her volcano had gone dormant.

End Notes

Primary Sources

EOH—Oral history by Eglé de Villelume-Sombreuil Gatins, 1976.

EMR—Eglé's written memoir, translated by author. 1988.

ELIB—Eglé's letters to her son and daughter-in-law during the liberation of Paris, 1944.

ICRC—International Committee of the Red Cross prisoner of war camp inspection reports.

JFGSTA—Joseph F. Gatins III passport files at U.S. Department of State.

SYLINS—Sylvia Gatins immigration/deportation file, U.S. Immigration and Naturalization Service.

JFGWEL—Joseph F. Gatins III correspondence with Atlanta lawyer Welborn Cody

JFGPOW—Prisoner-of-war correspondence, Francis to Sylvia.

JFGLOV—Love letters, Francis to Sylvia, from Saranac Lake, N.Y.

JOESIB—Voluminous e-mail correspondence between author and his brothers and sisters.

Chapter 1 – Wall Street Operator

1. **"living with his family in quiet luxury.** *The New York Times,* April 24, 1910, Page 1.

2. **"only a play of the big fellows."** *The Sunday Star,* Washington D.C., April 3, 1910, page 1. "Arrests 16 in Raids. Warrants Served on Alleged Bucket Shop Men."

3. **real estate appraised at $550,950.** Garrett, Franklin M. *Atlanta and Environs: A Chronicle of its People and Events.* 3 vols. (Athens: University of Georgia Press, 1954). II:634-635.

4. **Other prominent businessmen.** See *Slavery by Another Name,* by Douglas A. Blackmon. 2008. p. 348.

5. **rumored to be a heavy operator in the cotton market**. Crockett, Albert Stevens, *Old Waldorf Bar Days*, New York: Aventine Press, 1931.

6. **"Baby Titty."** *Ibid.*

7. **selling stock "short."** Simpson, Hope Gatins Curtis. Recollections of Joseph F. Gatins Sr.'s granddaughter, in personal telephone call to author. Gatins' short-selling practices also are alluded to in a suit he brought against a New York stock brokerage house in May, 1910, (see *The New York Times*, page 14, May 26, 1910).

Chapter 2 – Partying at the Ritz

8. **luxurious retreat for the very rich**. Roulet, Claude. *Ritz: Une histoire plus belle que la legende.* Quai Voltaire, 1998.

9. **One member of the Brady crowd at the Ritz**. Gatins, Eglé de Villelume-Sombreuil. Oral history, 1976. Tape-recorded interview in English with Tommy and Sophie Mason, October, 1976, at Richmond, Virginia. Author's partial transcription. Subsequently referenced as EOH.

10. **"I met him at a big party at the Ritz**." Weiland, Eglé Gatins. March 12, 2002 letter to author. Weiland suggests that the couple met for the first time on the "Island in the Bois de Boulogne," contrary to Grandmother's own recollections.

11. **so infected that it necessitated amputation.** Simpson, Hope Gatins Curtis. Personal letter to author, February 2, 1999. "As I remember hearing, Uncle Joe was a young boy and he was running upstairs, fell and from that he lost his arm." The story of the amputation is fleshed out a bit more by a lifelong Atlanta resident and family friend, Carroll Smith Offen. My grandfather had received a smallpox vaccination shortly before getting a broken arm set in a cast. The smallpox vaccination grew so infected that it necessitated amputation, according to Offen. According to 1945 correspondence from my father, my grandfather was 16 years old when the arm was amputated.

12. **nothing less than victory, won with flair and *panache*, would do to erase the long and highly divisive national nightmare occasioned by the Dreyfus Affair.** For a cogent summary of the Dreyfus scandal, see Robert Gildea's *Children of the Revolution: The French, 1799-1914. Harvard University Press.* 2008.

13. **some sense of self-sacrifice for her own mother's happiness.** E-mail correspondence with Nathalie Mason Fleury and Eglé Gatins Weiland, based on oral tradition of various Villelume-Sombreuil cousins in France.

14. **Grandfather Gatins brought two acquaintances as witnesses.** See wedding certificate.

15. **the unit's pathetic return to Paris.** Recollections of Grandmother Eglé in both EOH and EMR, the latter Grandmother's written memoir, originally dictated and transcribed in French in 1988, at Atlanta, Georgia, Author's translation to English.

16. **"Marriage of Mr. Joseph Gatins and Comtesse de Sombreuil in Paris."** From

an undated 1914 clipping in the Katherine Murphy Riley papers and photos maintained at the Kenan Research Center of the Atlanta History Center.

Chapter 3 – "I Don't Want You"

17. pugnacious, polo-playing bon vivant. Benjamin K. Gatins, nicknamed Champ, was no less colorful than my grandfather. He had a way with riding horses just like his one-armed brother, and often played rough-and-tumble polo for pick-up teams up and down the East Coast at the turn of the last century. He'd been a star halfback and fullback on Yale University's freshman football team in the years just before World War I, an inveterate gambler like his father, and a most colorful addition to the social scene wherever he landed.

He met his wife Dorothy, a Philadelphia debutante, at the age of 21, first on the piers of Atlantic City and Narragansett, Rhode Island, two of the favorite watering holes of the Gilded Age. He pursued her to the French Riviera during the winter polo season in Nice. She was but 17. Her parents, Philadelphia Mainliners, were said to be opposed to the match, and had shipped her off to Nice "to break off the intimacy which had led to the engagement rumors," as *The New York Times* explained it. But she got married somewhat surreptitiously to Ben on April 13, 1912. The headline in the next day's *Times* said it all:

DOROTHY WATERS SECRETLY WEDDED

Young Debutante Becomes Bride
Of B.F. Gatins, Despite
Parents' Opposition

NOW ON THEIR HONEYMOON

Gatins Followed Her When
Her Family Sent Her Abroad

Dorothy, *The Times* dutifully reported, left her family's Madison Avenue home "with only a handbag containing her jewels, met Mr. Gatins, and about 10:30 they procured a marriage license. "In the application she gave her age as 21 years. This is said to be at least three years older that she is commonly believed to be," the article continued. They found an assistant rector of Blessed Sacrament Catholic Church at 71st and Broadway to solemnize their union. They then spent their honeymoon in a Chicago hotel, where Ben, as his two daughters subsequenty retold the story, spent most of the time playing with a toy train set.

Little more than a year later, Ben was back in the news for being involved in an affray with the local constabulary of Narragansett Pier, Rhode Island, after he and another polo player were caught inside a cottage that did not belong to them. A loud argument ensued, and then a fight, with the police using nightsticks and shooting a pistol over Ben's head to subdue the unruly duo.

Ben and his pugilistic polo compatriot were "both in evening dress and their blood had made their shirt fronts red," *The Times* noted. No charges subsequently were filed by either side. Ben appeared in a polo match the next day, but was "struck by a polo ball in the face and severely injured in the fifth period of the match."

In 1918, he took his fighting to France, where as he saw brief service as a captain in the Infantry in the Aisne, Argonne and Meuse campaigns.

18. **"a beautiful young lady who had married an old judge."** EOH and EMR.

19. **"The Gatinses were very much Catholic."** EMR.

20. **a vivacious and gregarious Parisiènne had opened a highly successful millinery store.** New York City directories, 1909-10 and 1910-11. New York City Public Library.

21. **"I don't want you."** EOH.

22. **"but my mother-in-law wanted to keep me [in New York] for a family reunion."** EMR.

23. **joined James C. Brady, the New York moneyman…** This is James Cox Brady, not James Buchanan Brady, the swashbuckling gourmand and Wall Street investor known as "Diamond Jim Brady."

24. **"unfaithful to his wife on their honeymoon."** Based on confidential personal interview with old Gatins family friend in Atlanta. "My father knew him [Joe Gatins] and said he never liked him." Why not? "Unfaithful to his wife on their honeymoon."

25. **"I was won over by the feeling of the South…"** EMR.

26. **"helping to nurse him through a sudden illness that has alarmed his friends."** From undated clipping in *The Atlanta Journal* from 1914. Katherine Murphy Riley papers and photos. Kenan Research Center, Atlanta History Center.

27. **Model T driving and golf lessons.** Based on Martin T. Gatins photo album originally maintained as part of his personal papers. The album was lost when a Fedex delivery truck was stolen in New York in 2008.

28. **"You'd see all your friends rocking on their porches."** EMR. Grandmother Eglé's oral histories make particular mention of several additional close friends: Harry Atkinson and his wife, who lived across the street from the Terrace at the Ponce de Leon Apartments, as well as their daughter and son, Mary and Harry Jr. Other

social acquaintances mentioned included James and Emily Robinson, "who lived in a truly beautiful home in Druid Hills," as well as "a great friend of Joe's, James Alexander."

29. **"dubious distinction of being the state whose citizens (mostly white) illegally lynched the second-highest number of persons…"** See the *The New Georgia Encyclopedia* for a cogent summary of this horrendous practice, at: http://www.georgiaencyclopedia.org/nge/Article.jsp?id=h-2717

30. **any mention of the "big fire"** See Garrett, Franklin M. *Atlanta and Environs: A Chronicle of its People and Events.* 3 vols. (Athens: University of Georgia Press, Garrett 1954). II:700-705.

31. **"pursued one of his favorite hobbies, horseback riding…"** Stratemeyer, Marlene J. Telephone interview with author, February 17, 1999, and club documents, including *A History of the Elkridge Fox Hunting Club,* by J. Rieman McIntosh. According to Stratemeyer, Gatins joined the club officially on March 4, 1915 and transferred to a "non-resident membership" in October of that same year, which he maintained until his death on May 8, 1927. Eglé Gatins Weiland, my sister, recalled that Grandfather had found employment with a railroad, while others of us grandchildren believe he'd found a job with Alex Brown & Sons, the Baltimore-based brokerage and investment banking house, but the firm, and its successor brokerages, cannot today confirm record of such employment.

32. **"but my wife's people date back to the Crusades!"** From EMR, and two-page paper on the Villelume family antecedents maintained by Eglé. "The Villelumes, originally called Villem, definitely established themselves in France in 1100. They took part in the first Crusade. They thus have their escutcheons in the *Salle des Croisées* at the Chateau of Versailles."

33. **"most peaceful and enjoyable period of her brief, married life."** Gatins, Martin T. Recollection of author's brother. JOESIB

Chapter 4 – "Life was Intolerable"

34. **"decided that his child must be born in France—a huge error."** EMR.

35. **"the father being absent."** Extract of birth records. Ville de Versailles.

36. **sought to establish themselves as a normal family.** EMR, and Atlanta City Directories. Kenan Research Center, Atlanta History Center.

37. **teaching GIs French at Camp Gordon.** Garrett. II:712-721. The U.S. had joined the war on April 6, 1917. A universal draft day occurred on June 5. By mid-summer, construction of Camp Gordon was going full blast, including the laying of 13 miles of new water pipe. It opened on September 5. A total of about 230,000 men were trained there (more than 6,100 officers). Eglé's society friends, listed in her 1988 memoir, and in a contemporary clipping from one of Atlanta's newspapers, included Constance Draper, Isabel Tompkins, Mrs. Harry English and Edna Thornton.

38. **sought a commission as a lieutenant.** *The Atlanta Constitution,* April 23, 1917, "Commission asked in the U.S. Army by Joseph Gatins."

39. **failing to support his wife and child.** Gatins, Eglé de Villelume Sombreuil. Sworn affidavit, dated June 17, 1926, filed in support of a U.S. passport application. See U.S. Department of State response to Freedom of Information Act request, Case Control No. 2001.00087, CA/PPT/IML/R/RR—Gatins III, Joseph Francis. JFGSTA

40. **"America fundamentally altered its pattern of alcohol consumption."** White, William H. *Slaying the Dragon: The History of Addiction Treatment and Recovery in America.* 1998. A Chestnut Health Systems Publication.

41. **Eglé's separation and divorce filing.** My grandmother, according to passport applications maintained in the National Archives, applied for a U.S. passport on March 26, 1920, to "go see my family" in France, declaring "I am now living separate from my husband." See also, *Eglé de Villelume-Sombreuil v. Joseph F. Gatins Jr.* Fulton County, Georgia, court records. Civil case index, Volume S-2, page 93. Case No. 44864, filed April 7, 1920. The docket book entry suggests two law firms were involved in this case, McAdoo, Cotton & Franklin, and McDaniel & Black, but the court clerk's office is unable to find the case file, which remains missing from a box containing other such files from 1920.

42. **"because my husband did not and does not support my child and myself."** Sworn affidavit, dated June 17, 1926, filed in support of a U.S. passport application by Eglé Gatins.

43. **Battery Park Hotel details.** Weiss, Harry M., former executive director, The Preservation Society of Asheville & Buncombe County, Inc. Letter to author of April 14, 1999. "Your inquiry has allowed us to determine a more precise chronology of the redevelopment of the Battery Park site. Evidently, your father and grandfather were among the last visitors to the original hotel."

44. **for the then-fatal and virtually untreatable disease to run its course.** Department of Public Health, State of Georgia. Death certificate, Joseph F. Gatins Jr., May 8, 1927.

Chapter 5 – Burden of Family

45. **in China, where he was posted as a diplomat.** Recollection of Eglé Gatins Weiland.

46. **born in a hunting lodge at Crotoy, a beachfront resort in Normandy.** EMR.

47. **"not like the idea of being nice to other wives."** Recollection of Nathalie Mason Fleury, in e-mail to author of November 24, 2008.

48. **"magnetizers" said to have the power to cure evil…** See *The Wall Street Journal,* December 8, 2004. "French Magnetizer Convinces a Client Neighbor Is a Witch," by John Carreyrou.

49. **catechism was taught to local children in Breton.** EMR, and see introduction

to *Celtic Myths and Legends,* by Peter Berresford Ellis, New York: Carroll & Graf Publishers, 1999, for a cogent explanation of Breton language, and its connections to Irish and Gaelic.

50. **Both families, Villelume-Sombreuil and Madec, had been ennobled by French kings.** For greater detail, see supplement to Grandmother Eglé's oral histories, and correspondence with French National Archives.

51. **a wide circle of international acquaintances and the many girl friends.** EMR. Among those close, childhood chums were Lizie de Noue and Vera Galatzine, an Orthodox Russian girl also brought up at the convent school.

52. **"a store for women's dresses and hats, which was wildly successful."** See New York City directories at the New York Public Library for its location.

53. **unexpectedly hopped over to New York.** Although it seems clear Madame Jeanne de Villelume-Sombreuil came to Manhattan as early as 1909, the passenger records of The Statue of Liberty-Ellis Island Foundation Inc., which documents immigrant arrivals of that era, has no record of her disembarking in the United States until docking of the Oceanic on March 12, 1914.

54. **Eglé was to be introduced to a potential suitor, a very-well connected Swiss banker.** Recollection of Philippe Manset, author's godfather.

55. **eventually married her instead of Grandmother Eglé, in 1916.** See *Maison de Kerguelen,* by Yann de Servigny, Pont Médicis, Paris, 1997, at page 254 for date of this marriage.

Chapter 6 – Killybegs to Buckhead

56. **no one in my family knew of the McGettigan connection.** See microfilm record 188/43, AH 2875, Georgia Department of Archives and History, for Baptism and Confirmation records, Church of the Immaculate Conception in Atlanta, 1841-1871. It must be remembered that all the early records were recorded by hand, and subject to the handwriting vagaries of the officials recording the documents. One early U.S. Census document records the family under the heading Gatius—the 'n' in the name seeming like a 'u.' See also *Killybegs: Then and Now,* by Donald Martin, Dublin: Anvil Books, 1998.

57. **remaining in Atlanta, marrying two sisters who also emigrated from County Donegal.** See *The Famine Ships: The Irish Exodus to America*, by Edward Laxton, New York: Henry Holt & Co., 1996; and *Black '47 and Beyond: The Great Irish Famine,* by Cormac Ó Gráda, Princeton University Press, 1999, and *The Irish Catholic Diaspora in America,* by Lawrence J. McCaffrey, Catholic University of America Press, 1976. By most accounts, about one million Irish men, women and children were driven to the United States by hunger and disaster between 1846 and 1851. Another one million died in Ireland during the same period. See also *The Atlanta Constitution.* Saturday, September 16, 1916. Obituary for John Gatins on page 5, confirming the two Gatins brothers had married the two Cullen sisters. Microfilm records, Kenan Research Center, Atlanta History Center.

58. **"a founder of the Immaculate Conception Church—often referred to one of Atlanta's original 'pioneers.'"** Garrett. II:490.

59. **the "Moral Party" and the "Free and Rowdy Party."** *Ibid.* I:329.

60. **slaves were bought and sold and traded in Atlanta in some numbers.** See especially Garrett's Volume I for rich description of Atlanta's early days. Also, *Pioneer Citizens' History of Atlanta: 1833-1902*, Atlanta: Byrd Press, 1902, reprinted as a Heritage Classic Published by the Pioneer Citizens Society of Atlanta.

61. **about one-fifth were slaves.** See *The New Georgia Encyclopedia* at www.georgiaencyclopedia.org/

62. **"John Gatins.... appointed to the commissary department of the Confederate Army."** *The Atlanta Constitution* obituary article, dated September 16, 1916. Microfilm records, Kenan Research Center, Atlanta History Center.

63. **tantamount to a most public declaration of one's leanings during the conflict.** See *Secret Yankees: The Union Circle in Confederate Atlanta*, by Thomas G. Dyer, Johns Hopkins University Press, 1999.

64. **"I was Clerk in Capt. Hade's department at the time the cotton was taken."** Deposition of Joseph Gatins, Claim of John and James Lynch, Case No. 2502, General Jurisdiction, U.S. Court of Claims, Record Group 23, Federal Records Center, Suitland, Maryland.

65. **they would face massive desertion from the many Catholic soldiers in the Union forces if they fired the church.** See history of the Church of the Immaculate Conception, at www.catholicshrineatlanta.org/

66. **took his naturalization oath to uphold the U.S. Constitution, not the Confederacy, seriously.** *Ibid.* Court of Claims deposition.

67. **a member of the "Irish Volunteers."** *Atlanta Historical Society Bulletin*, 1927. Kenan Research Center, Atlanta History Center.

68. **having returned there [Savannah] to claim his bride, Bridget Cullen, in 1853.** *Marriage records*, Catholic Diocese of Savannah, Georgia. The diocese maintains a well-arranged, computerized file of birth, death and marriage records for early members of this diocese. I also sought to ascertain if this ancestor, after the sacking of Atlanta, followed Sherman on his destructive, slash-pillage-and-burn path to the coast as part of the motley crew of camp followers and civilians who went along for the ride. The search proved unsuccessful.

69. **Life was not easy for the young couple.** *Ibid.*

70. **Joseph Gatins filled in the blanks and signed the affidavit on April 8, 1868.** Voter Registration Book No. 7, commenced October 15, 1867. Drawer 296, Box 17, No. 5411. Georgia Department of Archives and History. Affidavits and lists of registered voters. A grand total of 6,709 voters took such election oaths by April 20 of 1868—with 3,755 identified as men of "color," and a minority, 2,944, as white. See also Garrett's Necrology, Franklin M. Garrett, Kenan Research Center,

Atlanta History Center for obituaries on both Atlanta "pioneers," Joseph and John Gatins. And *Pioneer Citizens' History of Atlanta: 1833-1902*, Atlanta: Byrd Press, 1902.

Chapter 7 – Peachtree to Wall Street

71. **in charge of the Central of Georgia's freight depot.** Atlanta City Directories. 1874. Kenan Research Center, Atlanta History Center. See also *Central of Georgia Railway and Connecting Lines: The Right Way,* by Richard E. Prince, Published by R.E. Prince, Millard, Nebraska. This slim, fascinating compendium details the growth of this once-powerful railroad, originally known as the Central Rail Road, subsequently as the Central Rail Road & Banking Company of Georgia, which built and bought the rail lines from Savannah to Macon, and then on to Atlanta, beginning in the late 1830s. Both immigrant white labor and Negro slaves built this railroad, whose main transport commodity was cotton, followed by lumber and naval stores.

72. **sold at foreclosure on August 25, 1895.** The Banking Department managed to operate as a separate enterprise until February 7, 1896, at which time its accounts were liquidated. *Ibid.* Page 23.

73. **died of causes unknown at the age of 17, in 1897.** Garrett. II:634-635, and Garrett's Necrology, and microfilm newspaper archives, Kenan Research Center, Atlanta History Center.

74. **"the cause of death for the nude man quickly being listed as caused 'by a fall from being overheated.'"** *Ibid.* The entire *Journal* article, page 1, Sunday, August 7, 1904, follows. The article in The Constitution was in the same vein, but with a few added details.

John L. Gatins, manager of the Southern Exchange, and one of the best known young men in Atlanta died a sudden and tragic death in Caldecott's Turkish bath houses at 101-2 Decatur Street Saturday evening about 5 o'clock.

Whether death was the direct result of a fall or whether heart failure caused both will never be known.

Mr. Gatins, whose office was in the Gould Building just above the bath house, went into the place shortly after 4 o'clock. He disrobed for a Turkish Bath and one of the attendants took him in charge. Later when the man said it was time for them to leave the steam room, Mr. Gatins declined to do so, saying he would remain in a short while longer.

(Continued...)

The man turned off the steam and went in another part of the bath house. At that time
Mr. Gatins was sitting on top of some marble
stairs in the room. That was the last seen of
him until he was heard to fall. When several
persons who heard his body strike the marble
floor of the bathhouse, he was unconscious and
in a few minutes was dead.

Skull Not Fractured

Just over the left temple was a bruised
place but there was no fracture.

This fracture was caused by his head coming
in contact with the corner of a marble washstand. The fall must have been a heavy one and
it is most likely that Mr. Gatins was standing
on the steps when he pitched forward striking
on his head. He was never conscious and could
give no account of how the accident happened.

Dr. G.E. Weems, of the staff of the Grady
hospital, was in the bath house at the time
and was one of the first to reach the dying
man. He announced at once that there was no
hope of his recovery as his pulse was barely
perceptible. Death came very shortly.

Attempted to Rise

There are two theories as to the fall, some
people thinking that Mr. Gatins was attacked
by heart failure, and attempting to rise, was
overcome and fell, striking his head. They
think that while the wound was sufficient to
cause death, that it would not have killed him
had his heart been in proper condition.

Paid all Creditors

Mr. Gatins was probably one of the best
known young men in the state, and had for
years been identified with stock and produce
exchanges. He was a member of the firm Murphy
& Co. and when that firm sold out to Baxter &

(Continued...)

Co., he remained manager of the Southern Exchange, which was a connection of the latter concern. The exchange suspended when the Baxter crash came, but in a short time Mr. Gatins paid every trader who had ever dealt with him in full. He then resumed business under the name of the Southern Exchange. He was prominent in society, and was an enthusiastic automobilist.

Mr. Gatins was 35 years of age and unmarried. He is survived by his father, a brother, Joseph Gatins of New York and one sister, Mrs. John Murphy of Atlanta.

Coroner Holds Inquest

An inquest was held Saturday night by Coroner Stamps, the verdict of the jury being to the effect that death was due to a fall, which was caused by being overheated.

Only a few witnesses were examined and the verdict was reached within an hour after the inquest was begun. Among those who testified are George C.A. Caldecott, proprietor of the bath establishment; J.R. Todd, who was called in to attend the wounded man and Ed Mead and Peter Banks, colored attendants.

According to the testimony of those connected with the bathrooms, Mr. Gatins entered the establishment about 4 o'clock in the afternoon. During the course of his bath, he remained in the steam room an unusually long time and continually called for more heat. Finally the attendants, fearing that he should be overcome, refused to comply with his requests and instead shut off the steam altogether and opened the door. According to the statements of the Negro attendants, Mr. Gatins refused to leave the room.

The attendants left the door for a moment and were startled a second later to hear a noise as if someone had fallen. Rushing to the door, they discovered Mr. Gatins lying upon the floor in an unconscious condition, with blood pouring from a wound over his right eye.

(Continued...)

While the witnesses differed in their opinion relative to the cause of the fall, the consensus of opinion was that he was temporarily overcome by the heat, and in attempting to rise lost his balance and was lunged forward.

Mr. Caldecott, proprietor of the bath establishment, was one of those who differed with this theory, testifying that he believed Mr. Gatins slipped upon the steps.

Close examination showed that the skull of Mr. Gatins had not been fractured. However, it was stated that the force of the fall was sufficient to cause concussion of the brain, and that this was probably the direct cause of death. On the other hand, death could have resulted from a general collapse produced by the fall, heart failure, internal injuries or other cause, and for this reason possibly the verdict of the coroner's jury was not more explicit.

Dr. Todd testified that he was called to the bath rooms to attend to Mr. Gatins but that he did not reach his side until several minutes after breath had left his body. He declared that the direct cause of death was purely a matter of conjecture. He stated that he found one of the Mr. Gatins' shoulders to be slightly burned, however supposed that it was caused by his "coming in contact with one of the hot pipes when he fell to the floor."

---

75. **"a convert and her church was her whole outside life."** Simpson, Hope Gatins Curtis. Recollection of granddaughter. Personal correspondence to author, February 2, 1999, and April 7, 2008.

Chapter 8 – Manhattan to Paris

76. **"well-known figure in society and sporting circles."** Obituaries in *The Atlanta Journal*, May 8, 1927, and *The Atlanta Constitution*, May 9, 1927. Kenan Research Center, Atlanta History Center. Also, Simpson, Hope Gatins Curtis, personal letter to author, February 2, 1999. "He went to England and rode with the Melton-Mowbray hunt, a very prestigious one. He and my father were top horsemen. How they got that way—I don't think they had any background in

horses—is quite amazing." See also *www.melton.uk/*. The town had a rich tradition in fox hunting.

77. **Atlanta really wanted to give him a send-off.** Atlanta society, then as now, seems to revere its bad boys and wild ones, and never more so than at their funerals. By then, all sins and transgressions seem forgiven. Christ The King Cathedral in Atlanta, for example, was similarly packed two generations of Gatinses later for the funeral of my brother Charles, the wild, "bad boy" of his generation of Gatinses.

78. **"open to all white males from any state."** See *Pandora*, University of Georgia yearbook, June 10, 1901, published by the Fraternities of the University of Georgia. Felix Hargrett Rare Book and Manuscript Library, University of Georgia Library System, Athens. See also *The University of Georgia: A Bicentennial History, 1785-1985*, by Thomas G. Dyer, Athens: University of Georgia Press, 1985, for coherent description of the two main literary societies in Athens and their influence on campus.

79. **surely was a grand tour of Europe.** *The Red and The Black*, May 27, 1901. Athens: Published by the Athletic Association of the University of Georgia. Brief note in "Local Mention" column: "Joe Gatins will sail for Germany on June 26." Microfilm collections, University of Georgia Library. Athens, Georgia.

80. **grandfather spent several years at Yale University.** Confirmed by Christine Weidemann, Yale University Library Manuscripts and Archives archivist in e-mail to author, March 23, 2001.

81. **joined a family construction firm.** New York City Directories. New York City Public Library.

Chapter 9 – Salons and Suffragists

82. **a residence with a decidedly fancy address.** EOH.

83. **"in the Salon Society that flourished in Paris between the world wars."** EOH and EMR. "I knew people like Paul Valéry, Claudel, Maurois, Léon-Paul Fargues, the lover of Paris, Dr. Henri Mondor, Mallarmé's biographer." She added that she was a close friend of Edmée de la Rochefoucauld, "with whom I busied myself with feminist questions, which fascinated me *(avec laquelle je m'occupais des questions feministes qui me passionaient.)*"

84. **The Rochefoucaulds eventually became Eglé's neighbors.** See Francine du Plessix Gray, "The Surrealists' Muse." *The New Yorker*, September 24, 2007. No. 11. Place des Etats-Unis was the home of the Vicomtesse Marie-Laure de Noailles, a patron of avant-garde style and artists, including Man Ray and Salvador Dali. Whether the vicomtesse ever crossed paths with Eglé, 10 years her junior, is a matter of conjecture, but each surely would have known that the other was a neighbor.

85. **"not to 'dispense with the modesty which becomes our sex.'"** See www. academielitterature.be/academie-membre-delarochefoucauld.php downloaded

on April 14, 2005, and www.museehistoirevivante.com/expositions/ lesfemmesaffichent/guide_expo.htm downloaded on March 26, 2005. For details on various authors in Grandmother's circles of acquaintances, see biographical sketches of French writers all available from www.google.com:

a. Paul Claudel (1868-1955). Member of the Académie Francaise. Poet and French diplomat.

b. Leon-Paul Fargue (1876-1947). Poet and writer. He ran in the Shakespeare and Company circles and is remembered most as an inveterate *boulevardier*, who cruised the bistros, boulevards and nightspots of Paris. He collaborated in inventing and deciphering Joyce's intricate wordplay in *Ulysses*.

c. André Maurois (1885-1967). Member of the Académie Francaise. Essayist and literary critic.

d. Henri Mondor (1885-1962). Member of the Academie Francaise. Surgeon and historian of science and literature.

e. Paul Valery (1871-1945). Member of the Académie Francaise. Poet, literary critic and essayist.

86. **"met Stein through "her great friend, Denise Azam...** Weiland, Eglé Gatins. Granddaughter's recollection in e-mail to author of April 14, 2005. JOESIB

87. **a bisexual beauty from Cincinnati.** Fitch, Noel Riley, *Sylvia Beach and the Lost Generation: A History of Literary Paris in the Twenties and Thirties.* New York, W.W.Norton & Company, 1983. At page 72.

88. **"I worked day and night to raise money for the poor."** *Atlanta Journal.* March 22, 1964.

89. **"What he [Teilhard] did not know was not worth knowing."** EMR and EOH. See also www.gaiamind.com/Teilhard.html, downloaded on March 27, 2005.

90. **stayed in Pontrésina, and enjoyed many Alpine treks.** Author's recollection and Gatins family photo albums.

91. **clung to all-black widow's weeds ...** Simpson, Hope Gatins Curtis, correspondence with author.

92. **By the mid-1920s, Fischer** was listed as the "administrateur délégué" of the Bankers Trust Co. office in Paris, per an affidavit filed by Grandmother in support of a U.S. passport application. EOH.

93. **only a slim file of Fischer's poems...** The file contains about 45-50 poems, all in French, some in varying degrees of editing, some hand-written, but most typewritten. One poem, undated, stands out for its thinly veiled allusions to physical and sexual desire:

> *Oui, je sais bien que je vous aime,*
> *Que je vous adore aujourd'hui,*
> *Chère, c'est de l'amour quand-même,*
> *Dut-il ne durer qu'une nuit*
>
> *Pourvu que les lèvres soient tendres*
> *Pourvu que les regards soient fous,*
> *Qu'on sente les désires se tender,*
> *Désirs d'amant puissants et doux.*
>
> *Si l'étreinte ne se relache,*
> *Si le râle ému ne se tait,*
> *Si la chair est faible et lâche,*
> *Non, en verité que nous fait*
>
> *Que demain, la fête finie,*
> *Nous nous perdions dans la nuit;*
> *Amour, qu'importe l'agonie*
> *Si nous nous aimons aujourd'hui!*

A rough, literal translation follows:

> *Yes, I know well that I love you,*
> *That I adore you today,*
> *Dear, it's still love*
> *Even if for one night.*
>
> *As long as lips are tender,*
> *As long as attraction be wild,*
> *Might we feel mutual desire*
> *Longing of lovers, strong and tender*
>
> *Whether I ever relax my hold*
> *Whether my emotion ever dims*
> *Whether my feeble senses betray me*
> *No, truly, what difference does it make*

(Continued...)

> *If tomorrow, the party over,*
> *We lose ourselves in the night*
> *Love, what difference the agony*
> *If we love each other today!*

Chapter 10 – Coming of Age

94. **taught formal table manners in rigorous fashion.** Author's childhood recollections. Keeping one's elbows off the dining room table was rigidly enforced, though not with knives, as I grew up.

95. **Real intelligent."** *Livret Scolaire* for Francis Gatins. École Tannenberg.

96. **"actually encouraged visits to Club 122."** Based on the recollections of my twin brother and sister, Martin Gatins and Eglé Weiland. JOESIB.

97. **tastes like Alka-Seltzer.** See Bottled Water Web at www.bottledwaterweb.com/bott/bt, downloaded on April 20, 2005.

98. **diagnosed with a case of pulmonary tuberculosis.** Georgia Department of Health, Bureau of Vital Statistics. Joseph Francis Gatins, Jr., death certificate, May 8, 1927. The cause of death is listed as pulmonary tuberculosis of six years duration. There is no mention of alcoholism.

99. **His *forte* as an international banker...** Manset, Philippe. Conversations with author, summer of 1966, Paris, France.

100. **"consolation-type prize..."** e-mail to author from brother Martin Gatins, November 8, 2007. JOESIB.

101. **insulate Francis from the grim reality of his grandfather's suicide.** Recollection of my sister Eglé Gatins Weiland in 2002 letter to author.

102. **slightly more rustic and simple place than the much flashier, neighboring resort of St. Moritz.** Based on photo albums kept by Eglé de Villelume-Sombreuil Gatins. Among the many Fischer relatives, members of the Zuber-Buler and Rudolph Gmür families remained close to the Gatins clan for generations hence.

103. **hint of danger.** The crevice episode is recalled by my sister Eglé; see Eglé No. 3 on Eglé No. 2 files, delivered to author in May, 2002.

104. **Piz Bernina, a most technically difficult mountain above Pontrésina ... Alpine climbing club.** Gmür, Rudolph, one of the Swiss cousins, in telephone conversation with author, at Pontresina, summer of 1989. For the peak's elevation, see also multiple references to the Piz Bernina at www.google.com. See also civilian identification card, showing Francis maintained membership in the Paris section of the "Club Alpin Francais" after the war.

105. **ideally suited to the world of academic research, ferreting out obscure facts.** Manset, Philippe. Conversation with author, summer of 1966, Paris, France.

Chapter 11 – Atlanta Interlude

106. my father-in-law had died. His eulogy, from family files, follows:

The death of Joseph Francis Gatins removes a leader long honored in the business realm and one whose strength of character and goodness of heart won a host of friends. A native Atlantian, born in 1855, he saw as a child the drama of the War Between the States and grew to manhood in the stressful times of Reconstruction. He was a comrade of those whose faith in a town that was fighting its way up from disaster formed its spirit and assured its future as a great and prosperous city. His own career was a record of courage against odds and of resourcefulness amid difficulties. Beginning as a railway clerk, he soon showed the initiative, far-sightedness and sound judgment that afterwards distinguished him in the world of affairs. Steadily, deservedly, he rose to positions of large trust, and then to leadership and fortune in enterprises of his own.

Though Mr. Gatins transferred his headquarters to New York years ago, he retained keen interest in Atlanta and was ever loyal to its welfare. His visits to the city of his earliest success and his oldest friends were frequent. Shortly before his death, in New York, he was here looking after his investments and renewing cherished acquaintances. His eighty-one years took nothing from the clarity of his mind or the appeal of his personality. He was active until the end, and still thoughtful of others. His former business associate and life-long friend, Mr. Thomas B. Paine, truly says that the passing of Joseph F. Gatins "has cast a gloom over every Atlantian that ever knew him," for "He was a prince of good fellows, a beloved friend, a devoted companion, one of the best known men in America, and one of the most esteemed."

---

107. **leaving his grandson a one-third ownership of the Georgian Terrace Hotel...**
See Fulton County Courthouse, Clerk of the Court, land records at Deed Book
337, page 402. Indenture filed February 14, 1912, in which Joseph F. Gatins Sr.
established the Trust Company of Georgia (later, SunTrust Bank), as the trustee
for the Georgian Terrace Property after his death, for the benefit of his three
children, Joe, Ben and Mary, and in the case of their death, to the benefits of
their children and descendants. *The Atlanta Constitution* of February 15, 1912 also
made due note of this gift, estimated to be worth about $1 million at the time.
This explains young Francis' financial interest in the Atlanta hotel property.

108. **rediscovered by the ever-watchful chroniclers of the Gatins family at Atlanta's
daily newspapers.** *The Atlanta Constitution*, clipping in Eglé de Villelume-
Sombreuil Gatins photo albums.

109. **"Members of the unmarried and married contingents were invited to meet the
honor guest."** *Ibid.*

110. **"known for its parties."** E-mail to author, May 18, 2005, from Martin Gatins.
See also Barnard, Susan Kessler. *Buckhead: A Place For All Time*, 1996. Hill Street
Press, Athens, Georgia. Pages 113-114. Conkey Whitehead moved to Europe
permanently after the divorce. JOESIB.

111. **party until the champagne ran out.** E-mail to author, May 18, 2005, from
Martin Gatins. JOESIB.

112. **"Murphys had to send someone else over to check on Katherine."** *Ibid.*
JOESIB.

Chapter 12 – "Dancing on a Volcano"

113. ***Chasseurs Alpins.*** French Ministry of Defense. Abstract of French military service
for Joseph Francis Gatins, with cover letter of August 28, 2001 to author.

114. **ended in premature death on March 16, 1926, only one year before Francis was
to lose his own estranged father.** Préfecture de la Seine. Abstract of minutes for
death records in the 16th arrondissement of Paris.

115. **"in order to sound more French and high class."** Series of e-mail exchanges with
my brothers and sisters, 2008. JOESIB.

116. **on a long red carpet...** Information relayed to author by his brother Martin, who
has maintained close ties to the Colombian side of the family. JOESIB

117. **Don Eloy Valenzuela.** *Ibid.*

118. **Sylvia... single and footloose, having broken her engagement to the Prince de
Broglie.** Beatrice de German-Ribon Manset. Letter to author, May 30, 2002.

119. **put a stop to the fling with Faure.** E-mail exchange with my brothers and sisters,
2008. JOESIB.

120. **who had been the randiest during that period.** *"Elle était absolument bandée."* She

was totally randy! Author's recollection of conversation at the family dinner table, circa 1977.

121. **art history course at The Louvre Museum.** From Sylvia's school records.

122. **Cambridge has no record of his ever having enrolled as a student at any level.** McGuire, Patricia, Archivist, King's College, Cambridge. Exchange of e-mail with author, 2007.

123. **"But she has a great figure."** Weiland, Eglé Gatins. E-mail communication with author, December 24, 2007. JOESIB.

124. **"Everyone was dancing on a volcano, but we were all dancing a lot."** EMR.

125. **"he has manifested his loyalty to France."** U.S. Department of State. Response to Freedom of Information Act request filed by author of December 20, 2000, releasing 86 of 87 documents relevant to the request. These papers contain a goldmine of information about Francis, as did a related legal file maintained by the Atlanta lawyer, Welborn B. Cody, who handled most of the young man's legal and business affairs during the pre- and post-war period.

126. **to clear some tax matters.** In a subsequent letter, Francis' Atlanta-based lawyer, Welborn B. Cody, wrote the State Department to explain the issue: "In this connection, I wish to advise that Mr. Gatins had no income sufficient to make a return covering the calendar year 1937, but did have such income that would require him to file a return for 1938. This return was recently filed and the tax paid." JFGWEL.

Chapter 13 – "War is Such a Curse"

127. **virtual who's who.** *The Atlanta Constitution*, November 19, 1939, page 6M. "Distress and Suffering in France Described by Mrs. Joseph Gatins," by Sally Forth. Here is the salient paragraph from the letter:

> *Edna, dear, I know that what I am asking you is most disagreeable, but please try to do it for me and for the France that you and I love. Please form a committee with the help of Mrs. James D. Robinson, Mrs. Katherine Ellis Newman, Mrs. Frank Adair, Mr. and Mrs. Robert F. Maddox, Sr., Mrs. William P. Hill, Mrs. H.M. Atkinson, Mrs. Henry Tompkins, Mrs. Jesse Draper, Mr. and Mrs. Ben Gatins, Mrs. James E. Hickey, Dr. and Mrs. Julian Riley, Former Governor and Mrs. John M. Slaton, Mrs. Rix Stafford, Charles Dannais, Jr., J.L. Riley, James Alexander, Sims Bray, and any of my friends who would like to respond to an appeal to help my poor people.*

128. **"Smile, everything is lovely."** From a series of 11 letters and one telegram from Joseph Francis Gatins III to Sylvia de German-Ribon, prior to his being captured. Author's translation to English. Sylvia's letters no longer exist.

129. **how to "fish" for chicken.** E-mail correspondence with author, April 6, 2008, from sister Sophie. JOESIB.

130. **taken prisoner, on June 14, 1940.** See French Ministry of Defense, abstract of French military service for Joseph Francis Marie Gatins, with cover letter of August 28, 2001.

131. **harder than stone.** Author's recollection of common dinner table conversation in the Gatins household.

Chapter 14 – *"These Were Terrible Times"*

132. **Eglé received a postcard notice from the International Committee of the Red Cross.** See author's correspondence with the archives section of the Geneva-based ICRC (International Committee of the Red Cross).

133. **regarding Charlic.** Eglé's memoir suggests her brother weakened after being shipped back to France, suffering from bronchitis picked up in a German prisoner-of-war camp. "Between the wars, Charlic had a top flight position as a foreign exchange trader at Banker's Trust, which he kept until this house was sold to Morgan," Eglé said. "For reasons I never understood, he refused to go with Morgan. No longer working, he stayed busy especially with matters of literature and theater," eventually buying a small printing firm responsible for printing theater programs.

134. **"not entitled to the formal protection of this government."** See U.S. Department of State Response to Freedom of Information Act request filed by author of December 20, 2000, releasing 86 of 87 documents relevant to the request. These contained every application my father ever made for a U.S. passport, dating to May, 1924. JFGSTA.

135. **Sylvia's scrapbook.** See Gatins, Sylvia de German-Ribon Gatins, red leather bound scrapbook, entitled *Francis & Sylvia, 8 Décembre, 1943*. The newspaper clippings are located inside the front cover of the book, which has the initials G.R.G on the scrapbook cover.

136. **"The book was full of names and addresses for all my friends…"** Author's recollection of long interview with father, circa 1956, when he recounted a good bit of his prisoner days for a "show and tell" session for the author's 5th-grade school class.

Chapter 15 – Prisoner of War No. 50-894

137. **German prisoner-of-war records apparently lost.** See German Wehrmacht Military Archives, Berlin, letter of February 2, 2002 to author, relaying that POW records had been seized and re-transferred to the French authorities, translated by Dr. Charles Sydnor, Richmond, Virginia. Also, French Ministry of Defense for abstract of French military service for Joseph Francis Gatins, with cover letter of August 28, 2001. It remains to be seen if any French POW records were seized by Soviet forces when they retook Stalag 325 at Rawa-Ruska.

138. **see German soldiers in a mirror, brushing their teeth.** *The Atlanta Journal.* July 10, 1951. *Around Town* column by Hugh Park.

139. **military bureaucracy also docked him for every piece of clothing lost in escape transition.** *Ibid.*

140. **arrived at Stalag VIII-C by July 3, 1940.** International Committee of the Red Cross and its tracing service, Geneva, Switzerland. Correspondence with author, December 6, 2001, attesting to Francis's arrival at Stalag VIII-C, with photocopy of his first POW "location card," written out in his own handwriting, dated, July 3, 1940. ICRC.

141. **another 37,000 [prisoners] scattered in some 1,300-to-1,500 work details across Silesia and Austria.** ICRC. Stalag VIII-C Red Cross inspection report of December 3, 1940, in French. Author's translation to English.

142. **redeemable only at camp canteens, which had lemonade and malt beverages for sale and, sometimes, fresh produce.** *Ibid.*

143. **a high morale reigns.** *Ibid.*

144. **"sometimes we have a hard time realizing that we are prisoners."** *Ibid.*

145. **French POWs are too lazy to use urinals.** ICRC. Stalag VIII-C Red Cross inspection report of November 27, 1944 by Doctors Thudichum and Rossell. Author's translation from French to English.

146. **"more and more painful."** According to a close friend and former fellow newsman assigned by the U.S. military to interview American prisoners of war after the conflict was over, the key thing to remember about the camps was "that these were not very pretty places to be." Author interview with Charles E. Cox, Richmond, Virginia, March 14, 2008.

147. **head to Hungary.** See April 22, 1947 letter from Joseph Gatins to Atlanta lawyer Welborn Cody, detailing attempted escape to Hungary. JFGWEL. As for the stay at Stalag X-B, the only confirmation is provided by the International Committee of the Red Cross and its International Tracing Service in a letter to the author of November 5, 2001, relaying results of a file search in German military archives. None of Francis' letters from Stalag X-B, if there were any, survived the war.

Chapter 16 – Eglé's Private Resistance

148. **"all were sent to camps, where most of them perished, as you know."** See Marrus, Michael R., and Paxton, Robert O., *Vichy France and the Jews*. Stanford University Press. 1995. Originally published in French. Largely based on review of German archives, the book starkly details the fawning, anti-Semitic collaboration many French and their government willingly gave to the occupiers.

149. **She said that you could hear the babies and children crying.** Weiland, Eglé Gatins. E-mail to author, January 26, 2002. JOESIB.

150. **"a terrible odor infected the place."** Mathey-Jenais, J.M. Contemporary account, relayed in an article by George Wellers, appearing in *La Revue du Centre de Documentation Juive Contemporaine*, April-June, 1967.

151. **"with nervous cries and shrieks, kids crying and even adults at the end of their rope."** *Ibid.*

152. **she made a weekly trek to the Basilica of the Sacred Heart, on a hillside overlooking Montmartre.** E-mail to author from my sister Sophie Mason, April 6, 2008. JOESIB.

153. **that garnered her the highest award possible for French civilians,** the *Legion d'Honneur*. Grande Chancellerie de la Legion d'Honneur, Paris. Correspondence with author, October 21, 2001, providing copies of Eglé's nomination papers to be named *Chevalier de le Legion d'Honneur*.

154. **on some very formal occasions, she would wear the Legion's medal itself.** Gatins family recollections. JOESIB.

Chapter 17 – Deaf-Mute Escape to Hamburg

155. **transferred from Stalag II-B to Stalag X-B at Sanbostel.** International Committee of the Red Cross. Correspondence with author from the agency's International Tracing Service, November 5, 2001, relaying results of a file search in the Deutsche Dienstelle, the German military archives, translated by Dr. Charles Sydnor, Saltville, Virginia.

156. **became a notorious death camp.** Suggested in Wikipedia, the Internet encyclopedia.

157. **"everywhere the dead and dying sprawled around the slime of human excrement."** From Clifford Barnard's *Two Weeks in May 1945*, as referenced in the Wikipedia entry. Quaker Home Service. 1999.

158. **Tuberculosis was rampant ...** International Committee of the Red Cross, inspection reports for Stalag X-B, August 6, 1942 by Drs. Schirmer, Lehner and Wenger, and November 21, 1942 by Dr. Masset and Mr. Freidrich. ICRC.

159. **"I was free just two weeks when I was caught in Hamburg and sent to a concentration camp in Poland."** JFGSTA. See "Affidavit by Native American to Explain Protracted Foreign Residence," in support of a U.S. citizen's registration

application filed by my father at the U.S. Embassy in Paris on December 19, 1944, made available to the author in response to Freedom of Information Act request filed by author of December 20, 2000. The understated fashion in which my father related these events on paper carried over to real life. He was prone to minimize his adventures and understate the duress that he had experienced.

160. **anecdotal evidence suggesting he used the false identity papers to present himself as a deaf-and-dumb, guest worker from France.** Author's recollection and author's conversation with old family friend in Atlanta, John C. Calhoun, *circa* 2002, confirmed in correspondence with Calhoun, July 2, 2002.

161. **successful escapes only "possibly number 85,000."** See *World War II in Europe: An Encyclopedia,* by David T. Zabecki, at pp. 1204, *et. seq.* and article on Escape and Evasion by Alexander Molnar Jr.

Chapter 18 – Hell in the Ukraine

162. **habitually tried to hush him up, in vain.** Author's recollections.

163. **about 15,000 of the Soviet prisoners died of hunger, disease or flat-out murder there.** Principal Soviet Inquiry Commission into Hitlerian Crimes in Poland. Report of the Inquiry into the town of Rawa-Ruska of 24-30 September, 1944, translated from the Polish to the French and then to English by the author. This report was collected and published by *Ceux de Rawa-Ruska,* a French World War II veterans organization that maintains a most informative website relating to Stalag 325, at http://rawa-ruska.net/rawa02.htm.

164. **shot to death, and dumped into common graves.** *Ibid.*

165. **rude awakening even before landing at the Ukraine punishment prison.** International Committee of the Red Cross correspondence of May 16, 1961 with members of the French veterans group, *Ceux de Rawa-Ruska,* at www.rawa-ruska. net.

166. **"The soil, the walls and some of the 'sleeping boards' were covered with vermin."** *Ceux de Rawa-Ruska.* The website is now largely maintained by prisoners of war descendants. See *Historique de camp de Rawa-Ruska.* Author's translation to English.

167. **"And thus always hope."** The crest and motto can be found on Grandmother Eglé's silver set.

168. **red triangles, which, under the Nazi camp classification system, were reserved for political prisoners.** United States Holocaust Memorial Museum, and its website, http://www.ushmm.org/. See online article, "Classification System in Nazi Concentration Camps."

169. **"work on railcars, or put to work by the railroad administration of the Reich."** See International Committee of the Red Cross inspection report for Stalag 325 Rawa Ruska, dated August 16, 1942. See also inspection reports for Rawa-Ruska and its work detachments of February 7, 1943 (both for main camp);

for work detachment No. 2001, near Lemberg [L'viv,] of February 6, 1943; an undated, special companion report for the same detachment detailing the specific, individual complaints of a French POW, Jean Chabry, who had been brought to the attention of the Red Cross; for work detachment No. 2048F, at Jezernia, near Tarnopol, dated February 8, 1943; for Zweilager Tarnopol, dated February 8, 1943; for work detachment No. 2047, Berezowica, dated February 9, 1943; and for the main camp at Lemberg [L'viv,] again on August 25, 1943. ICRC.

170. **The prison commandant was nicknamed Tom Mix.** *Ceux de Rawa-Ruska.* Website. See *Historique de camp de Rawa-Ruska.* Author's translation to English, and Chevallier, Paul. *Les Chemins qui Menaient a Rawa-Ruska.* Editions des Ecrivains. Paris, 2000.

171. **we ate the dog of our tormentor.** *Ibid,* Chevallier, pp. 173-174.

172. **root cellar had been placed on top of a charnel house.** Jarny, Raymond. *L'Enfer de Rawa Ruska: Chronique de guerre, d'evasions et d'espoir.* Presses de Valmy. Paris. 2000, p. 349.

173. **"Russian-style" latrines.** Author's recollection. My father well remembered the open nature of these latrines and the jokes the soldiers told each other about this experience: "You eat like a bird, but you shit like a steer." (*"Tu manges comme un oiseau, mais tu schies comme un boeuf."*)

174. **French prisoners staged something of a full-dress parade through the camp, singing the French national anthem,** *La Marseillaise. Op. Cit.,* Jarny.

175. **a "hymn" for Rawa-Ruska, whose wry title, "Up-the-Ass," bespoke volumes about their feelings.** See *Ceux de Rawa-Ruska,* at http://rawa-ruska.net/rawa02.htm.

176. **Rawa-Ruska … a "seminary" for the hard-core and the untamable.** From Gatins family papers. This typewritten note, undated and unsigned, looks like a formal statement that a former Rawa-Ruska prisoner might have provided to the news media, or in testimony before a tribunal. It is not possible today to know who wrote it.

177. **would have been impossible to fix the numerous inconveniences described in the preceding report.** ICRC. Inspection report of February 7, 1943 for "Stalag 325, 'Zitadelle' Lemberg [L'viv] (formerly at Rawa-Ruska)."

178. **mere threat of a transfer to the** *Gouvernement Général* **has a decidedly salutary effect on prisoner discipline.** *Ibid.*

179. **impossible to tell how many never made it back from far-away commando detachments.** *Ceux de Rawa-Ruska* website.

180. **"some of our guards, who had participated in this operation, quite good-humoredly explained to us that 2,000 Jews had been killed that night."** Nuremberg Trial Proceedings, Vol. 6, January 29, 1946. See the Avalon Project, Yale Law School, http://www.yale.edu/lawweb/avalon/imt/imt.htm.

181. **singling out Jewish prisoners for especially harsh treatment …** Late in the war, the Nazi regime singled out American prisoners with obviously Jewish features or last names for segregation in special detachments that were exercises in brutality.

By 1944, the Nazi hierarchy set up prisoner slave camps, such as the Berga work detachment of Stalag IX-B, where most of the American G.I.s held prisoner there were Jewish, and subjected to brutally dehumanizing conditions. Of 350 American prisoners detailed to Berga, 73 died. See Roger Cohen's *Soldiers and Slaves: American POWs Trapped by the Nazis' Final Gamble*, Knopf, 2005.

182. **Scapini… twice prosecuted after the war.** See news articles appearing in *Le Monde*, July 25-28, 1952, and the Scapini entry in the *Dictionnaire de la Politique Francaise*, Henry Coston Publications, 1979.

Chapter 19 – "His Mind Went Crazy"

183. **'yes, but let's have some dessert.'"** Martin T. Gatins tape-recorded interview with author, June 13, 2001, at Satolah, Georgia.

184. **early slaughter included murder by shooting, burning, clubbing, drowning or burying alive, as well as by grenade or mobile gas vans.** For a detailed view of these actions in and around Rawa-Ruska and L'viv, where such murder units were stationed, see *The Einsatzgruppen Reports*, edited by Yitzhak Arad, *et. al.* Holocaust Library, New York, 1989. Also, the growing testimony being gathered by Father Patrick Desbois, a French priest, and grandson of a French prisoner of war at Rawa-Ruska, on the *Einsatzgruppen* killings of Jews in the Ukraine. Desbois and his team have uncovered some 600-plus common graves used for these shootings and documented an additional 1.5 million murders, approximately, under this pre-camp death program. Information about Father Desbois efforts is widely publicized and available in news articles and websites, including the Centre de Documentation Juive Contemporaine in Paris and the www.yahadinunum.org website.

185. **brandy distillery, used to enslave and control local peasantry.** From *The Enigma of Ukraine: Culture or Nation State*, by M. Raphael Johnson, appearing in *The Barnes Review* magazine at www.barnesreview.org.

186. **sheer scale of the Holocaust murders in the Triangle of Death camps is staggering.** These totals do not include the 33,000–39,000 murders committed in this area as part of Operation Ernterfest (Nov. 3-5, 1943), in which the Nazis sought to eradicate evidence of the Holocaust extermination camps.

187. **"gold coins from 34 countries; 2,910 kilograms of gold bars; 18,734 kilograms of silver bars; 16,000 diamond carats, and more."** See a second book by Yitzhak Arad, *Belzec, Sobibor, Treblinka: The Operation Reinhard Death Camps.* Indiana University Press, 1987. The latter, besides enumerating the carnage, makes detailed and specific reference to the enormous economic plunder that accompanied these killings (right down to suitcases full of gold teeth yanked from the bodies). At pp. 159-164.

188. **take potshots at the babies on the other side, like a skeet shoot.** Jarny, Raymond. *L'Enfer de Rawa Ruska: Chronique de guerre, d'evasions et d'espoir.* Presse de Valmy. Paris. 2000. At pp. 390-392.

189. **The smell is unbearable when the wind comes back our way.** *Ibid,* page 370. I have found no other suggestion or evidence of a death camp-style crematory at Rawa-Ruska, similar to the ones built at the Reinhard camps, but the Nazis did employ special pyres like those later used to try to eradicate evidence of the killings and mass graves left all over the Ukrainian landscapes.

190. **where I witnessed a terrible scene.** *Ibid,* at page 352.

191. **some 500,000 Galician Jews.** See *Historique de camp de Rawa-Ruska,* on the French Rawa-Ruska POW veterans group's website, relating to a visit to L'viv in 2003. The entry displays a picture of a plaque at the Kleparov freight depot, written in English: "Kleparov. The last stop of L'vov's Jews before being expelled and put to death in gas chambers of Belzetz [sic]. The station served as passage for all Galician Jews on their way to death. About 500,000 Jews passed here in trains from March, 1942 till the beginning of 1943."

192. **"Deprived of air and water, with no sanitary facilities, forced to spend endless hours traveling or waiting in stations in the packed freight cars, many died en route."** Arad, Yitzhak. See pp. 63-67. *Op. Cit.*

193. **impossible to avoid the sickening, sweetish smell of death.** Translation by Dr. Charles Sydnor of a German non-commissioned officer's journal entries from Rawa-Ruska, August 31, 1942.

194. **"That evening, all that was left were the women, the carts and the straw."** Desbois, Patrick. *Porteur de Mémoires: Un prêtre revele la Shoah par balles."* Editions Michel Lafon, Neuilly-sur-Seine, 2007.

195. **truckloads of Jews are brought to their mass grave and executed six at a time by six shooters with machine pistols.** *Ibid,* at page 316, and author's and sister Sophie Gatins Mason's interview with Father Desbois, Atlanta, Georgia, February 26, 2008.

196. **"when his mind went crazy."** Martin T. Gatins' tape-recorded interview with author, June 13, 2001, at Satolah, Georgia.

Chapter 20 – Last Stalag

197. All references in this chapter derive from Francis' letters to Sylvia. JFGPOW.

Chapter 21 – Surreal in Berlin

198. **"a more scientific way of escaping."** *The Atlanta Journal,* July 10, 1951, *Around Town* column by Hugh Park.

199. **almost 225,000 French prisoners opted for the "transformation" process by June of 1944, (out of a total of 956,101).** See *La Captivité: Histoire des prisoners de guerre Francais, 1939-1945,* by Yves Durand, available in the archives of the Centre de Documentation Juive Contemporaine, Paris.

200. **living practically as he pleased in Berlin."** *The Atlanta Journal,* July 10, 1951, *Around Town* column by Hugh Park.

201. **"I can't thank you enough. It really made me happy."** Only two letters of my father's correspondence to Eglé survive. The rest of them, although once in possession of the author's brother Martin, are lost. Each letter in this series includes the envelopes, with 55 Deutschmarks worth of stamps (depicting Adolph Hitler's image).

202. **"Does not respond to summons."** French Ministère de la Défense, archives section, letter to author of July 26, 2002.

Chapter 22 – Wartime Wedding

203. **endless Métro rides from one end of Paris to the other.** Author's recollections.

204. **"Expect financial complications in the long term..."** Undated handwriting analysis and horoscope kept by my mother.

205. **of French nationality "and non- Jewish."** Madame DuFour, notary. Typewritten marriage contract papers drawn up for Mr. Gatins and Miss de German-Ribon, November 25, 1943.

206. **laws aimed at the "economic Aryanization" of Jewish properties.** See report of the Mission Matteoli, the blue-ribbon panel appointed by the French government in 1995 to study the issue of the economic "spoliation" of French Jews. The equivalent of more than $1.35 billion euros were stolen. See also Weisberg, Richard H. *Vichy Law and the Holocaust in France,* 1996, New York University Press, New York.

207. **a large diamond surrounded by eight smaller, faceted diamonds.** E-mail correspondence between author and his brother Martin, a Cartier senior vice-president in New York. December 20, 2007. The engagement ring is exactly the same design as rings subsequently made by the Cartier luxury jewelry house, but Cartier's artisans definitely did not make it in 1943, according to Cartier records. The diamonds, moreover, were not top quality, perhaps reflecting the realities of the diamond trade under the occupation. JOESIB.

208. **particularly effusive about Francis' escape.** The typewritten copy of the mayor's speech was pasted into Sylvia's wedding scrapbook, a red leatherbound album with the initial G.R.G.

209. **wedding cake .... so tasty the hungry guests gobbled it all up...** E-mail correspondence with author from sister, Sophie Gatins Mason, April 6, 2008. JOESIB.

210. **wedding witnesses.** From marriage bann secretly filled out and published by the parish authorities at Chaillot on December 8, 1943.

211. **a mildly sensational article about the wedding.** The clipping was pasted into a leatherbound scrapbook kept by my mother, entitled Francis et Sylvia, and dated the same day as the wedding banns were published, December 8, 1943.

212. **studiously kept a list of all the wedding gifts.** List was saved in Sylvia's wedding papers.

213. **dined that same wedding night at Maxim's.** Author's interview with old family friend, John C. Calhoun in 1997.

Chapter 23 – Wartime Honeymoon

214. **"the dinner table at La Chezotte was lined with German machine pistols."** Author's recollection.

215. **talk a German patrol out of arresting a youngster from a nearby farm...** Gatins family recollection.

216. **buried all the shotguns and rifles in the garden beds...** Author's recollection. The collection of armaments was thoroughly rusted when it was dug out of the garden after the war—totally unusable.

217. **a constant search for victuals...** Author's recollections and e-mail correspondence with brother Miguel. JOESIB.

218. **made to dig their own graves and, without trial or hearing, shot dead...** See Parrotin, Marc. *Immigrés dans la Resistance en Creuse.* Editions Verso. Ahun, France. 1998. This book is out of print, but can sometimes be found in bookstores of La Creuse. The four Italian laborers eventually were identified as Pierre Rinaldi of Marbinigno, Italy; Pierre Capelleto; and two others whose first names could not be determined, Collegaro and Bertoli.

219. **smell of the dead bodies was so pungent...** Collective Gatins family recollections.

220. **local doctor...shot dead by a German officer in the courtyard of the local elementary school in Ahun...** *Op. Cit.* Parrotin.

221. **more than 450 others gave their lives to the same cause in this remote department....** *Op. Cit.* Parrotin.

222. **to me, the site appeared remarkably peaceful.** From author's visit to the site in the summer of 2002.

Chapter 24 – Knocking Over the Anthill

223. **They read like a diary, recording daily events from the mundane to the earth-shattering.** Grandmother's liberation letters were typed into readable formal by my sister Eglé in 2007-2008. Author's translation to English.

224. **miliciens included ultra-collaborationists, toughs and some smattering of "respectable bourgeoisie and even the disaffected aristocracy."** Ousby, Ian. *Occupation: The Ordeal of France, 1940-1944.* Cooper Square Press, 2000.

225. **"for the purpose of obtaining a valid American document in order to join**

the American Army." U.S. Department of State. Response to Freedom of Information Act request filed by author of December 20, 2000, releasing 86 of 87 documents relevant to the request. See especially, at pages 40 through 40-C, Francis's "Affidavit by Native American to Explain Protracted Foreign Residence," in support of a U.S. citizen's registration application filed at the U.S. Embassy in Paris on December 19, 1944. JFGSTA.

Chapter 25 – Tubercular in Love

226. **bought a house.** Located at 106 and 1/2 Park Avenue in Saranac.

227. **"all your perfume and your virginity."** The Saranac love letters bluntly allude to Sylvia's giving herself to Francis on their wedding night at the Lancaster Hotel in Paris, where, it seems, the sexual pleasure was all his. But the correspondence also suggests Sylvia subsequently learned to glory in the joy of mutual sexual satisfaction.

228. **"Pity to have given him the name Miguel!"** I had no idea I had an extra middle name until I had to produce my birth certificate sometime after high school. Up until then, I thought I was called Joseph F. Gatins, Jr.

229. **"I've seriously started writing my memoirs, in an attempt to get them published and to make a bit of money."** To my knowledge, my father never put his memories to paper or, if he did, they are long lost. In letter No. 77, the next to last in this series, apparently on November 28, 1946, he noted he "tried to write my memoirs. But the cold cuts out all inspiration. I can only read with one hand outside the covers. I'm totally wiped out."

Chapter 26 – Not White Trash

230. **The Georgian Terrace … experienced something of an economic and financial renaissance during World War II.** *The Atlanta Journal-Constitution*, May 17, 2001. Article by Jim Auchmutey.

231. **"This hotel marks a distinct step forward in southern hoteldom."** *The Atlanta Journal*, October 3, 1911. The hotel was designed by an architect from New York, William Lee Stoddard, who was also retained to design another nearby Gatins property at 468 Peachtree, a "bachelor apartment house," according to *The Atlanta Constitution* of October 18, 1912.

232. **placed [the hotel] in trust for his three children and their descendants in 1912.** Fulton County, Georgia, Deed Records, Atlanta, Georgia, at Deed Book No. 337, page 402.

233. **$57,200 was being held on his behalf.** Equivalent to about $677,000 in today's dollars.

234. **report the sighting of a former prisoner of war that he thought might be**

"used by the Russians as an espionage agent in the United States." The FBI declassified the interview report on August 1, 2008 and made it available pursuant to author's Freedom of Information Act request. The one-page "FBI Espionage Memorandum" was dated December 31, 1947, forwarded from the Special Agent in Charge of the Atlanta office to then FBI director Herbert Hoover, whom history has shown to have been totally paranoid about the possibility of Communists in the U.S. government.

Chapter 27 – International Interlude

235. **INS effort, involving voluminous documention, formal hearings and findings, filings of some 16 different birth and marriage certificates and the like...** Contained in U.S. Department of Justice Immigration and Naturalization Service, January 31, 2003 response to author's Freedom of Information Act request. SYLINS.

236. **Sylvia had brought her own funds to the marriage, most of them invested in holdings in Colombia...** See *Sylvia Account Book*, a handwritten, monthly accounting of her Colombian investment holdings during the period July, 1943—December 31, 1955.

237. **"let us hope that we will be soon as the bar of the P.D.C. [Piedmont Driving Club]."** Spalding went on to become the top editor of *The Atlanta Journal*. At the time, the club was open only to about 1,000 white men, most of them business or social lions known locally as the "Big Mules." The term "big" also often represented a function of age for males in the deep South. In my youth, I often was called "little Joe," for example, to differentiate me from my father, "big Joe."

238. **"I hope I will find a job in spite of the fact that I am getting pretty old, and that since I left college, I never had a chance to settle down to business."** From one of Francis' letters to lawyer Welborn Cody. JFGWEL.

239. **Might have been having an affair in New York during the period.** Recollection of the late Dorothy Gatins Brewster, daughter of Ben and Dorothy Gatins, Francis' cousin, shared with author during a visit to New York.

240. **"Enough, with the prayers!"** Recollection of Gatins family friend in Atlanta, Joan Zillessen.

241. **landed at Shannon.** A jet flight from New York to Paris can take less than seven hours today. It was an 18-hour adventure in the 1950s, entailing refueling stops in Newfoundland and Ireland before reaching Paris. The Gatins family most often flew big, Lockheed Constellations, four-engine prop planes with three tails that, at night, could be seen to spit out blue flames from its exhausts. These early trans-Atlantic prop flights were also deemed dangerous enough that the Gatins family split itself in two the first time it flew to Paris. Daddy took three of the children, while Mommy took the three others on a separate, later flight. It was also a heady time for adventure of aviation, generally, in which men dressed in coats and ties and brought their shaving gear for such trips to look right upon deplaning.

242. **Scapini.** See *Dictionnaire de la Politique Francaise,* Volume III, Henry Coston, Paris. 1979, at page 648. Scapini was arrested in 1945 and initially freed the following year. He fled to Switzerland, but was returned and tried in France and sentenced to five years hard labor in 1949. The accusations and that verdict were thrown out, however, and he was subsequently found not guilty of lesser charges that he "demoralized the French military and the French nation" and "harmed the national defense." (See trial coverage in *Le Monde,* 25-28 July, 1952).

243. **yellow-brick house.** Located at 2525 Rivers Road.

Chapter 28 – Culture Shock

242. **another part of the extended Gatins clan.** Besides Joe and Ina Gatins, there was also Aunt Nell Gatins, a teacher who did so well that she rose to become the first woman public school principal in Atlanta's history. This Joe's brother, John Gatins, has enlisted during World War II and was killed during the D-Day invasion in Normandy. Another colorful Gatins characters was Bill Gatins, this Joe's oldest brother, a house was by day, who by night, entertained Atlanta on the radio in the 1930s with Bill Gatins' Jug Band (he also played tenor banjo). According to Wayne W. Daniel, author of *Pickin' on Peachtree: A History of Country Music in Atlanta, Georgia,* Bill became known as one of the "best-known hillbilly personalities of the Atlanta area." In a subsequent wave of immigration from Ireland, yet another Joseph Gatins came to New York from Killybegs in the early 20th Century, apparently fleeing trouble with British forces. That branch of the McGettigan-Gatins clan also flourished, providing a multitude of firefighters, policemen, accountants and lawyers to New York-area governments and municipalities. But the Gatinses in Atlanta had no idea of the existence of those New York Gatinses until a chance meeting of one Dan Gatins, a distant cousin, with Martin's wife in Atlanta in the 1990s. Uncle Ben also ran into that new immigrant at a New York hospital, but at the time refused to countenance the idea that they were related!

244. **Butterball and Whitey.** In French, Bouboule and Blanchette. Per e-mails of February, 2009, with siblings. JOESIB.

245. **found it in our genetic code to be fleet of foot and fearless on the gridiron.** My organized football career, such as it was, ended as an all-state guard in the Rhode Island prep league. I was not big enough for college ball.

246. **hiked us unmercifully up and down nearby mountain paths, sometimes above the snow line, sometimes breaking into bawdy French Army marching songs.** One example of these French marching songs:

> *Y'était un grenadier—qui revenait de Flandres.*
> *Y'était si courvertu—qu'on y voyait son membre.*

(Continued...)

> *Tambour battait — la Générale!*
> *Tambour battait toujours — la nuit comme le jour.*
> *La Générale se bat — ne l'entendez vous pas?*

A rough translation:

> *Was a grenadier, coming home from Flanders.*
> *So few clothes left, you could see his member.*
> *Drum roll rolling — the General alarm!*
> *Drum roll forever rolling — night and day.*
> *Drum roll rolling — can't you hear it tolling?*

These ditties were used to count cadence on military parades and are very similar to the "Jody songs" once used by the U.S. Army to do exactly the same. "Jody" was the man left behind after draftees were enlisted into basic training. One example, recalled by the author from his basic training at Ft. Benning, Georgia:

> *Ain't no use — in lookin' back,*
> *Jody done got yo Cadillac!*
> *Ain't no use — in lookin' blue,*
> *Jody done got yo sister, too!*

Chapter 29 – Tabasco in Buckhead

247. **enclave of black residents known as Johnson Town.** See *Buckhead: A Place For All Time*, by Susan Kessler Barnard. Hill Street Press, Athens, Georgia, at pp. 79-80, *et. seq.*

248. **waving a switchblade around the P.D.C. bar.** That switchblade was part of Francis' fairly large knife collection.

249. **"taking care of Francis tonight."** E-mail correspondence with author from brother Martin, May 9, 2008. JOESIB.

250. **vigorous argument with friends about whether George Washington had smoked pot...** Recollection of Stuart Witham in conversation with author, Spring, 2008.

251. **"crying like a fountain"** *Il pleurait, pleurait, pleurait, il pleurait comme une Madeleine. Il pleurait, pleurait, pleurait. Il pleurait comme une fontaine.*

252. **"declaim a doggerel "Rebel Song…"** Sims Bray Jr., provided the full text of the Gatins-Bray "Rebel Song," noting that his father sang it at his wedding, too. "After he finished singing, I looked around the room to see a bunch of wide-open jaws and eyes that displayed utter disbelief at what they had just seen and heard," Bray Jr. said.

The Good Old Rebel Song (*Sims Bray version*)

I'm a good ole rebel & that's just what I am,
For this fair land of freedom, I do not give a damn,
I'm glad I fought agin it, I only wish we'd won.
I don't want no pardon for anything I done.
I hates the Constitution and the uniform of blue,
I hate the Freedmen's bureau and everything they do.
I hate the striped banner dripping with our blood,
Lying, thieving Yankees, I fought all I could.
Three hundred thousand before they conquered us.
They died of Southern fever and Southern steel and shot,
I wish it was three million instead of what we got.
I can't take up my musket and fight 'em any mo,
But I ain't gonna love 'em, and that is certain sho.
And I want no pardon for what I was and am,
And I won't be reconstructed, and I don't give a damn!

Various versions of the "Good Old Rebel" lyrics apparently have been around since the late 1860s. It was then published and sung by various veterans of the defeated Confederate forces in 1914, and later republished and used by various singers, including Ry Cooder.

253. **Daddy served as navigator on this trip—by looking down below and following Interstate 75.** Mary Branch Close. Letter to author, June, 2008.

254. **"instinct shooting" techniques.** For details of "Lucky" McDaniel's prowess, see http://en.wikipedia.org/wiki/Lucky_McDaniel#Biography or *Lucky McDaniel's Secrets to Shooting*, by Lucky McDaniel and Bill Reece, Columbus, Georgia, Waldrup Printing Company, 1980.

255. **each indulgence putting us a step closer to eternal bliss.** The practice of securing plenary indulgences generally was discontinued after Vatican II, but it has

increased significantly under the current conservative pope, Benedict XVI. They are no longer for sale outright, however. See *The New York Times*, February 10, 2009, article by Paul Vitello, "For Catholics, a Door to Absolution Is Reopened."

256. **"If I ever see you again, I'll cut your balls off."** In French, *"Petit salaud, si jamais j'te retrouves, j'te coupes les couilles."* Author's recollection.

257. **"They called her Chanel No. 5."** Author's recollection and e-mail correspondence with siblings Eglé and Miguel, August, 2002. JOESIB.

258. **Attempt escape alone.** *The Atlanta Journal,* Tuesday, July 10, 1951. Hugh Park column.

259. **rock-and-roll from Elvis and Jerry Lee Lewis, rhythm-and-blues from the likes James Brown and The Famous Flames, or Dr. Feelgood and the Interns.** I have an endearing memory of this "race music," as rhythm-and-blues music was called in the early 1960s. Picture this: Better than a hundred teenaged white boys and girls, dressed in Sunday best for the Atlanta Cotillion Christmas dance, jitterbugging and doing the Twist like mad to an all-black band at the upscale Cherokee Town & Country Club (formerly the Grant family estate, on West Paces Ferry Road). The drummer was sweating, the brass and saxophone sections were strutting in unison while the lead guitarist picked the strings with his tongue. "Baby, shake that thing!" the vocalist screamed. When I first head the Beatles several years later, I thought their music sounded strange.

Chapter 30 – New Realities of the 1960s

260. **called "soldier's heart" during the American Civil War, et. seq.** L. Weisaeth, *The European History of Psychotraumatology*, 2002, in *Journal of Traumatic Stress*, 15, 443-452.

261. **continue to demonstrate post-traumatic symptomology...** See doctoral thesis of January, 1999, by Julie M. Brody, entitled "An Assessment of Nazi Concentration Camp Survivors for PTSD and Neurological Concomitants," in the archives of the U.S. Holocaust Memorial Museum.

262. **by feelings of detachment...** E-mail to author from Sophie Gatins Mason, May 21, 2001. JOESIB.

263. **small monthly allotment received from the French government...** Grande Chancellerie de la Legion d'Honneur. Correspondence with author, providing copies of Charlic's nomination papers to be named *Chevalier de le Legion d'Honneur.*

264. **She confronted her brother, who got very huffy and told her finances were "none of a woman's business."** Recollection of Martin T. Gatins, in e-mail to author, November 22, 2008. JOESIB.

265. **"Now, it's over. You're going to come live with us in Atlanta."** Grandmother's return to Atlanta entailed her securing a permanent visa (as a French citizen) to live in the U.S., which occasioned yet another bureaucratic squabble with

American authorities. Eglé notes in her memoirs that the matter was "fairly complicated," all the more so since a vice-consul handling the matter at the U.S. Embassy in Paris "hated me for reasons that I never understood." Francis appealed the matter to a U.S. Senator from Georgia, though, who loathed embassy people and facilitated her emigration to her late husband's native soil. After that, the matter was quickly smoothed over and Eglé secured permission to enter the country and pass her remaining furniture collection through customs.

266. **Her engagement ring also was sold to pay everything off.** Recollection of Martin T. Gatins, in e-mail to author, November 22, 2008. JOESIB.

267. **made of brass artillery shells from World War I.** Grandmother Eglé brought over another wartime memento from France, this one a fearsome set of brass knuckles given her mother by an American G.I. convalescing in a French hospital during World War I.

268. **she feared she might experience another suicide in the family.** Author's recollection of a terrible night in the Gatins household, summer of 1964.

269. **Charles and I, with our father's help, found summer jobs.** My construction jobs were due to the generosity of Joe Hutchison, principal in a large general contracting firm, and a good friend of the family, as well as Alfred Kennedy, who owned the machine shop. Charles got his office work via G. Albert Lawton, president then of an Atlanta-based life insurance company.

270. **In a soul-wrenching effort to put food on the table, she also decided to secretly sell off some of the Colombian emerald jewelry.** My mother was both devastated by the decision to sell the jewelry—and also proud at the same time to have taken this drastic step to help ensure the family's survival. Author's recollection of a tearful, long-distance phone call from his mother.

271. **a portfolio of blue chip securities...** From family tax return for 1958.

272. **and to introduce Sophie to French society.** A good childhood friend from that period in Atlanta, George "Jorge" Lawton, also accompanied us on that trip to France.

273. **he literally seemed gray.** Recollection of sister Eglé in letter to author, May, 2002. JOESIB.

Chapter 31 – Tempest Fugit

274. **Francis and Sylvia became grandparents.** Here's how it happened. I married Frances Moeller White, with one son, Demian; Charles, my late brother, married Laura Bird, and had three children, Julia, Charles and Sophie; Sophie, married Thomas D.S. Mason, and had two daughters, Nathalie and Anne-Stewart; Martin married Dianne Clark and they had four children, Phillip, Audrey, Jeannette and John; Eglé married Kurt Weiland, creating three children, Martin Hugo, Christian and Beatrice; Miguel's marriage to Ruby Aubert brought two more children to the fold, Joseph Francis Gatins V and Rémy. Miguel's first marriage to Rhonda Dawes was childless.

275. **and regular delivery of care packages.** Besides tins of homemade cakes from Sylvia, I especially remember generous packages of food from Dr. Ciro and Rita Scotti, parents of a prep school friend in Rhode Island. My friend, young Ciro, had introduced me to his family (six daughters, five sons!) in senior year, an Irish-American-Italian clan worthy of my own in size and sweep and complexity. The sisters proved intriguing. For reasons I never really understood, the Scotti parents welcomed me as an extra son, putting out mounds of home-cooked pasta, cooking huge breakfasts (served in bed to me by Mrs. Scotti sometimes), and giving parched prep school boys access to an open bar on weekend leaves. It was a very warm home, one that took the edge off the turmoil in Atlanta, and that forged friendships lasting to this day.

276. **more smoking and drinking…** Karestan C. Koenen, et. al., Persisting Posttraumatic Stress Disorder Symptoms and their Relationahip to Functioning in Vietnam Veterans: A 14-year Follow-up, in *Journal of Traumatic Stress,* February, 2008. pp 49-57, Volume 21, No. 1.

277. **"All this from just one child!"** Recollection of close family friend, Denise Simons-Carmichael.

278. **financial help of her friends, and an annuity from her brother Charlic's printing company in Paris.** One of the delicious ironies involving the printing company was that its employees had purchased it for a song in 1963 after Charlic's death, with a slight percentage of gross sales to be turned over to Grandmother for life. As it turned out, the business thrived and the payments to Eglé grew accordingly—but the owners could not believe she was still alive more than 20 years later. They even went so far as to petition the French consul in New Orleans to certify that she was still living! Grandmother thoroughly enjoyed these episodes, and took pains to ensure that the firm paid every franc she was owed with the help of an *"homme d'affaires"* in Paris.

279. **two FBI agents came knocking at the door one Sunday morning, much to the children's consternation.** Based on e-mail correspondence with my brothers Martin and Miguel, April 2008. JOESIB. I sought access to any FBI report that might still exist about this interview, but the agency said it had not found any papers relating to this investigation.

280. **Lucarotti's claim to criminal fame.** That French Connection, as it were, prompted me some few years later to pen a memorial list of everyone who had spent the night in the library guest room and its famous "old brown bed," an A-list of family relatives, rogues, party-goers, couples, strangers, girl friends, boy friends, and various overnight guests who passed out there.

281. **provide him with a new suit from Brooks Brothers.** E-mail correspondence from my brother Miguel, April 2008. JOESIB.

282. **"the ghost of Mr. Gatins."** Author's e-mail correspondence with Susan Dedeyn, August, 2008.

283. **didn't know how boring we were…"** From Caroll Smith Offen, as recalled by Eglé G. Weiland in e-mail to author, April 10, 2008. JOESIB.

284. expiring at the age of 97... Eglé's great-granddaughter, Nathalie Mason Fleury, read the eulogy at Christ the King Cathedral in Atlanta, January 30, 1990.

My great-grandmother, Eglé, loved. She loved unconditionally and unselfishly. She loved life. She knew much grief in her life, but rather than dwelling on self-pity, she used times of trial to grow in her faith. Suffering for my great-grandmother became a wellspring of compassion that overflowed to touch people's lives. She loved life but never held onto it greedily—she shared her life, lived for others. Because she did not try to cheat age and time, she transcended generations. It is my belief that Mé's 97 years on this earth were a gift to teach us about love. Her life and experiences gave her perspective that few of us can truly appreciate. Here is a woman who can remember the Empress Eugénie, Widow of Napoleon III, walking in the Tuileries. In her lifetime, my great-grandmother saw history repeat itself. She knew war. In the First World War she wrote in her memoirs of the day her brother's regiment left for the front. She described the beauty of the young men on horseback in the costume of the French dragoons, riding off to war with lances in their hand. She also saw these men return emaciated in their tattered rags wounded and broken. My great-grandmother especially ministered to those who confronted war. She saw her son fight in the Second World War and her grandson fight in the Vietnam War. My great-grandmother was a healer. During the Second World War, she served as a volunteer nurse for the Red Cross. She also risked her life as a courier of false identity papers for the Resistance during the German Occupation of Paris. She was ready to sacrifice her life, if need be, for others.

My great-grandmother was a person of great generosity. If she had a penny in her hand, she always found a way to give a dollar to others. My sister and I can remember how she would serve Cokes to the garbage men. She would get Anne Stewart [Nathalie's sister] to invite

(Continued...)

the mailman into the house so she could give him some extra money. She often anticipated people's needs giving them not always what she wanted to give them, but what she thought would give them pleasure. She gave generously with no strings attached.

Not only did Mé give of her resources, she gave of herself. When I was a baby, she kept my crib in her house. As I got older, I remember how she would tirelessly read me Tintin comic books. She would permit Anne Stewart and me to play beauty parlor with her hair and play dress-up with her clothes. I remember how we used to have tea together in the mornings and after school—how she would nurse me and baby me when I had a cold, reprieve me for skipping my French lessons, and comfort me as I cried into her lap after a hard day at school.

We see grief for we are in a mirror and perceive but dimly. But Mé is face to face with God and she understands fully what can only appear cloudy to us, for she has been fully understood as she sought during her life to fully understand others. I think of Mé and I remember a story she used to tell about her cousin, who led a cavalry charge against the German airplanes in World War I. For me, Mé's life epitomizes this Don Quixote image—in generations of 'me-ness,' she lived for others. In a world that preaches selfishness, she was generous—in a world full of hate, my great-grandmother represented love.

Selected Bibliography

Newspapers

The Atlanta Constitution
Atlanta Georgian & News
Atlanta Journal
The Atlanta Journal-Constitution
Deseret Morning News
Le Monde
New York Herald American
New York Journal-American
The New York Times
New York World Telegram
The Wall Street Journal
(Washington) The Evening Star
(Washington) The Sunday Star
Washington Herald
The Washington Post
Washington Times
Washington Tribune

Atlanta Research

Atlanta Historical Society. *Atlanta Historical Society Bulletin, 1944, Vol. VII. The Irish Influence in Early Atlanta.* 1944.

Barnard, Susan Kessler. *Buckhead: A Place for All Time.* 1996.

Bauerlein, Mark. *Negrophobia: A Race Riot in Atlanta, 1906.* 2001.

Bayor, Ronald H. *Race & the Shaping of Twentieth-Century Atlanta.* 1996.

Blackmon, Douglas A. *Slavery by Another Name: The Re-Enslavement of Black Americans from the Civil War to World War II.* 2008.

Bolton & Culclasure, editors. *The Confessions of Edward Isham: A Poor White Life of the Old South.* 1998.

Blass, Kimberly S. & Rose, Michael. *Atlanta Scenes: Photojournalism in the Atlanta History Center Collection.* 1998.

Bryant, James C. *Capital City Club: The First One Hundred Years, 1883-1983.* 1991.

Cash, W.J. *The Mind of the South.* 1941.

Coleman, Kenneth, general editor. *A History of Georgia, Second Edition.* 1991.

Daniel, Wayne W. *Pickin' on Peachtree: A History of Country Music in Atlanta, Georgia.* 2001.

Davis, Burke. *The Southern Railway: Road of Innovators.* 1985.

Dinnerstein, Leonard. *The Leo Frank Case.* 1966, 1987.

Dray, Philip. *At the Hands of Persons Unknown: The Lynching of Black America.* 2002.

Dyer, Thomas G. *Secret Yankees: The Union Circle in Confederate Atlanta.* 1999.

Ellison, Janet Correll, editor. *On to Atlanta: The Civil War Diaries of John Hill Ferguson, Illinois Tenth Regiment of Volunteers.* 2001.

Garrett, Franklin M. *Atlanta and Environs: A Chronicle of Its People and Events. Vols. I & II.* 1954.

Goodson, Steve. *Highbrows, Hillbillies and Hellfire: Public Entertainment in Atlanta, 1880-1930.* 2002.

Grant, Donald L. *The Way It Was in the South: The Black Experience in Georgia.* 1993.

Greene, Melissa Fay. *The Temple Bombing.* 1996.

Haggler, Carol Louise. *Irish Immigrants in Atlanta, 1850-1896.* Emory University Master's Thesis, 1968.

Henderson, Lilian. *Roster of the Confederate Soldiers of Georgia.*

Inscoe, John C. and Kenzer, Robert C., editors. *Enemies of the Country: New Perspectives on Unionists in the Civil War South.* 2001.

Kemble, Frances Anne. *Journal of a Residence on a Georgia Plantation in 1838-1839.* 1961, 1984.

Kuhn, Clifford M. *Contesting the New South Order: The 1914-15 Strike at Atlanta's Fulton Mills.* 2001.

Martin, Harold. *Atlanta and Environs: A Chronicle of Its People and Events, Vol. III.* 1987.

Mason, Herman. *African-American Entertainment in Atlanta.* 1998.

Mason, Herman. *Black Atlanta in the Roaring Twenties.* 1997.

Selected Bibliography

Merritt, Carole. *The Herndons: An Atlanta Family*. 2002.

Mills, Gary B. *Southern Loyalists in the Civil War: The Southern Claims Commission*. 1994.

Oney, Steve. *The Dead Shall Rise: The Murder of Mary Phagan and the Lynching of Leo Frank*. 2003.

Piedmont Driving Club. *The First Hundred Years: Piedmont Driving Club, 1887-1987*. 1987.

Pioneer Citizens Society of Atlanta. *The Pioneer Citizens' History of Atlanta, 1833-1902*.

Prince R.E. *Central of Georgia Railway and Connecting Lines: The Right Way*. 1976.

Roberts, Gene & Klibanoff, Hank. *The Race Beat: The Press, the Civil Rights Struggle and the Awakening of a Nation*. 2006.

Rose, Michael. *Atlanta: A Portrait of the Civil War*. 1999.

Gladney, Margaret Rose, editor. *How Am I to Be Heard? Letters of Lillian Smith*. 1993.

Shavin, Norman and Galphin, Bruce. *Atlanta: Triumph of a People*. 1982.

Trudeau, Noah Andre. *Southern Storm: Sherman's March to the Sea*. 2008.

Winn, Les. *Ghost Trains & Depots of Georgia (1833-1933)*. 1995.

Simpson, Brooks D. & Berlin, Jean V., editors. *Sherman's Civil War: Selected Correspondence of William T. Sherman, 1860-1865*. 1999.

Taliaferro, Tevi. *Historic Oakland Cemetery*. 2001.

Tuck, Stephen G.N. *Beyond Atlanta: The Struggle for Racial Equality in Georgia, 1940-1980*. 2001.

Workers of the Writers' Program of the Works Progress Administration in the State of Georgia, introduced by Spalding, Phinizy. *Georgia: The WPA Guide to its Towns and Countrysides*. 1940.

Robber Barons and the Gilded Age

Chernow, Ron. *The House of Morgan: An American Banking Dynasty and the Rise of Modern Finance*. 1990.

Crockett, Albert Stevens, *Old Waldorf Bar Days*. 1931.

Josephson, Matthew. *The Robber Barons*. 1934.

Livingston, Bernard. *Their Turf: America's Horsey Set & Its Princely Dynasties*. 1973.

McIntosh, J. Rieman. *A History of the Elkridge Fox Hunting Club, The Elkridge Hounds, The Elkridge-Hartford Hunt Club*. 1978.

McIntosh, J. Rieman. *Elkridge Fox Hunting Club: Stories of the Hunts*. 1978.

Mercer, Lloyd J. *E.H. Harriman: Master Railroader*. 1985.

Morrell, Parker. *Diamond Jim: The Life and Times of James Buchanan Brady*. 1934.

World War I, the Lost Generation and World War II

Balfour, R.E. *The Action Française Movement.* 1930.

Fitch, Noel Riley. *Sylvia Beach and the Lost Generation: A History of Literary Paris in the Twenties and Thirties.* 1983, 1985.

Manchester, Willliam. *The Arms of Krupp, 1587-1968.* 1968.

May, Ernest R. *Strange Victory: Hitler's Conquest of France.* 2000

Meyer, Ahlrich. *L'Occupation Allemande en France, 1940-44.* 2002.

Némirovsky, Irene. *Suite Française.* 2004.

Ousby, Ian. *Occupation: The Ordeal of France, 1940-44.* 2000.

Parrotin, Marc. *Femmes de la Resistance en Creuse.* 1997.

Parrotin, Marc. *Mémorial de la Resistance Creusoise.* 2000.

Parrotin, Marc. *Immigrés dans la Resistance en Creuse.* 1998.

Roulet, Claude. *Ritz: Une histoire plus belle que la légende.* 1998.

Tuchman, Barbara W. *The Guns of August.* 1962.

Tuchman, Barbara W. *The Proud Tower: A Portrait of the World Before the War 1890-1914.* 1962.

Holocaust Research

Arad, Yitzhak. *Belzec, Sobibor, Treblinka: The Operation Reinhard Death Camps.* 1987.

Arad, Yitzhak, Kralowski, Shmuel and Spector, Shmuel, editors. *The Einsatzgruppen Reports: Selections from the Dispatches of the Nazi Death Squads; Campaign Against the Jews in Occupied Territories of the Soviet Union, July 1941.-January 1943.* 1989.

Bartov, Omer. *Erased: Vanishing Traces of Jewish Galicia in Present-Day Ukraine.* 2007.

Birnbaum. Pierre. *Un Mythe Politique: La "Republique Juive."* 1988.

Bradsher, Greg. *Holocaust-Era Assets: A Finding Aid to Records at the National Archives at College Park, Maryland.* 1999.

Browning, Christopher R. *Ordinary Men: Reserve Police Battalion 101 and the Final Solution in Poland.* 1992.

Chevallier, Paul. *Les Chemins qui Menaient à Rawa-Ruska.* 2000.

Compiled by Aroneanu, Eugene. *Inside the Concentration Camps: Eyewitness Accounts of Life in Hitler's Death Camps.* Translated by Thomas Whissen. 1996.

Chabord, Marie-Thérese and Pouessel, Jean. *Inventaire des Archives du Commisariat Géneral aux Questions Juives et du Service de Restitution des Biens des Victimes des Lois et Mesures de Spoliation.* 1998.

Cohen, Roger. *Soldiers and Slaves: American POWs Trapped by the Nazis' Final Gamble.* Knopf. 2005.

Selected Bibliography

Desbois, Patrick. *Porteur de Mémoires: Sur les Traces de la Shoah par Balles.* 2007.

Goldhagen, Daniel Jonah. *Hitler's Willing Executioners: Ordinary Germans and the Holocaust.* 1996.

Gutman, Yisrael and Krakowski, Shmuel. *Unequal Victims: Poles and Jews During World War II.* 1986.

Jarny, Raymond. *L'Enfer de Rawa-Ruska: Chronique de Guerre, d'Evasions et d'Espoir.* 2000.

Heberer, Patricia and Matthaus, Jurgen, editors. *Atrocities on Trial: Historical Perpsectives on the Politics of Prosecuting War Crimes.* 2008.

Kahane, David, translated by Michalowicz, Jerzy. *Lvov Ghetto Diary.* 1990.

Kingston, Paul, J. *Anti-Semitism in France during the 1930s. Organisations, Personalities and Propaganda.* 1983.

Klarsfeld, Serge. *La Shoah en France, Vols I, II, III & IV.* 1983.

Lower, Wendy. *Nazi Empire-Building and the Holocaust in Ukraine.* 2005.

Marrus, Michael R. and Paxton, Robert O. *Vichy France and the Jews.* 1981.

Mehjlman, Jeffrey. *Legacies of Anti-Semitism in France.* 1993.

Peschanski, Denis. *La France des Camps: L'Internement, 1938-1946.* 2002.

Rajsfus, Maurice. *Opération Etoile Jaune.* 2002.

Rhodes, Richard. *Masters of Death: The SS Einsatzgruppen and the Invention of the Holocaust.* 2002.

Rubenstein, Joshua and Altman, Ilya. *The Unknown Black Book: The Holocaust in the German-Occupied Soviet Territories.* 2008.

Silverman, Willa. *The Notorious Life of GYP: Right Wing Anarchist in fin-de-siècle France.* 1995.

Weisberg, Richard H. *Vichy Law and the Holocaust in France.* 1996.

Schelvis, Jules. *Sobibor: A History of Nazi Death Camp.* 2007.

Winter, Miriam. *Trains.* 1997.

Miscellaneous

Black, Robert C. III, *The Railroads of the Confederacy.* 1998.

Bullard, Mary R. *Robert Stafford of Cumberland Island: Growth of a Planter.* 1995.

Coleman, Kenneth, general editor. *A History of Georgia—Second Edition.* 1991.

Coué, Jean. *René Madec: Le Nabab du Grand Moghol.* 1997.

Cook, Adrian. *The Armies of the Streets: The New York City Draft Riots of 1864.* 1974.

Dames, Michael. *Mythic Ireland.* 1992.

De Baudus, Florence. *Le Lien du Sang.* 2000.

de Servigny, Yann. *Maison de Kerguelen.* 1997.

Dunne, Dominick. *Justice: Crimes, Trials and Punishments.* 2001.

Dyer, Thomas G. *The University of Georgia: A Bicentennial History, 1785-1985.* 1985.

Ellis, Peter Berresford. *Celtic Myths and Legends.* 1999.

Ellis, Peter Berresford. *A Brief History of the Druids.* 1994.

Ferguson, Niall. *The War of the World.* 2006.

Fitts, Robert K. *Inventing New England's Slave Paradise: Master/Slave Relations in Eighteenth-Century Narragansett, Rhode Island.* 1998.

Freeman, Philip. *The Philosopher and the Druids: A Journey Among the Ancient Celts.* 2006.

Georgia Humanities Council. *The New Georgia Guide.* 1996.

Gildea, Robert. *Children of the Revolution: The French, 1799-1914.* Harvard University Press. 2008

Gleeson, David T. *The Irish in the South, 1815-1877.* 2001.

Greenberg, Sue & Kahn, Jan. *Asheville: A Postcard History, Vol. I.* 1997.

Hepburn, Lawrence R., editor. *Contemporary Georgia.* 1987.

Hogan, Michael. *The Irish Soldiers of Mexico.* 1997.

Latimer, Sallie W. *Narragansett in Vintage Postcards.* 1999.

Laxton, Edward. *The Famine Ships: The Irish Exodus to America.* 1996.

Lewis, David Levering. *God's Crucible: Islam and the Making of Europe, 570-1215.* 2008.

Martin, Donald. *Killybegs: Then & Now.* 1998.

McCaffrey, Lawrence, J. *The Irish Catholic Diaspora in America.* 1976.

McDaniel, Douglas Stuart. *Asheville.* 2004.

McQuigg, Jackson, Galloway, Tammy & McIntosh, Scott for the Atlanta History Center. *Central of Georgia Railway.* 1998.

Miller, Zell. *Great Georgians.* 1983.

Ó Gradá, Cormac. *Black '47 and Beyond: The Great Irish Famine.* 1999.

Painter, Sidney. *French Chivalry.* 1940.

Phillips, Ulrich B. *American Negro Slavery.* 1918, 1966.

Reagan, Alice E. *H.I. Kimball, Entrepreneur.* 1983.

Russell, Preston and Hines, Barbara. *Savannah: A History of her People Since 1733.* 1992.

Seabrook, Charles. *Cumberland Island: Strong Women, Wild Horses.* 2002.

White, Willliam L. *Slaying the Dragon: The History of Addiction Treatment and Recovery in America.* 1998.

Selected Bibliography

Useful Websites

Atlanta History Center.
 http://www.atlantahistorycenter.com/
The Avalon Project (Nuremberg trials collection at Yale Law School)
 http://avalon.law.yale.edu/subject_menus/imt.asp
Ceux de Rawa-Ruska.
 http://rawa-ruska.net/rawa01.htm#01
Centre de Documentation Juive Contemporaine.
 http://www.memorialdelashoah.org/
Georgia Archives.
 http://sos.georgia.gov/archives/
The New Georgia Encyclopedia.
 http://www.georgiaencyclopedia.org/nge/Home.jsp
Federal Open Government Guide.(The Reporters Committee for Freedom of the
 Press.) http://www.rcfp.org/fogg/index.php
The Inflation Calculator.
 http://www.westegg.com/inflation/
International Committee of the Red Cross.
 http://www.icrc.org/
The National Archives (Southeast Region).
 http://www.archives.gov/southeast/
United States Holocaust Memorial Museum.
 http://www.ushmm.org/
U.S. Department of State (FOIA Section).
 http://www.state.gov/m/a/ips/

Author's Note and Acknowledgments

❧　　❧　　❧

The rationale for this story originated in Atlanta on December 18, 1983, the very cold, sunny morning that my father died in my arms. The death nurse at the hospital stripped him of his wedding band and a gold bracelet. The latter ended up on my wrist. When I woke up the next morning, the bracelet felt like a vise, twisting and tugging at my left arm, as if he was not quite ready to relinquish his ties to life on earth.

I'd essentially lived away from home since sent away to school more than two decades earlier, but I realized that morning as never before that I was intricately tied to blood. I knew that I'd eventually try to flesh out the history of a family whose twists, turns, adventures and secrets, like those of so many families, was fast being erased by the passing of the generations. My five brothers and sisters and I all plowed through papers and old photographs hidden here and there in Daddy's papers and throughout the house after he died. I found one photo that struck me particularly, of a one-armed man holding a baby in the crook of his left arm. Who was this child, who the one-armed man? The baby was my father. The one-armed man was my paternal grandfather, who had faded out of the family picture a few short years after his marriage. He had died a sad death about 20 years before I was born. By the mid-1990s, my mother Sylvia, Grandmother Eglé, and my brother Charles also had died. I took up the photo again and, with the benefit of early retirement from the news business, began trying to untangle the complicated and often-secretive skein that is my family history. I went looking for a one-armed grandfather, but uncovered a lot more. It could have been the stuff of fiction.

I found my Gatins grandmother and through her and with her, new lenses opened onto the complicated chiaroscuro that was my own father—a tapestry colored primarily by his experiences in World War II—and his difficult, but also enduring and richly textured relationship to my mother, and their eventual return to Atlanta. Maybe I found a bit of myself, too.

If I have any regrets, it is that I found much more archival information about the lively and often-irritating Gatins men than I did about the remarkably strong women who accepted their name, like my Grandmother Eglé. All together, though, they represented universal human traits and actions at interesting times in interesting places, instructing us to the human condition both then and now.

I do hope readers will enjoy this history as much as I did researching it and writing it. I found it a true learning experience, somewhat cathartic, in that the writing eventually required dredging up personal memories and feelings, not all of them pleasant, that I had been professionally trained to keep out of the hundreds of articles I had written during a newspaper career, and shed new light on how parental patterns of behavior seem to be passed down from one generation to the next. At times, it was difficult to maintain a necessary distance from characters so intimately tied to my own story.

I had immensely valuable help from my surviving brothers and sisters in exploring these feelings and recollections and turning them into an accurate reminiscence. This book could not have been written without the active aid and support of Sophie Gatins Mason, Martin Thomas Gatins, Eglé Gatins Weiland and Miguel Ribon Gatins. They each gave generously of their time, answering incessant e-mail correspondence, deciphering the hieroglyphics of 19th and 20th Century handwriting, finding and forwarding family files, photos and correspondence and fleshing out their own pertinent memories of different times and places. My nieces Nathalie Mason Fleury and Anne-Stewart Mason Forbes, who were old enough to know and remember some of the principals, also added salient detail to the whole, as did my wife Fran and son Demian, and my aunts, the late Dorothy Brewster and Hope Simpson, the latter my godmother.

But it is not the book they would have penned. Each of us has different memories of different times in the family's story, with slight, but meaningful degrees of separation. That became increasingly clear as I proceeded. This non-fiction historical biography of family and family events—not a memoir in the usual sense of the word—rests entirely on my own interpretation of the facts, as do all the translations from French documents and letters to English.

In the end, I believe I got the highlights right, the dates and chronologies finally in correct order as I peeled back the layers of this big Vidalia onion that was my family's history. It also was an exercise in stretching and extending long-dormant memory (and quickly writing it down before it faded again). I take particular satisfaction in completing the story of a real-life adventure that my own father had vowed to write but never set to paper and that, in so doing, I was able to open his life and that of Grandmother Eglé as I never fully knew them when they were still alive.

I also must recognize the patience and attention to detail shown by a platoon of librarians and archivists, including the staff of the Kenan Research Center, Atlanta; Margaret Scholl, of the Privacy Team, U.S. Department of State, Washington. D.C.; the reference librarians of the Newspaper & Periodical Reading Room, Library of Congress, Washington, D.C.; staff of the National Archives, Washington, D.C.; archival staff of the Hargrett Rare Book and Manuscript Library and staff of the microfilm reading room, University of Georgia Libraries, Athens, Georgia; Harry Weiss, former executive director, The Preservation Society of Asheville & Buncombe County, Inc., Asheville, North Carolina; archival staff of the Centre de Documentation Juive Contemporaine, Paris, France; the archivists of the U.S. Holocaust Memorial Museum Library, Washington, D.C., and the staff of the Stacks at *The Atlanta Journal-Constitution.*

Very special thanks must go to Peter Black, chief historian at the Holocaust Memorial Museum's Center for Advanced Holocaust Studies, who was both encouraging and patient in dealing with a novice in the dark business of Holocaust research, and proved invaluable in steering me to documentary archives in Europe. Dr. Charles Sydnor, former president of Emory and Henry College, also gave of his valuable time in this process, translating several key documents from German to English.

Dr. Thomas Dyer of the University of Georgia in Athens, also put his own facility in German to the task and, more importantly, discovered and confirmed the pro-Yankee bent of the first Gatins ancestor in Atlanta. His counsel was invaluable as was that of Dr. John Inscoe, another historian at the University of Georgia, editor of *The New Georgia Encyclopedia.*

This book would not have seen the light of day without the expert help of J. L. Saloff of Saloff Enterprises, who showed patience in completing this book's design.

Honor Woodard was responsible for the photo selection and layout as well as the cover design, for which I am truly grateful. She also listened patiently when this project was still in its "talking stages," and helped immensely in getting this collection of sometimes dim memories to the light of day.

A platoon of other friends and acquaintances also lent aid to this task, either by reading parts of the manuscript or the whole, counseling me about the book trade, hearing me talk about this tale or answering questions about the Gatins family. This list includes Sims Bray Jr., the late John C. Calhoun, Thomas Rain Crowe,

Charles E. Cox, the late Rudolph Gmür, Dietrich Hoecht, Patricia Kyritsi Howell, Robinette Kennedy, George "Jorge" Lawton, Eston Melton, Carroll Smith Offen, Karen Pietrowicz, Johanna Rucker, Ran Shaffner, Ciro Scotti, R.A. Scotti, Randolph P. Smith, Thomas A. Silvestri, Francis Tancrède and Joan Zillessen.

Finally, giving credit where true credit is due, this book could not have been written without the special editing and pushing and counsel of my wife, Fran. She has sustained me in both good times and hard, and convinced me to bail out of the news business for sanity's sake. Truth be told, it wasn't much fun anymore. She deserves a lion's share of the credit for seeing this work to fruition, which is why this book is dedicated to her, a true friend and mate.

Index

❧   ❧   ❧

Miscellanea

About the Type

The main text of this book is set in Adobe Caslon Pro, an adaptation by the American calligrapher Carol Twombly of the original type designs by British engraver William Caslon during the years 1734-1770, which, in turn, had been influenced by old style Dutch Baroque typefaces of the 17th Century. Benjamin Franklin hardly used any other typeface, and the first printings of the American Declaration of Independence and Constitution were set in Caslon.

About the Cover

The cover was designed by Honor Woodard. It includes a photo of Eglé Gatins and her son Francis in Paris in the early 1920s and one of many letters he sent her from Germany during World War II. Francis, imprisoned for more than three years in POW camps, was working in Berlin at the time as a "guest worker" of the Reich under the false identity of Joseph Garrat. Several weeks later, he made a final, successful escape from Nazi control. The rosary, one of the many belonging to Eglé, is emblematic of the many prayers said on his behalf during these turbulent times.

About the Author

Photo by Honor Woodard

Joseph Gatins for many years was a reporter and special projects editor with *The Richmond Times-Dispatch*, Richmond, Virginia, now retired. He lives with his artist-author wife Fran in the mountains of north Georgia, staying grounded by hiking nearby national forests, working an organic vegetable garden and occasionally throwing a few clay pots.

CPSIA information can be obtained at www.ICGtesting.com
Printed in the USA
239421LV00001B/2/P

9 780578 027791